VIRGINIA GENEALOGICAL RESEARCH

by

George K. Schweitzer, Ph.D., Sc.D.
407 Regent Court
Knoxville, TN   37923

Typed by
Anne M. Smalley

ISBN 0-913857-06-8

TABLE OF CONTENTS

Chapter 1. VIRGINIA BACKGROUND........................5
  1. VA geography...5
  2. Early Colonial VA....................................9
  3. Later Colonial VA...................................12
  4. The Revolution......................................15
  5. Early statehood.....................................17
  6. The middle period..................................18
  7. The Civil War.......................................21
  8. Reconstruction and after.........................24
  9. Suggested reading..................................27
 10. The VA counties.....................................27
 11. The VA independent cities........................30

Chapter 2. TYPES OF RECORDS........................37
  1. Introduction..37
  2. Bible records.......................................39
  3. Biographies...41
  4. Birth records.......................................43
  5. Cemetery records...................................45
  6. Census records......................................46
  7. Church records......................................52
  8. City directories....................................56
  9. City and county histories........................56
 10. Colonial record compilations....................57
 11. Court records.......................................62
 12. DAR records...64
 13. Death records.......................................64
 14. Divorce records.....................................66
 15. Emigration and immigration......................67
 16. Ethnic records......................................69
 17. Gazetteers, atlases, and maps...................70
 18. Genealogical indexes & compilations for VA.......72
 19. Genealogical periodicals........................75
 20. Genealogical societies...........................77
 21. Historical societies..............................78
 22. Land records..78
 23. Manuscripts...82
 24. Marriage records...................................83
 25. Military records: Colonial.......................86
 26. Military records: Revolutionary War............87
 27. Military records: 1812–1860......................91
 28. Military records: Civil War......................94
 29. Mortuary records...................................97
 30. Naturalization records...........................97

31. Newspaper records.................................99
32. Published genealogies for the US................100
33. Regional records................................101
34. Tax lists......................................104
35. Wills and probate records......................106

Chapter 3. RECORD LOCATIONS.........................109
 1. Court houses...................................109
 2. The major facilities...........................110
 3. The VA State Library & Archives................111
 4. The VA Historical Society Library..............118
 5. The Alderman Library of the University of VA...119
 6. The National Archives..........................122
 7. The Library of Congress........................124
 8. The Daughters of the American Revolution
    Library......................................125
 9. Genealogical Society of UT Library & Its
    Branches.....................................126
10. Regional libraries............................129
11. Large genealogical libraries..................131
12. Local libraries...............................132
13. Bookshop.....................................133

Chapter 4. RESEARCH PROCEDURE & COUNTY LISTINGS.....135
 1. Finding the county............................135
 2. Recommended approaches........................137
 3. The format of the listings....................140
 4. Accawmack County.............................142
 5. Accomack County..............................142
 6. Albemarle County.............................143
 7. Alexandria County............................144
 8. Allegheny County.............................144
 9. Amelia County................................144
10. Amherst County...............................145
11. Appomattox County............................145
12. Arlington County.............................145
13. Augusta County...............................146
14. Bath County..................................147
15. Bedford County...............................148
16. Bland County.................................148
17. Botetourt County.............................148
18. Brunswick County.............................149
19. Buchanan County..............................149
20. Buckingham County............................150
21. Campbell County..............................150
22. Caroline County..............................151

23. Carroll County.....................................151
24. Charles City County.............................152
25. Charles River County............................152
26. Charlotte County.................................152
27. Chesterfield County..............................153
28. Clarke County.....................................153
29. Craig County......................................153
30. Culpeper County..................................154
31. Cumberland County...............................154
32. Dickenson County.................................155
33. Dinwiddie County.................................155
34. Dunmore County...................................156
35. Elizabeth City County...........................156
36. Essex County......................................156
37. Fairfax County....................................157
38. Fauquier County..................................158
39. Fincastle County.................................158
40. Floyd County......................................158
41. Fluvanna County..................................159
42. Franklin County..................................159
43. Frederick County.................................160
44. Giles County......................................160
45. Gloucester County................................161
46. Goochland County.................................161
47. Grayson County...................................162
48. Greene County.....................................162
49. Greensville County...............................162
50. Halifax County....................................163
51. Hanover County...................................163
52. Henrico County...................................164
53. Henry County......................................165
54. Highland County..................................166
55. Isle of Wight County............................166
56. James City County................................166
57. King and Queen County..........................167
58. King George County..............................167
59. King William County.............................168
60. Lancaster County.................................168
61. Lee County..169
62. Loudoun County...................................169
63. Louisa County.....................................170
64. Lower Norfolk County............................170
65. Lunenburg County.................................170
66. Madison County...................................171
67. Mathews County...................................171
68. Mecklenburg County..............................172

69. Middlesex County.....................................172
70. Montgomery County...................................173
71. Nansemond County.....................................173
72. Nelson County..174
73. New Kent County......................................174
74. New Norfolk County...................................174
75. Norfolk County.......................................175
76. Northampton County...................................176
77. Northumberland County................................176
78. Nottoway County......................................177
79. Old Rappahannock County..............................177
80. Orange County..177
81. Page County..178
82. Patrick County.......................................178
83. Pittsylvania County..................................179
84. Powhatan County......................................179
85. Prince Edward County.................................180
86. Prince George County.................................180
87. Prince William County................................181
88. Princess Anne County.................................181
89. Pulaski County.......................................182
90. Rappahannock County..................................182
91. Richmond County......................................183
92. Roanoke County.......................................183
93. Rockbridge County....................................184
94. Rockingham County....................................185
95. Russell County.......................................185
96. Scott County...186
97. Shenandoah County....................................186
98. Smyth County...187
99. Southampton County...................................187
100. Spotsylvania County.................................187
101. Stafford County.....................................188
102. Surry County..188
103. Sussex County.......................................189
104. Tazewell County.....................................189
105. Upper Norfolk County................................190
106. Warren County.......................................190
107. Warrosquoyoake County...............................190
108. Warwick County......................................190
109. Washington County...................................191
110. Westmoreland County.................................191
111. Wise County...192
112. Wythe County..192
113. York County...193

Chapter 1

VIRGINIA BACKGROUND

1. Virginia geography

The commonwealth (state) of Virginia (VA), the first to be settled of the original thirteen colonies, is located in the central region of the eastern seaboard of the US. In shape it resembles a triangle (see Figure 1), the base being about 440 miles, the long sloping side on the west being about 380 miles, and the sharply rising side on the east being about 220 miles. In addition to this main section of the state, a small area of the southern portion of the Delmarva Peninsula belongs to VA. This portion, known as the Eastern Shore, rests east of the center of the eastern coast of VA, just across Chesapeake Bay. The state is bordered on the west by WV and KY; on the south by TN and NC; on the east by the Atlantic Ocean, Chesapeake Bay, the Potomac River, and MD, and on the north by MD, DC, and WV. The capital of the state is located at Richmond in the central-east area, and the state is divided into 100 counties plus 41 independent cities (not subject to county administration). The principal cities of VA (with their approximate populations in thousands) are Norfolk (286K), VA Beach (257K), Richmond (220K), Arlington (153K), Newport News (147K), Hampton (131K), Chesapeake (115K), Alexandria (109K), Portsmouth (108K), and Roanoke (100K). Arlington and Alexandria are together in the northeast section suburban to Washington, DC. Norfolk, VA Beach, Newport News, Hampton, Chesapeake, and Portsmouth are clustered in the extreme southeastern corner of the state. And Roanoke is located in the southwestern area.

An understanding of the progressive settlement of the state is greatly enhanced by an examination of the geographic regions and features. These are pictured in Figure 1. The eastern coastal plain, called the Tidewater, is generally quite flat and sometimes swampy. Four rivers cut into this plain: the Potomac (across which lies MD), the Rappahannock, the York, and the James, all of them draining into Chesapeake Bay. About 55 miles to the west the Tidewater plain gives way to a rise of about 300 feet all along what is known as the Fall Line, which passes north to south through

Key to Figure 1

A = Alleghany Mountains
Ap = Appomattox River
B = Blue Ridge Mountains
Ba = Bannister River
Bl = Blackwater River
C = Clinch River
CB = Chesapeake Bay
D = Dan River
DC = District of Columbia
E = Eastern Shore
H = Holston River
J = James River
KY = Kentucky
M = Mattaponi River
MD = Maryland
Me = Meherrin River
N = New River
NA = North Anna River
NC = North Carolina
NN = Northern Neck

No = Norfolk
Nt = Nottaway River
P = Peninsula
Pa = Pamunkey River
Po = Potomac River
R = Roanoke River
Ra = Rappahannock River
Rp = Rapidan River
S = Staunton River
SA = South Anna River
Sh = Shenandoah River
Sm = Smith River
SS = Southside
SV = Shenandoah Valley
TN = Tennessee
UP = Upper Peninsula
V = Valley Of VA
WV = West Virginia
Y = York River

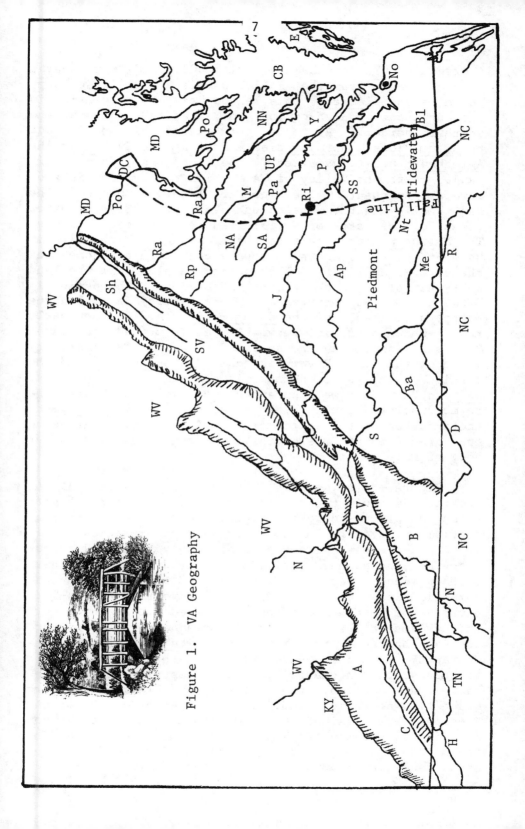

Figure 1. VA Geography

Alexandria, Fredericksburg, Richmond, and Petersburg. Extending west from the Fall Line is a rolling country known as the Piedmont, this region being 40 miles wide in the north but broadening out to about 180 miles at the southern border. At the western extreme of the Piedmont the Blue Ridge Mountains rise and along the WV border the Allegheny Mountains rise. Between the two mountain ranges rests the Valley of VA, which really consists of several component valleys cut by lower mountains. The major valley is the Shenandoah Valley. Several other areas of VA are often referred to with special names. The Northern Neck refers to the peninsula which sits in between the Potomac and Rappahannock Rivers. Sometimes the term is applied to the peninsula plus all the land northwest of it back to the WV border. The peninsula between the Rappahannock and York Rivers is called the Northern Peninsula or the Upper Peninsula. The peninsula region which sits in between the York and the James Rivers is simply known as the Peninsula. The territory south of the James River is called Southside, and the portion of VA west of Roanoke is generally referred to as Western VA. In some instances you will encounter the terms Upper and Lower. They refer to rivers, Upper being the area nearer the source of the river, and Lower being the area nearer where the river empties into a larger body of water.

Figure 1 also depicts the major rivers of VA. An understanding of the coastal regions and the river patterns is of considerable importance to the history and settlement of early VA and to travel and migration within it. The waterways were the most widely employed avenue into VA, and pioneer families usually settled on or near streams since they were the major transportation and communication lines in the early years. Ribbon-like patterns of settlement often developed along the rivers and streams. The Tidewater is drained by the Potomac, the Rappahannock, the York (and its tributaries, the Mattaponi and the Pamunkey), and the James (and its tributary, the Chickahominy), all emptying into Chesapeake Bay, and by the Nottaway and Blackwater Rivers which flow south into NC. The upper regions of the Piedmont are drained by the Potomac, the Rappahannock (and its tributary, the Rapidan), the North Anna and the South Anna (both emptying into the Pamunkey), and the James (and its tributary, the Appomattox). The broad expanse of the Piedmont along the NC border is drained by the Smith, the Dan, the Banister, the Roanoke (Staunton), and the Meherrin, all flowing south into NC, and then into the Atlantic Ocean. The Valley is drained in the north by the northward-flowing Shenandoah (which empties into the upper Potomac), in the center by the James and the Staunton (Roanoke), and in the south by the New, the South Fork and the North Fork of the Holston, and the Clinch.

2. Early Colonial VA

On or about 06 May 1607, 105 men, employees of the royally-chartered London Company (later also called the VA Company), entered Chesapeake Bay in three ships. After about two-and-a-half weeks of exploring the lower James River, they came ashore and built a stockade, thus establishing a settlement which they called Jamestown. During the next 2-3 years, starvation, disease, and Indian attacks took a terrible toll on the original settlers and on two other groups which came late in 1607 and in October 1608. In 1609, several hundred more colonists arrived to bring the total population at Jamestown to about 500, but by spring 1610 only 60 remained alive. In June, 300 men came, more in early spring 1611, and still more in the late summer, some women, livestock, and food accompanying them. Late in 1611, some settlers moved upriver from the swampy Jamestown to an island (now Farrar's Island) where they established a town which was called Henrico. The leader of VA, about this time, abandoned the communal plan (all land worked in common, all food distributed from a common store) and started assigning plots of land to individuals so they could grow crops for their own use. The results were rapid increases in production and morale. In 1612, the beginnings of a fast-developing and profitable raising of tobacco for export were made. By 1616, 351 English colonists were in VA, including 65 women and children. There were also 216 goats, 144 cattle, 6 horses, and many hogs and poultry. In the nine years since the first settlement (1607-16), about 1650 had come to VA, about 1000 had died, and about 300 had returned to England. But by now, the colony had stabilized and it was obvious that it would be permanent. In the next three years, further settlers increased the population to over a thousand. By 1619, VA had been divided into four districts called plantations: James City, the City of Henrico, Charles City, and Elizabeth City. Each plantation included a central settlement plus some surrounding settlements, some of which were called hundreds (because they included 100 men). This year of 1619 was extremely important because of four important events: a governing assembly of representatives from the plantations started meeting, black slaves were brought in, the indentured-servant system was inaugurated (a white laborer's passage to VA was paid in exchange for 4-5 years of service), and there was the arrival of 1261 persons including families, 100 apprentices, and 90 young women (all of whom were promptly married), bringing the total population to about 2500. The headright system also increased the number of immigrants. Under it, anyone who paid for his, his family's, and his servants' passages to VA received 50 acres per person.

On 22 March 1622 a coordinated series of attacks were made by the Indians on settlers all along the James River, over 350 deaths and much property loss resulting. Jamestown, having been warned by a friendly native, was able to repel the raiders. Numerous retaliatory expeditions against the Indians were launched. The Indians were slain, their villages were burned, and their stores and crops were destroyed. In 1622-4, disease and starvation again ran rampant, such that in early 1625 only 1095 survivors inhabited VA. They were what was left of 7549 who had come 1607-24. In 1624, the king dissolved the VA (London) Company, and the settlements became a Crown Colony, with a somewhat weakened General Assembly meeting irregularly. In the years following, further settlement took place as colonists pushed up the James and York Rivers, occupied the banks of Chesapeake Bay, and built primitive roads into forests. The General Assembly in 1634 divided VA into eight shires (counties): Accawmack (later Northampton), Charles City, Charles River (later York), Elizabeth City, Henrico, James City, Warrasquoake (later Isle of Wight), and Warwick River (later Warwick). County courts were set up, and commissioners, clerks, sheriffs, constables, justices of the peace, and coroners were designated. Appeals of county court cases could be made to the newly-established General Court or to the General Assembly (which was elected by all freemen). By 1635, the population was approximately 5000. The year 1639 witnessed the royal approval of the elected Houses of Burgesses and the governor's Council (together making the General Assembly) as the legislative branch of VA's government. The Church of England [Episcopal] was the state church and therefore was the official church of Colonial VA. As early as 1624, there were 13 parishes, and 22 clergymen had been sent from England. The churches functioned as places of worship, centers of social activity, enforcers of morality, and certifiers and record keepers for the rites of passage (christenings, marriages, deaths). Each parish was governed by an elected vestry who chose the minister under the supervision of the bishop. In addition to the church, people met at the county seat on court day, at the militia musters, and at the race tracks. As of 1641, the population was about 7500. About 70% of them had come as indentured servants or apprentices and had become freemen and small farmers. There were approximately 250 blacks, most being indentured servants rather than slaves.

In early 1642, William Berkeley came to VA as governor, and shortly thereafter civil war broke out in England between the King and the Parliament. Berkeley saw to it that VA remained loyal to the crown, and many royal refugees came to the colony. In 1644, another series of Indian attacks occurred, over 500 settlers being killed, especially in the outposts. Retaliation was swift, and the Indians sued for peace. In 1645, the General Assembly authorized several frontier forts around which settlers gathered and from which explorers and traders penetrated hundreds of miles into the back country. Among the emigrants who came to VA in the period 1640-70, there were about 100 whose families would dominate the political life of VA through the Revolutionary War period. Included were the family names: Beverley, Burwell, Byrd, Carter, Cary, Digges, Fitzhugh, Grymes, Harrison, Lee, Ludwell, Mason, Nelson, Page, Randolph, Wormeley. There was a sharp separation between these gentlemen-families and the ordinary small farmers of the colony. After the King's beheading in 1649 by the victorious Puritans, VA prepared to resist, but commissioners from Parliament negotiated a peaceful submission with Governor Berkeley retiring. From then until 1660, the English Government left VA essentially free to run its own affairs, and they prospered in the rapidly expanding tobacco trade. This era of prosperity ended in 1660 when the King was restored to England's throne. Parliament made laws restricting VA trade to England and the use of English ships, which caused tobacco to pile up and prices to drop, a depression resulting. Discontent, especially among the ruined small farmers, spread and the restored Governor Berkeley's arrogant favoritism for the large planters, his progressive weakening of the General Assembly, plus his refusal to permit settlers to retaliate against Indian attacks brought on Bacon's Rebellion in 1676. Under the leadership of Nathaniel Bacon, the ordinary people attempted to wrest control of the government from Berkeley. When Bacon died suddenly, the leaderless rebellion was viciously and ruthlessly put down by Berkeley, whose actions brought about his recall to England. In 1670 voting requirements had been tightened so that only property owners (freeholders) could vote.

In July 1682, the depression of the tobacco industry began to let up, as the colonists were again allowed to market their product in Europe. The situation in VA now was made up of the ruling group (the large land-holding plantation proprietors) and a vast number of common people who held a few hundred acres of land which they farmed. They were very prosperous in these years, but the increasing importation of slaves to work the plantations would squeeze them out economically. After the Glorious Revolution of 1688 in England, a new monarch who showed genuine concern for VA came to the throne. Settlements were now spreading beyond the Fall Line, Indian attacks were abating, Huguenot refugees from France were coming in, the College of William and Mary in Middle Plantation (Williamsburg) was chartered in 1693, and the capital was moved from Jamestown to Williamsburg in 1699. In 1700 the population numbered about 72,000.

3. Later Colonial VA

In 1710, Alexander Spotswood became VA's chief executive. His twelve years in office probably represent the most notable gubernatorial period in colonial times. He supervised the burgeoning growth of Williamsburg, tried to stop the importation of slaves, advocated more humane treatment and education of Indians, brought Germans over to work the iron mines, attempted to prevent landgrabbing by the rich, supported the opening up of the western sections of the state, and launched expeditions against the coastal pirates. VA's leaders on into the

1730s and 1740s, especially Lt. Gov. William Gooch, continued to foster migration beyond the Blue Ridge Mountains (into the Valley) and even beyond the Alleghenies. Part of the later motivation for this was to claim the areas before France could. The major routes the pioneers followed into the back country were up the James, Rappahannock, and Roanoke Rivers and their tributaries. During these times, Germans and Scotch-Irish were descending from PA into the Shenandoah Valley. As the decade 1740-50 came to a close, western land was being taken up quite rapidly. By the early 1750s, settlers in sizable numbers were pushing into southwest VA. Many of the westward-moving people were dissenters (non-Episcopalians), but for the most part, they were allowed to practice their own faiths, especially since Williamsburg was so far away and Episcopal clergy were essentially not to be found on the frontiers. The major religious faiths were Presbyterian (Scotch-Irish), Lutheran and German Reformed (both German), Mennonite, Welsh Baptist, and English Quaker. One important issue that came to a head in 1749 was the matter of the Fairfax Proprietary. This was a large area of land between the Potomac and Rappahannock Rivers and extending back into the Alleghenies. It had been given to an ancestor of Thomas Lord Fairfax, but VA had been granting lands in it to settlers. An appointed panel of commissioners addressed itself to Lord Fairfax's complaint and ruled that the grants were valid but that the taxes on the land must be paid to Fairfax. The period 1700-50 is sometimes called VA's Golden Age. In the east the aristocracy prospered as their plantations grew in size and production such that they dominated the social, economic and political scene. The growth of the plantations was fed by large-scale slave importation to provide workers. The slave population rose from 7000 in 1700 to about 120,000 in 1756. The many small farmers in the east were squeezed out of business, but many migrated west to join those pouring in from other states.

In 1751, Robert Dinwiddie took over as chief administrative officer of VA. The major events of his term (1751-8) centered around the French and Indian War. In the years preceding 1751, the French and the English had both been trying to colonize the OH Valley, the OH Company grant furthering English exploration in the region and bringing them in contact with the French. Dinwiddie sent George Washington in 1753 to tell the French that they were on land claimed by England, but the French ignored the message. Dinwiddie then in early 1754 dispatched Washington with a small force to drive the French away from the Forks of the Ohio (now Pittsburgh). Washington encountered and defeated a small group of French at Great Meadows (near where PA, VA, and WV now join), then was himself attacked and defeated by a larger force of French and Indians. Aid was sought from Great Britain, and General Edward Braddock and two regiments came to VA. Braddock, with Washington as his aide plus some VA militia, was killed and his forces defeated when he attempted to take Fort Duquesne (later Pittsburgh) from the French and their Indian allies. Washington escaped, was made commander of VA forces, and moved very effectively against French-incited Indian attackers all along the frontier. In 1758, renewed British efforts brought about the capture of Fort Duquesne (Washington playing an important role), and then other French outposts progressively fell, Quebec in 1759, and Montreal in 1760, terminating the war. The Treaty of Paris of 1763 granted all of Canada to Great Britain.

In 1765, the British Parliament passed the Stamp Act putting a tax on all legal documents, newspapers, pamphlets, and some other items. Opposition in the colonies was vigorous, the colonists asserting that legislation governing them should not be passed without their being represented. Parliament repealed the Stamp Act in 1766, but replaced it with the Townshend Acts which put a duty on tea, paper, glass, and paint imported into the thirteen colonies. The colonies again asserted that only their own legislatures had a right to levy taxes on them. In 1770 all the duties were repealed except the one on tea. Committees to cooperate with each other in opposing the British were set up in the various colonies. Tea was not coming into VA, but in late 1773, Bostonians threw a shipment in the harbor in protest. In retaliation, the British blockaded Boston until it would pay for the tea. The other colonies, including VA, sent in food and money for the relief of Bostonians. Parliament then provided for Quebec to annex the territory northwest of the Ohio River, a territory Virginians had fought for. The VA Governor Dunmore dissolved the Assembly when they denounced the blockade of Boston, but they met anyway, suggesting a convention of all the colonies. This First

Continental Congress met 05 September 1774. The Delegates adopted a Declaration of Rights and indicated that
Parliament had abridged several in the decade preceding.
Indian attacks on the frontier were becoming so frequent
that Dunmore commissioned Andrew Lewis and over 800 VA
Valley frontiersmen to move against them. At Point
Pleasant (where the Ohio and Kanawha Rivers merge), they
defeated the Shawnees and drove them west. The frontier
was thereby stabilized, and a blow against the Quebec
annexation was made.

4. The Revolution

On 23 March 1775, a VA convention meeting in Richmond, under the impact of a stirring speech by Patrick
Henry, voted to prepare the colony for defense against
anticipated British action. On 18 April 1775, the situation in Boston led to an armed clash between British
soldiers and MA militia at nearby Lexington and Concord.
In early May the Second Continental Congress convened in
Philadelphia, electing Washington to command the Continental Army. In this same month, Governor Dunmore fled
to a British warship in the York River, later moving to
the Norfolk harbor. A July convention provided for
troops to be raised, militia to be trained, and a Committee of Safety to take charge of the colony. Dunmore
landed a force near Norfolk and was defeated by the 2nd
VA regiment. He then proceeded to shell and burn Norfolk, and what he hadn't destroyed, the withdrawing VA
forces burnt in February 1776. After shore batteries
shelled his ships several times, Dunmore finally departed
for England in July 1776. No further significant military action took place in VA until 1779, but VA contrib-
uted 26,678 to the Continental Army and well over 4000
served in the militia. The British conducted numerous
raids along the coast of Chesapeake Bay and the Atlantic
Ocean. Many people loyal to England (Loyalists), particularly merchants and planters, departed, but many remained. Treatment of Loyalists (Tories) was mild at first,
but became harsher as the war heated up. The death
penalty was carried out on those who aided the enemy, and
the properties of Loyalists were confiscated.

An elected VA Constitutional Convention met in
Williamsburg 06 May 1776. This convention on 15 May
instructed the VA delegation to move adoption of a Decla-

ration of Independence by the Continental Congress. On
12 June 1776 the VA convention adopted George Mason's VA
Bill of rights, and on 29 June adopted his VA Constitution. Then came the news that the Continental Congress
had approved Jefferson's Declaration of Independence on
04 July 1776.   The scene of warfare in these days was
largely in the north with the capture of Ticonderoga (10
May 1775) and the battle of Bunker-Breed's Hills (17 June
1775).   The invasion of Canada by the Continental forces
and the attempt to take Quebec (1775-6) ended in dis-
aster.   This was followed by the loss of New York City
(15 September 1777) and then Philadelphia (04 October
1777) to the British.   The next major event was the
colonists' victory at Saratoga (17 October 1777), which
led to France's entry in the war against the British.
The terrible winter spent by the Continental Army at
Valley Forge (1777-8) followed. In 1778-9 George Rogers
Clark and 180 VA and KY riflemen took the Northwest
Territory from British forces and the area was organized
by VA as IL County. In 1780 the VA capital was moved to
Richmond.   The British had occupied Savannah since late
1778, and in May 1780 they took Charleston.   Then using
these two towns as bases, they moved inland and soundly
defeated the Americans at Camden, SC (August 1780).   In
October, a group of frontiersmen defeated a British force
at Kings Mountain, SC/NC.   After sailing up the James
river, Benedict Arnold and 1600 men marched on Richmond,
took it (January 1781), burned it, then withdrew.   After
suffering sizable losses at Cowpens, SC (17 January 1781)
and at Guilford Courthouse, NC (15 March 1781), General
Cornwallis led his British troops into VA to join forces
with British General Philips who was coming from the base
at Portsmouth. A French force under Lafayette arrived at
Richmond just as Philips was coming up from the south.
Philips moved away to meet Cornwallis at Petersburg. The
VA General Assembly and VA Governor Jefferson had moved
to Charlottesville when Richmond came under threat.
Knowing this, Cornwallis dispatched a contingent to
capture them, but being forewarned, they escaped, re-
assembling at Staunton.

Cornwallis had now moved his merged forces to Yorktown. On 05 September 1781, Washington's Continentals and
Rochambeau's French Army rapidly moved south toward VA,
just after French Admiral DeGrasse had put his fleet at
the entrance to Chesapeake Bay. The British fleet tried

to dislodge DeGrasse, but they were repelled. When
Washington and Rochambeau arrived north of Yorktown,
Cornwallis found himself trapped. After a couple of
weeks of seige, on 17 October Cornwallis surrendered.
The war was over, and American Independence had been
gained. The formal peace treaty was signed 03 February
1783.

5. Early Statehood

During the war, VA had moved toward religious freedom, had removed entail (limits on who could inherit an
estate) and primogeniture (inheritance by only the first-
born son), had liberalized the legal code, had abolished
slave importing, and had established 19 counties in the
west. In 1782, a law providing for emancipation of
slaves was passed (it lasted 10 years), and in 1786 a law
providing for complete religious freedom was enacted. In
1784 VA ceded to the US the Northwest Territory. The
year 1787 saw the meeting of a convention in Philadelphia
which drafted a Constitution for the US, approval by nine
states being required for its acceptance. In June 1778,
a state convention met in Richmond, and on the 26th
ratified the document. Washington was unanimously
elected the first US President in 1789 and was re-elected
in 1792. VA ceded a portion of its Potomac land to the
US for the DC in 1789, and three years later, KY County
of VA was admitted to the US as the 15th state. The end
of the century was marked by the death on 14 December
1799 of George Washington. As of 1800, VA ranked first
in population, wealth, and influence among the thirteen
original states plus the three newly-formed ones. VA had
played an exceptionally important part in the birth of
the US by giving to the latter half of the 18th century a
large number of notable soldiers and statesmen. One
needs only to recall George Washington, Thomas Jefferson,
James Madison, James Monroe, John Marshall, George Mason,
Richard Henry Lee, Patrick Henry, George Wythe, Edmund
Pendleton, Peyton Randolph, and George Rogers Clark.

For about 40 years after the Revolution, VA was in
considerable economic distress due to the after effects
of the war and the severe depletion of the soil by
tobacco growing. This distress promoted migration of
many Virginians into and beyond the regions that are now
the states of KY, TN, OH, IN, and MI. In 1800 Jefferson

was made US President, and was elected to a second term
in 1804. In 1800 and again in 1802, slave revolts in and
around Richmond and Norfolk were narrowly averted when
the plots were discovered. In 1801 John Marshall began a
34-year tenure as Chief Justice of the US. The purchase
of the vast LA Territory from France in 1803 doubled the
land area of the country, and the 1804-6 expedition of
Virginians Lewis and Clark to the Pacific Coast became
the basis of the US claim to the Oregon Territory. James
Madison came to the presidency of the US in 1809 and
served through 1817.

After a long series of British attacks, seizures,
and depredations on American ships, the US declared war
in 1812.   Efforts to invade Canada in 1812 led to American defeat at Detroit and repulsion at Niagara River.
Even though there were several US naval victories in
1812, Britain asserted its sea supremacy in 1813 by
capturing or bottling-up most US ships. In January 1813
at Raisin River (south of Detroit), American forces were
again beaten, but in September Admiral Oliver Perry won a
notable victory on Lake Erie.   This was followed by the
action of US General William Henry Harrison who drove the
British out of Detroit, then pursued and defeated them at
Thames River.   When Great Britain in 1813 attempted to
take Carney Island (which guarded the approach to Norfolk
and Portsmouth), they were driven off by VA militia and
US sailors. The British then attacked Hampton, took it,
and committed atrocities on its peoples. In August 1814,
a large British army moved from Canada into upper NY
state, but had to retreat when their accompanying fleet
was defeated near Plattsburg in September.   August of
1814 also saw an enemy expedition enter Chesapeake Bay,
win a victory at Bladensburg, burn the capitol in Washington, then be halted by Fort McHenry just outside of
Baltimore, MD. VA militiamen were called up when Washington was taken, but did not fight since the enemy did
not try to invade VA.   After much negotiation, a peace
treaty was signed 24 December 1814, but before news of it
reached New Orleans, General Andrew Jackson decisively
defeated the British there on 08 January 1815.

6. The Middle Period

James Monroe of VA became President of the US in
1817 and remained in office until 1825.   Notable among

the events of his administration were the MO Compromise, the settlement of Canadian-US boundary disputes, confirmation of US possession of FL, and the Monroe Doctrine (no new colonization and no European interference in the Americas). The MO Compromise was an early signal of the growing slavery problem in the US. Its main section was an agreement that MO entered the Union as a slave state and slavery would be prohibited in the LA Purchase north of 36 degrees 30 minutes. In 1825 the University of VA opened its doors, this being of significance for public education in the entire nation. From 1825-45, VA's influence on national affairs declined, this being paralleled by exhaustion of much land, the population drain to the west, very few immigrants, a general economic decline, backwardness in primary education, the paucity of manufacturing, and the inefficiency of slave labor. Not until the late 1840s were there notable upturns especially in manufacturing and agriculture, the use of lime and fertilizers along with the reaper assisting the latter.

In 1829-30, finally responding to complaints of western counties over under-representation in the legislature, and the lack of roads, canals, ferries, and bridges, a convention was called to review the state constitution. The eastern counties, which were in control, refused most of the requests, but granted a few concessions, some increases in representation, a somewhat broadened suffrage, and some curtailment of executive power. In 1831, sixty white persons were killed in Southampton County by a slave insurrection led by Nat Turner. The perpetrators were captured and paid the death penalty but the fear quickened VA's legislature to enact harsher restrictive laws relating to blacks. The failure of the legislature to deal constructively with the issue by providing for a gradual abolition may be due to the tremendous business of marketing VA slaves to the cotton states. The decade of 1830-40 saw considerable activity in road and canal building, as well as in some short railroad construction. The patenting of McCormick's reaper in 1834 was to give rise to considerable wheat raising activity, especially in the Valley, VA ranking 4th among the states for quite some time. In 1841, two Virginians were sent to Washington, William Henry Harrison as President, and John Tyler as Vice President. Upon the death of the President after one

month, Tyler succeeded him. Before he left office in
1845, his plan for annexation was accepted by TX. This
annexation, added to previous frictions, was the immediate cause of the Mexican War. When General Zachary
Taylor occupied Point Isbel at the mouth of the Rio
Grande, Mexico saw it as an act of aggression. When
Mexican troops crossed the Rio Grande and bombarded Fort
Taylor, the US declared war on 12 May 1846. Taylor drove
the Mexicans back across the Rio Grande, Santa Fe was
taken by General Kearny, and California switched to
American rule. In February 1847, Taylor and Mexican
President Santa Anna clashed at Buena Vista in what
appeared to be a draw, but at the end, the Mexicans
withdrew. The final campaign of the war began in March
1847 when General Winfield Scott landed at Vera Cruz,
then began a drive to Mexico City. After successively
taking Cerro Gordo, Contreras, Casa Mata, Molino del Rey,
and Chapultepec, US troops entered Mexico City on 14
September 1847. Terms of the treaty of 01 February 1848
provided for Mexico's cession to the US of two-fifths of
its territory.

Another state constitutional convention in 1850-1
was more responsive to the western counties than the one
of 1829-30 had been. The right to vote was given to
white males; a capitation tax to support schools was
enacted; the governor, lieutenant governor, judges,
legislators, and county officials were to be elected by
vote; and representation in the House of Delegates was
determined by a population basis and in the Senate by a
combined population-property basis. Interest in public
education had been having an increasing impact, which was
evidenced in 1855 by the presence of common schools in
ten counties and four cities. Since the previous century
there had been numerous small private academies and this
had grown into the hundreds by 1855. In 1860, they
employed 700 teachers and ministered to 13,000 students.
VA, as much of the US, was essentially rural. The
largest city was Richmond (38,000), then Norfolk (about
15,000). Alexandria, Abingdon, Fredericksburg, Lexington, Lynchburg, Petersburg, and Big Lick (Roanoke) were
small towns. The majority of the 1,600,000 population
lived on farms, some large, most small. The percentage
of slaves had declined from 48% to 1830 to 30% in 1860.

VA in its colonial days had often opposed the importation of blacks. As a state, it had been a pioneer in
prohibiting the slave trade, its delegates to the US
Constitutional Convention having sought to have such a
prohibition written in. With regard to what to do with
slaves already in VA, the people generally favored emancipation provided the slaves were removed from the state.
However, this concept gave way to intolerance evidenced
when the 1835-6 Assembly passed a law mandating severe
punishment for those circulating any written material
denying that masters had property rights in slaves. Even
so, there were abundant representations of opposite
views, many critics of slavery being quite outspoken.
However, the pro-slavery defenders outnumbered them in
the 1840s and 1850s, clergymen and laymen alike defending the institution of human servitude. In practically all
towns of VA, the slave market stood in a prominent place.
The institution had become woven into the cloth of the
state's economy and social structures.

7. The Civil War

On 16 October 1859, John Brown and 22 associates
captured the US military arsenal at Harper's Ferry, VA
(now in WV), Brown seeing this as an initial step in
country-wide uprising to liberate the southern slaves.
Col. Robert E. Lee and his aide Lt. J. E. B. Stuart
leading a company of Marines retook the arsenal and Brown
was subsequently hanged. This incident was prophetic of
the violent Civil War that was about to be unloosed on
the US. For years the Northern and Southern states had
been progressively becoming divided by a number of
issues: sectional rivalry, industrial against agricultural interests, economic and trade regulation, and
Federal centralization against states' rights. Compromises had been worked numerous times, but they became
increasingly unavailable as the 1850s wore on, and conflict loomed large. When Abraham Lincoln was elected
President in 1860, the south clearly remembered his
statement of policy that a government cannot endure
permanently half slave and half free. Before his inauguration, SC seceded from the Union on 20 December, and was
joined by AL, FL, GA, LA, MS, and TX (the cotton states,
the deep south) by 01 February 1861. A government of the
Confederate States of America was formed at Montgomery,
AL, with Jefferson Davis as President. VA, hopeful of

avoiding war, called a convention of all states on 04 February, but the seven seceded states refused to attend. In a state convention on 13 February, VA continued to try to find a route to peace, and on 04 April voted against secession. On 12 April 1861 SC began bombardments of the Federal Fort Sumter on an island in the harbor of Charleston. The next day the fort surrendered. President Lincoln on 12 April issued a call for 75,000 volunteers to put down the armed rebellion, and unwilling to furnish troops to move upon SC, VA's convention voted 88-to-55 to secede. In short order, the convention offered Robert E. Lee (who had refused the command of the US Army on 18 April) the post as commander of VA's military forces, and he accepted on 22 April. By 24 May 1861 three more southern states had joined the Confederacy. The two sides, Union and Confederate, began to mobilize their men and resources, and four years of horrible conflict began. We will now give an overview of the war, then we will discuss VA's part in it in a bit more detail.

The intention of the Union came to be the defeat of the Confederacy by invasion and the forcible return of them to the Union. The history of the Civil War can be seen as the fulfillment of five strategies by the Union: (1) the blockading or capture of southern ports to cut off supplies, (2) the taking of the Confederate capital Richmond by attack from the north, (3) the splitting of the Confederacy by driving down and up the MS River, (4) the further splitting of the Confederacy by driving from the northwest corner of TN down the TN and Cumberland Rivers to Nashville to Chattanooga to Atlanta to Savannah, and then, if necessary (5) driving north from Savannah into SC, then NC, then assaulting Richmond from the south.

Strategy (1), the sea blockade was accomplished early in the War with blockades or captures of most Atlantic Coast ports, capture of New Orleans 28 April 1862, and the capture of Fort Pulaski 12 December 1862, effectively closing the port of Savannah. Strategy (2), the drive toward Richmond from the north, failed again and again, the Confederacy even making two counterinvasions to threaten Washington, until success began to be had by Grant in 1864 by brunt of overwhelming numbers. Strategy (3), the drives to take the MS River, chiefly involved the Union victory at Shiloh on 06-07 April 1862, the capture of New Orleans 28 April 1862, the taking of Memphis 06 June 1862, the conquest of Vicksburg 04 July 1863, and the fall of Port Hudson 09 July 1863. Strategy (4) the drive from northwest TN to Savannah, involved taking control of the TN and Cumberland Rivers by capturing Fort Henry 06 February 1862 and Fort Donelson 16 February 1862, winning at Shiloh 06-07 April 1862, capturing Chattanooga after recouping the Confederate Chickamauga victory of 19-20 September 1863 in the battles of Lookout Mountain and Missionary Ridge 24-25 November 1863, marching toward Atlanta in May-July 1864, capturing Atlanta 02 September 1864, defeating a Confederate attack in the rear at Nashville 16 December 1864, then taking Savannah 22 December 1864. Strategy (5), the drive north from Savannah, was accomplished by the taking of Charleston and Columbia in February 1865, pushing into NC, and forcing the capitulation of one of the remaining two Confederate armies at Durham Station, NC 26 April 1865. The other major army had capitulated, after having been driven from Richmond, at Appomattox on 09 April 1865. These ended the conflict except for two surrenders of Confederate forces of AL-MS and of trans-MS forces in May 1865.

It is obvious from the above account that Strategy (2) was fought out in VA and adjacent states. We now direct our attention to this, realizing that more Civil War battles were fought in VA than in any other state. Lee set himself to the massive tasks of preparing VA for a prolonged war, and he knew that the Union would move on VA as soon as possible, since the Confederate capital had been relocated to Richmond on 20 May 1861. In addition Richmond's Tredegar Iron Works were vital to arms production, its flour mills were among the nation's largest, and the Shenandoah Valley was to be the granary of the Confederacy. At the beginning of the War the genius of VA's military leaders (Robert E. Lee, Thomas J. [Stonewall] Jackson, J. E. B. Stuart) delivered setback after setback to the Union Armies as they attempted to take Richmond: at the first battle of Bull Run (21 July 1861), in the Seven Days Battles of the Peninsula Campaign as the Federals moved up the James-Rappahannock peninsula (April-July 1862), in Jackson's Shenandoah Valley attacks at Kernstown (23 March 1862), McDowell (08 May 1862), Front Royal and Winchester (23-25 May 1862), Cross Keys and Port Republic (8-9 June 1862). These latter battles, constituting the Shenandoah Campaign constantly forced the US authorities to divert much manpower from attempts against Richmond to keep Jackson from using the Valley as an attack route on Washington. The second battle of Bull Run was a brilliant victory for Lee. This made possible his invasion of MD and southern PA, which led to the bloody battle of Antietam, where Lee's forces were stopped on 17 September 1862. On 18-19 September, Lee moved back into VA.

The repulsions of Federal invasions continued at Fredericksburg (13 December 1862), and Chancellorville (02-04 May 1863), which encouraged Lee to make another invasion of the north. This time the Potomac was crossed at the top of the Shenandoah Valley, Lee moving into the region of Harrisburg and Chambersburg, PA. On 01-03 July, the greatest battle of the Civil War was fought at Gettysburg, PA. Lee withdrew on 04 July, the Confederates having lost about 25,000 dead, missing, and wounded and the Union about 23,000. This marked the beginning of the end for the Confederacy in VA. Bloody battles in which the US troops under Grant gradually bottled up the outnumbered Southerners then occurred: the Wilderness campaign fought in the tangled woods about 10 miles west of Fredericksburg (May-June 1864), the long drawn-out seige of Petersburg (1864-5), the victories in and laying waste of the Shenandoah Valley by Sheridan (September 1864-March 1865), the abandonment of Richmond (03 April 1865), and the surrender of the remnant of Lee's Army at Appomattox (09 April 1865). Other surrenders (Mobile, AL, Durham Station, NC, Citronella, AL, Tallahassee, FL, Chalk Bluff, AR, anu New Orleans, LA) rapidly brought the War to an end.

8. Reconstruction and after

Shortly after the War, VA was made into Military District No. 1 and General John M. Schofield was placed in command of the region and its occupying Union troops, with Francis H. Pierpont as provisional governor. the Federal Reconstruction Acts had disenfranchised practically all Virginians who had previous experience in state government. In 1867, a constitutional convention met in Richmond, this meeting being dominated by Radicals (carpetbaggers, scalawags, blacks). They drafted a state constitution providing for taxes, free public schools, black suffrage, a secret ballot, exclusions of many VA whites from the vote, and disqualification of most whites from holding office. A committee, with Schofield's support, secured permission from the Federal authorities to vote on the last two items separately. They were rejected, but the remainder of the constitution was passed. Radical control was then ended when VA elected to office its own moderate party led by William Mahone, a former Confederate general. In 1870, the Assembly ratified the 14th and 15th amendments to the US Constitution, and VA was readmitted to the Union. VA had escaped much of the retribution of Reconstruction experienced by other southern states, but thousands of its youth had been killed or crippled, its dwellings and fields had been devastated, its currency rendered worthless, its people impoverished, its industry disabled, its slave labor lost, its plantations dissolved, its morale plunged into despair, and its debt increased to over 45 million.

The major issue of the next two decades was the debt. As fruit farming, seafood gathering, lumbering, dairy farming, cattle raising, flour milling, and tobacco culture began to pick up, the economy slowly moved toward recovery. During these years, two parties addressed themselves to the debt issue. The Funders stood for payment in full, regardless of the adverse effect on public education: the Readjusters led by Mahone wanted to reduce the debt payments and to foster education. The Readjusters came to power in 1879, readjusted the debt, and enacted education laws which moved VA ahead of other southern states. But, in reaction to Mahone's dictatorial political behavior, the Democratic Party was revived in 1883, and won the elections that year. The party kept most of the good reforms of the previous administration, but enacted carefully-drafted laws to perpetuate their own rule. The Democrats held control over the state for more than 80 years, with the blacks becoming and remaining politically powerless over most of the time. After 1880, northern investors began supporting VA business and industry. The discovery of coal in 1873 in the southwest area of the state led to increased coal mining, railroad construction, and factory development. And Newport News began a spectacular rise to an important ship-building city and port. When the Spanish-American War broke out in 1898, thousands of VA men

volunteered. Major events in this brief conflict included the defeat of a Spanish Fleet at Manila, defeat of
another at Santiago de Cuba, and the taking of Santiago.
The result was the freeing of Cuba, and the ceding of
Puerto Rico, Guam, and the Phillipines to the US.

In 1901, a constitutional convention met in Richmond, and in 1902 produced a new constitution. Its
intent was to reduce the black vote, and this it accomplished with rigorous literacy tests, taxes, and queries.
In the first decade of the new century, notable advances
in education, public health, road-building, agricultural
services, and black welfare were made. In 1912, another
native son of VA, Woodrow Wilson, was elected to the US
Presidency, and in 1916 was elected again. World War I
began in 1914, and the US entered the War in early 1917,
the defeat of Germany coming in late 1918. VA was heavily involved, both in the large number of enlistees it
provided, in the importance of the ports of Norfolk,
Portsmouth, and Newport News, and in the importance of
the army and navy installations around Hampton Roads.
The powerful state Democratic machine which Thomas S.
Martin and James Cannon, Jr. had headed was taken over in
1926 by Harry Flood Byrd when he was elected governor.
He was appointed US Senator in 1933 and was continually
reelected until 1965. As governor, he put the state on a
debt-free economy, which made it possible for VA to
absorb the economic shock of the Depression (1930s)
better than many other states. The state's economy was
built largely on food, textiles, and tobacco which still
had a market. In World War II (1935-45), VA again con-
tributed men and women, military training installations,
industries, and the Hampton Roads shipyards. In the
postwar period, VA showed great progress in tobacco
product manufacture, apple growing, poultry raising,
lumbering, coal and iron mining, cattle raising, road
construction, and recreational park development.

Major attractions in VA which are of special inter-
est to genealogists include those near Tazewell (Old Fort
Witten), near Wytheville (Fort Chiswell Monument), in
Danville (Last White House of the Confederacy), near
Roanoke (Booker T. Washington Monument), in Lexington
(Lee's Tomb and Jackson's Grave), at Red Hill (Patrick
Henry's Grave), near Charlottesville (Monticello, Ash
Lawn, Madison's Grave), at New Market (Civil War Battle-

field), near Haymarket (Manassas Battlefield), near
Alexandria (Mount Vernon), near Stafford (Rising Sun
Tavern), in Richmond (White House of the Confederacy,
Confederate Museum, St. John's Church, Richmond Battlefield Park), at Appomattox (Civil War Park), in Petersburg (Battlefield Park), Yorktown, Jamestown, Williamsburg, and near Fredericksburg (National Military Park).

9. Suggested Reading

A knowledge of history is extremely important as an
aid to the genealogist who wishes to search out every
possible source of information on a VA ancestor. A
practically indispensable book for this is:
__V. Dabney, VA, THE NEW DOMINION, Doubleday, Garden
  City, NY, 1971.
Other single-volume works on VA history include:
__L. D. Rubin, VA, A BICENTENNIAL HISTORY, Norton, New
  York, NY, 1977.
__M. W. Fishwick, VA, A NEW LOOK AT THE OLD DOMINION,
  Harper, New York, NY, 1959.
__M. P. Andrews, VA, THE OLD DOMINION, Doubleday, Garden
  City, NY, 1937.
__J. E. Cooke, VA, A HISTORY OF THE PEOPLE, Houghton-
  Mifflin, Boston, MA, 1911.
Some multi-volume works which might prove useful to you
are:
__P. A. Bruce, VA, REBIRTH OF THE OLD DOMINION, Lewis
  Publ. Co., New York, NY, 1929, volumes 1-2 (volumes 3-4
  biography).
__R. A. Brock, VA AND VIRGINIANS, Reprint Co., Spartan-
  burg, SC, 1973 (1888), 2 volumes.
__P. A. Bruce, L. G. Tyler, and R. L. Morton, HISTORY OF
  VA, American Historical Society, New York, NY, 1924,
  volumes 1-3 (volumes 4-6 biography).
__R. R. Howison, A HISTORY OF VIRGINIA, Carey & Hart,
  Philadelphia, PA, 1846-8, 2 volumes.

10. The VA Counties

Out of the eight original VA counties (or shires)
formed in 1634 plus another in 1648, there eventually
came 172 counties. As of 1950, the Commonwealth of VA
had come to contain exactly 100 of these counties, 13 had
become extinct, 9 now being in KY, and 50 now in WV,
which split from VA in 1863 during the Civil War. Figure

2 shows the 100 VA counties, the abbreviations with the counties corresponding to their names. To locate a county, simply find its abbreviation in the following alphabetical list. The abbreviation appears in parentheses after the name of the county. Then notice the symbols after the parentheses. These symbols tell you in what part of the state you will find the county. The sections of the state are the far west (FW), the midwest (MW), the north central (NC), the south central (SC), the north east (NE), the south east (SE), and the Eastern Shore (ES). The small map in the upper left hand corner of Figure 2 will show you where on the large map to look.

The counties are: Accomack(Ac) ES [1], Albemarle (Al) NC [8], Allegheny(Ag) MW [9], Amelia(Am) SC [21], Amherst(Ah) SC [8], Appomattox(Ap) SC [8], Arlington(Ar) NE [9], Augusta(Au) NC [9], Bath(Ba) MW [9], Bedford(Be) MW [2], Bland(Bl) FW [10], Botetourt(Bo) MW [9,10], Brunswick(Br) SC-SE [2], Buchanan(Bu) FW [10], Buckingham(Bc) SC [8], Campbell(Ca) SC [2], Caroline(Co) NE [9], Carroll(C) MW [10], Charles City(Cc) SE [2], Charlotte (Ch) SC [2], Chesterfield(Cs) SE [8], Clarke(Cl) NC [9], Craig(Cr) MW [10], Culpeper(Cu) NC [9], Cumberland(Cm) SC [8], Dickenson(Di) FW [10], Dinwiddie(Dn) SE [2], Elizabeth City(Ec) SE [4], Essex(E) NE [9], Fairfax(Fa) NE [9], Fauquier(Fq) NC [9], Floyd(Fl) MW [10], Fluvanna(Fv) SC-NC [8], Franklin(Fr) MW [2], Frederick(Fd) NC [9], Giles(Gi) MW [10], Gloucester(G) SE [3], Goochland[Go] Sc-NC [8], Grayson(Gr) FW [10], Greene(Gn) NC [9], Greenville(Gv) SE [2], Halifax(Ha) SC [2], Hanover(Hn) SE [3], Henrico(He) SE [8], Henry(Hr) MW [2], Highland(Hi) MW [9], Isle of Wight(I) SE [6], James City(J) SE [5], King and Queen(Kq) NE-SE [3], King George(Kg) NE [9], King William(Kw) SE[3], Lancaster(La) NE-SE [9], Lee(Le) FW [10], Loudon(Lo) NE [9], Louisa(Lu) NC [3], Lunenburg(Ln) SC [2], Madison(Ma) NC [9], Mathews(Mt) SE [3], Mecklenburg(Me) SC [2], Middlesex(Mi) SE [9], Montgomery(Mo) MW [10], Nansemond(Na) SE [4], Nelson(Ne) SC [8], New Kent (Nk) SE [3], Norfolk(No) SE [4], Northampton(Nr) ES [1], Northumberland(Nt) NE [9], Nottoway(Nw) SC [2], Orange (Or) NC [9], Page(P) NC [9], Patrick(Pa) MW [2], Pittsyslvania(Pi) MW-SC [2], Powhatan(Po) SC [5], Prince Edward(Pe) SC [2], Prince George(Pg) SE [2], Prince William(Pw) NE [9], Princess Anne(Pc) SE [4], Pulaski(Pu) MW [10], Rappahannock(Ra) NC [9], Richmond(Ri) NE [9], Roanoke(Ro) MW [10], Rockbridge(Rb) MW [9], Rockingham

29

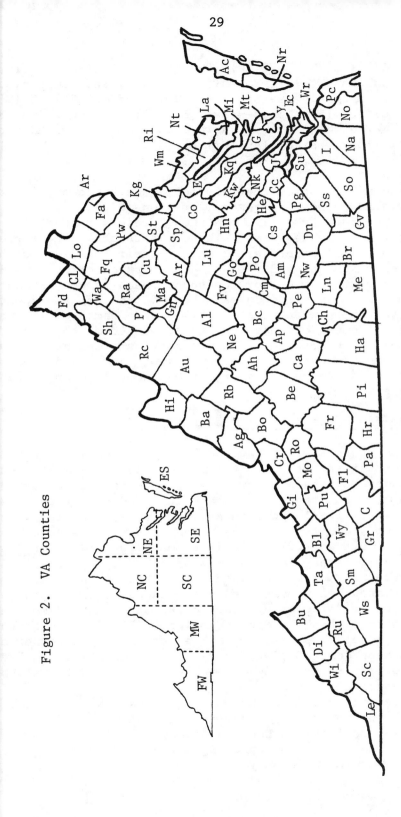

Figure 2. VA Counties

(Rc) NC [9], Russell(Ru) FW [10], Scott(Sc) FW [10],
Shenandoah(Sh) NC [9], Smyth(Sm) FW [10], Southampton(So)
SE [6], Spotsylvania(Sp) NE [9], Stafford(St) NE [9],
Surry(Su) SE [5], Sussex(Ss) SE [5], Tazewell(Ta) FW
[10], Warren(Wa) NC [9], Warwick(Wr) SE [7], Washington
(Ws) FW [10], Westmoreland(Wm) NE [9], Wise(Wi) FW [10],
Wythe(Wy) FW [10], York(Y) SE [3].

You will notice that following each county is its
abbreviation, then its general area on Figure 2, then a
number in brackets [ ]. This number refers to one of the
ten charts presented next. These charts show the forma-
tions of the counties, tracing their origins to the
counties which preceded them. The superscript e indicates that the county or the county name is now extinct,
and the asterisk * indicates that parts of the county
came from more than one county. The names of all the
ancestral counties may be obtained from the county
listings in Chapter 4. The superscript c indicates that
the county has been completely taken over and dissolved
into an independent city or cities (see the next section
for details).

11. The VA Independent Cities

The state of VA not only has counties, but in
addition there are now 41 Independent Cities. These
independent Cities are largely separate from the counties
in that when they were made Independent Cities, they
established local governments of their own including
their own courts. This means that the genealogical
searcher must not only look into county records, but must
also examine the City records if the City had been made
independent prior to the dates the searcher is interested
in. Listed below are the past and present Independent
Cities of VA followed by the date of establishment in
parentheses, then the county in which it exists is given.
In some cases, especially in the southeastern corner of
VA, Independent Cities have replaced counties and have
taken over their records. A bit more detail will be
given concerning these.
   Alexandria(1852) [known early as Hunting Creek,
      then Belhaven] in Arlington County
   Bedford(1968) in Bedford County
   Bristol(1890) [name changed from Goodson, 1852] in
      Washington County

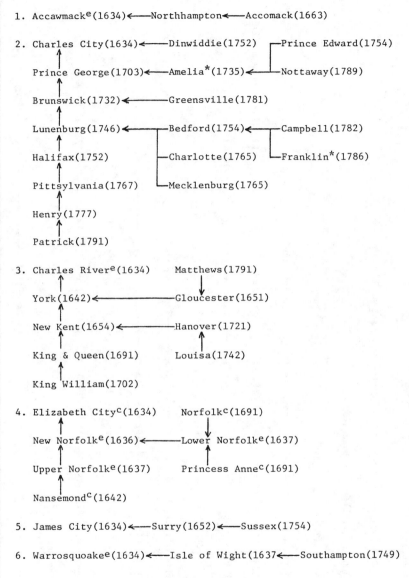

1. Accawmack^e(1634)◄——Northhampton◄——Accomack(1663)

2. Charles City(1634)◄——Dinwiddie(1752)   ┌—Prince Edward(1754)

   Prince George(1703)◄——Amelia*(1735)◄——┴—Nottaway(1789)

   Brunswick(1732)◄————Greensville(1781)

   Lunenburg(1746)◄————Bedford(1754)◄——┌—Campbell(1782)

   Halifax(1752)   ┌—Charlotte(1765) └—Franklin*(1786)

   Pittsylvania(1767) └—Mecklenburg(1765)

   Henry(1777)

   Patrick(1791)

3. Charles River^e(1634)   Matthews(1791)

   York(1642)◄————————Gloucester(1651)

   New Kent(1654)◄————Hanover(1721)

   King & Queen(1691)   Louisa(1742)

   King William(1702)

4. Elizabeth City^c(1634)   Norfolk^c(1691)

   New Norfolk^e(1636)◄————Lower Norfolk^e(1637)

   Upper Norfolk^e(1637)   Princess Anne^c(1691)

   Nansemond^c(1642)

5. James City(1634)◄——Surry(1652)◄——Sussex(1754)

6. Warrosquoake^e(1634)◄——Isle of Wight(1637◄——Southampton(1749)

7. Warwick River^e(1634)◄——Warwick^c(1642)

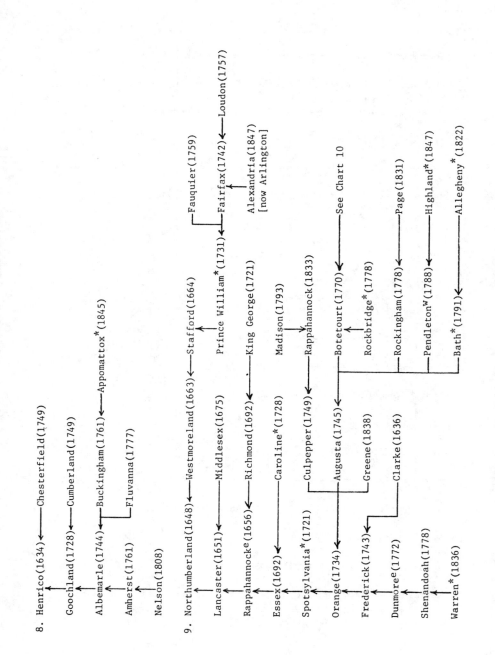

8. Henrico(1634) ← Chesterfield(1749)

Goochland(1728) ← Cumberland(1749)

Albemarle(1744) ← Buckingham(1761) ← Appomattox*(1845)

Amherst(1761) ← Fluvanna(1777)

Nelson(1808)

9. Northumberland(1648) ← Westmoreland(1663) ← Stafford(1664) ← Fauquier(1759)

Prince William*(1731) ← Fairfax(1742) ← Loudon(1757)

Alexandria(1847) [now Arlington]

Lancaster(1651) ← Middlesex(1675)

Rappahannock^e(1656) ← Richmond(1692) ← King George(1721)

Essex(1692) ← Caroline*(1728) ← Madison(1793)

Spotsylvania*(1721) ← Culpepper(1749) ← Rappahannock(1833)

Orange(1734) ← Augusta(1745) ← Botetourt(1770) ← See Chart 10

Greene(1838)

Rockbridge*(1778)

Frederick(1743) ← Clarke(1636)

Rockingham(1778) ← Page(1831)

Dunmore^e(1772) ← Shenandoah(1778)

Pendleton^w(1788) ← Highland*(1847)

Warren*(1836)

Bath*(1791) ← Allegheny*(1822)

10.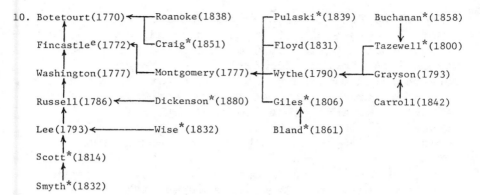

Buena Vista(1892) in Rockbridge County
Charlottesville(1888) in Albemarle County
Chesapeake(1963) produced by a merger of Norfolk County and the City of South Norfolk, all now known as Chesapeake
Clifton Forge(1906) in Allegheny County
Colonial Heights(1948) in Dinwiddie County
Covington(1954) in Allegheny County
Danville(1890) in Pittsylvania County
Emporia(1967) in Greensville County
Fairfax(1961) in Fairfax County
Falls Church(1948) in Fairfax County
Franklin(1961) in Southampton County
Fredericksburg(1879) in Spotsylvania County
Galax(1954) in Carroll County
Hampton(1908) in Elizabeth City County until 1952, at which time Hampton annexed Elizabeth City County, all now known as Hampton
Harrisonburg(1916) in Rockingham County
Hopewell(1916) in Prince George County
Lexington(1966) in Rockbridge County
Lynchburg(1852) in Campbell County
Manassas(1975) in Prince William County
Manassas Park(1975) in Prince William County
Martinsville(1928) in Henry County
Newport News(1896) in Warwick County (and part of Elizabeth City County) until 1952, when Warwick County became the independent City of Warwick, then in 1958 the independent Cities of Newport News and Warwick merged, all now called Newport News
Norfolk(1845) in Norfolk County until 1963, at which time Norfolk County and the independent City of

South Norfolk merged to form the independent City of Chesapeake, Norfolk now sits adjacent to the independent Cities of Chesapeake and Portsmouth

Norton(1954) in Wise County

Petersburg(1850) [about 1645 known at Fort Henry, then Peter's Point] at junction of Chesterfield, Dinwiddie, and Prince George Counties

Poquoson(1975) in York County

Portsmouth(1858) in Norfolk County until 1963, at which time Norfolk County and the independent City of South Norfolk merged to form the independent City of Chesapeake, Chesapeake now sits adjacent to the independent Cities of Norfolk and Portsmouth

Radford(1892) [name changed from Central City in 1890] in Montgomery County

Richmond(1782) [known as Falls of James River in 1609] in Henrico County

Roanoke(1884) [name changed from Big Lick in 1882] in Roanoke County

Salem(1968) in Roanoke County

South Boston(1960) in Halifax County

South Norfolk(1921) in Norfolk County until 1963 when Norfolk County and the independent City of South Norfolk merged to form the independent City of Chesapeake, all now called Chesapeake

Staunton(1871) in Augusta County

Suffolk(1910) in Nansemond County until 1972 when Nansemond County became the independent City of Nansemoned, then in 1974 the independent City of Suffolk merged with the independent City of Nansemond, all now called Suffolk

Virginia Beach(1952) in Princess Anne County, then in 1963 Princess Anne County was annexed by the independent City of Virginia Beach, all now called Virginia Beach

Waynesboro(1948) [name changed from Teasville in 1797] in Augusta County

Williamsburg(1722) [called the Settlement between Archer's Hope and Queenes Creeks very early, then in 1632 renamed Middle Plantation, then in 1699 Williamsburg] in James City County (and part of York County)

Winchester(1874) [at first called Frederickstown] in Frederick County

In light of this somewhat complex City-County relationship in VA, you must always take care to look into
the records of any independent City that had been established in the county where your ancestors lived. It is
important to do this even if your forebears did not live
in the City, since they may have had business and/or
legal dealings in the City and/or with persons who lived
in the City. Of course, if the City was not established
(see parenthetical dates above) until after your ancestors were gone, you need not investigate the City
records. Another item that you need to exercise some
caution about is this. Some of the VA counties carry the
word City in their names: Charles City County, Elizabeth
City County, and James City Counties. Be careful to
recognize that these are counties, not independent
Cities. Finally, please pay special attention to independent Cities which have replaced counties: (1) Norfolk,
Portsmouth, and Chesapeake replacing Norfolk County in
1963, (2) Hampton replacing Elizabeth City County in
1952, (3) Newport News replacing Warwick County in 1952-
8, (4) Suffolk replacing Nansemond County in 1972-4, and
(5) Virginia Beach replacing Princess Anne County in
1963.

Good references for further study on VA county form-
ation, organization, and development are:
__J. R. V. Daniel, A HORNBOOK OF VA HISTORY, VA Depart-
  ment of Conservation and Development, Richmond, VA,
  1949.
__M. W. Hiden, HOW JUSTICE GREW: VA COUNTIES, AN ABSTRACT
  OF THEIR FORMATION, University Press of VA, Charlottes-
  ville, VA, 1957.
__M. P. Robinson, VA COUNTIES: THOSE RESULTING FROM VA
  LEGISLATION, VA State Library, Richmond, VA, 1916.
__J. C. Gioe, THE VA LOCATOR, Ye Olde Genealogie Shoppe,
  Indianapolis, IN, 1982.

Abbreviations

ALUV	Alderman Library, University of VA
AMS	Anne M. Smalley
BLGSU	Branch Library(ies), Genealogical Society of UT
CH	Court House(s)
DARL	Daughters of American Revolution Library, Washington
GKS	George K. Schweitzer or Genealogy Kinship Sources
GSU	Genealogical Society of UT, Salt Lake City
LL	Local Library(ies)
LOC	Library of Congress
RL	Regional Library(ies)
SLCWM	Swem Library, College of William & Mary, Williamsburg
VHSL	VA Historical Society Library, Richmond
VSL&A	VA State Library and Archives, Richmond

Chapter 2

TYPES OF RECORDS

1. Introduction

The commonwealth (state) of VA is relatively rich in genealogical source materials, even though there are notable gaps in the early years, and there are problems with the loss of records in the Richmond Civil War fire and in court house (CH) fires, which were fairly common in the 18th and 19th centuries. A great deal of work has been done in accumulating, preserving, photocopying, transcribing, abstracting, printing, and indexing records. The best overall collection in or near the state is the VA State Library and Archives (VSL&A) in Richmond. They have large holdings of historical, biographical, and genealogical books, microfilms (city records, county records, state records, federal records, newspapers, censuses, military records, manuscripts), old newspapers, periodicals, manuscripts, Bible records, church records, colonial records, maps and atlases, and original documents, plus numerous indexes and finding aids. The VA Historical Society Library (VHSL), which is also in Richmond has historical, biographical, and genealogical books, old newspapers, periodicals, manuscripts, personal, family, and business papers, and Bible records. Two subsidiary genealogically-related libraries also deserve mention. The first is the Alderman Library at the University of VA (ALUV) in Charlottesville. This library has extensive collections of historical and biographical books, manuscripts, family, personal, and business papers, newspapers, church records, and several special VA historical collections. The second is the Swem Library of the College of William and Mary (SLCWM) in Williamsburg, which specializes in Colonial VA and has good holdings in manuscripts, letters, family papers, governmental papers, and other materials.

Just across the Potomac River from Alexandria, VA are three very important genealogical research facilities. The National Archives (NA) contains many federal records, both originals and copies, which bear upon VA and its people. The Library of Congress (LOC) has an extremely large collection of published materials, including a great deal pertinent to VA. In the US capital city there is also the Daughters of the American Revolution Library (DARL), which holds many local, state, and federal VA records, particularly ones relating to tracing Revolutionary War participants and their descendants, as well as numerous compilations of genealogical data not generally available in many other places.

The Genealogical Society of UT (GSU) in Salt Lake City, the largest genealogical library in the world, holds a large number of books and microfilmed copies of books and original records relating to VA. The microfilms are made available to you through their numerous Branch Libraries of the Genealogical Society of UT (BLGSU) which are located all over the US. Included among these branch libraries are seven in the state of VA.

In addition to the above collections, there are VA record collections in a number of large genealogical libraries (LGL) around the county, especially those in states near VA. Other collections, usually with emphasis on a section of VA, are located in several regional libraries (RL) in VA. Further, the county court houses (CH) in the 100 VA counties and the city buildings in several of the independent cities have many original records, particularly after 1865 (some of those before that having been deposited in VSL&A). Finally, local libraries (LL) in the county seats and independent cities often have good materials relating to their own areas. All of the libraries, archives, and repositories mentioned above will be discussed in detail in Chapter 3.

In this chapter, the many types of records which are available for VA genealogical research are discussed. Those records which are essentially national or statewide in scope will be treated in detail. Records which are basically county or city records will be mentioned and treated only generally, but detailed lists of them will be given in Chapter 4, where the major local records available for each of the 100 VA counties and several cities will be presented.

2. Bible records

During the past two hundred years it was customary for families with religious affiliations to keep vital statistics on their members in the family Bible. These records vary widely, but among the items that may be found are names, dates and places of birth, christening, baptism, marriage, death, and sometimes military service. Compilations of such Bible records have been made by the Daughters of the American Revolution (DAR) and by other agencies and individuals for various VA counties and areas. Bible records in the form of loose leaf transcriptions and copies have also been gathered by several libraries in VA, especially VSL&A and VHSL. Bible records which are not parts of compilations or special collections may be available in manuscripts which have been gathered in libraries, in published genealogies, and in genealogical periodical articles. These last three types of records will be discussed separately in other sections of this Chapter. So, this section will be devoted to Bible record compilations, both those which have been published and those collections of loose document copies which are gathered together in files or notebooks and indexed at various libraries.

Published compilations of Bible records are generally found in four main forms: books, typed compilations, handwritten compilations, and microfilms of all of these. Many of these published collections are listed in two major reference works:
__J. D. and E. D. Stemmons, VITAL RECORD COMPENDIUM, Everton Publishers, Logan, UT, 1979.
__M. J. Brown, HANDY INDEX TO THE HOLDINGS OF THE GENEA-LOGICAL SOCIETY OF UT, Everton Publishers, Logan, UT, 1971.
These references indicate that the major sources of Bible records for VA are VSL&A, VHSL, DARL, GSU, and BLGSU. In addition LL in the counties and independent cities sometimes have Bible record compilations. In Chapter 4, those counties and independent cities for which extensive Bible records exist are indicated. Instructions regarding locating the repositories and then finding the Bible records in them will be presented in Chapter 3.

In addition to county and city compilations of

records, there are some multi-county and state-wide compilations of Bible records. Included among them are:

__BIBLE RECORDS OF VA FAMILIES DEPOSITED WITH THE VA HISTORICAL SOCIETY, The Society, Richmond, VA, 1954.

__DAR of CA, BIBLE AND FAMILY RECORDS, Genealogical Records Committee of CA, DAR, Washington, DC, 1942-54, volumes 1-23.

__DAR OF FL, FAMILY, BIBLE AND CEMETERY RECORDS, The Society, Clearwater, FL, 1971-2.

__DAR OF FL, ORIGINAL BIBLE RECORDS AND WILLS, The Society, Tampa, FL, 1957-8.

__DAR OF KY, KY INSCRIPTIONS, BIBLE, AND FAMILY RECORDS, The Society, Lexington, KY, 1948.

__DAR OF LA, LA BIBLE RECORDS, COLLECTION OF BIBLE AND FAMILY RECORDS, The Society, Washington, DC, 1951 ff, several volumes.

__DAR OF VA, BIBLE RECORDS OF VA, The Society, Washington, DC, 1972.

__DAR OF VA, VA BIBLE RECORDS, listed in numerous volumes with titles such as VA BIBLE RECORDS, BIBLE RECORDS OF VA, FAMILY AND BIBLE RECORDS OF VA, RECORDS OF THE VA GENEALOGICAL RESEARCH COMMITTEE, VA FAMILY RECORDS, VA GENEALOGICAL RECORDS, MISCELLANEOUS RECORDS, all published by various Chapters of the VA DAR, all in the DAR Library, Washington, DC, publication dates, 1932 ff. [Many in VA State Library and Archives, Richmond, VA.]

__H. E. Hayden, VA GENEALOGIES, Genealogical Publishing Co., Baltimore, MD, 1979 (1891).

__M. A. Lester, OLD SOUTHERN BIBLE RECORDS, Genealogical Publishing Co., Baltimore, MD, 1974.

The large collections of Bible records in several libraries are listed in guidebooks to or indexes in these libraries:

__L. H. Hart, III, GUIDE TO BIBLE RECORDS IN THE VSL&A, The Library, Richmond, VA, 1985.

__TYPESCRIPT INDEX TO BIBLE RECORDS, VSL&A, Richmond, VA, several volumes, alphabetical by surname.

__CARD INDEX TO BIBLE RECORDS, VHSL, Richmond, VA, alphabetical by surname.

__LIBRARY CATALOG, DARL, Washington, DC, look under both state and county, then under surname.

__INDEX TO BIBLE RECORDS, ALUV, Charlottesville, VA, alphabetical by surname.

3. Biographies

There are several major national biographical works which contain sketches on nationally-eminent Virginians. If you suspect or know that your ancestor was that well-known consult:

__NATIONAL CYCLOPEDIA OF AMERICAN BIOGRAPHY, White Co., New York, NY, 1893-present, over 54 volumes, cumulative index for volumes 1-51.

__DICTIONARY OF AMERICAN BIOGRAPHY, Scribners, New York, 1928-37, 20 volumes, cumulative index.

__J. G. Wilson and J. Fiske, APPLETON'S CYCLOPEDIA OF AMERICAN BIOGRAPHY, Appleton, New York, NY, 1887-1900, 7 volumes.

__THE 20TH CENTURY BIOGRAPHICAL DICTIONARY OF NOTABLE AMERICANS, Gale Research, Detroit, MI, 1968, 10 volumes.

__AMERICAN BIOGRAPHY: A NEW CYCLOPEDIA, American Historical Society, New York, NY, 1916-33, 54 volumes, cumulative index for volumes 1-50.

__ENCYCLOPEDIA OF AMERICAN BIOGRAPHY, NEW SERIES, American Historical Co., West Palm Beach, FL, 1934-present, 4 volumes.

Most of these works and about 340 more have been indexed in a 3-volume set which gives the sources of over 3 million biographies, all arranged in alphabetical order of the names:

__M. C. Herbert and B. McNeil, BIOGRAPHY AND GENEALOGY MASTER INDEX, Gale Research Co., Detroit, MI, 1980-1, 8 volumes, with SUPPLEMENTS.

Several good biographical compilations for the commonwealth of VA or for sections of it exist. These volumes list persons who have attained some prominence in the fields of law, agriculture, business, politics, medicine, engineering, science, military, teaching, public service, or philanthropy. Your first effort should be directed to a very important compendium which indexes over 750 biographical, genealogical, and historical works, giving 6,000 family names and 18,000 references. These references are to books, journals, magazines, and newspapers. The compendium is:

__R. A. Stewart, INDEX TO PRINTED VA GENEALOGIES, Genealogical Publishing Co., Baltimore, MD, 1970 (1930). [750 books, 6,000 family names, 18,000 references.]

You can then turn your attention to the more notable of
the VA biographical works, many of which are indexed by
Stewart:

__R. A. Brock, VA AND VIRGINIANS, Reprint Co., Spartan-
burg, SC, 1973 (1888), 2 volumes.
__R. B. True, THE BIOGRAPHICAL DICTIONARY OF EARLY VA,
1607-60, Association for Preservation of VA Antiqui-
ties, Jamestown, VA, 1982. [120,000 entries, very
important!]
__A. Brown, GENESIS OF THE US, Houghton, Mifflin, Boston,
MA, 1890, volume 2. [Biographies of Virginians con-
nected with founding of VA, 1605-16.]
__P. A. Bruce, VA: A REBIRTH OF THE OLD DOMINION, LEWIS
Publ. Co., Chicago, IL, 1929, volumes 3-5.
__P. A. Bruce, L. G. Tyler, R. L. Morton, and others,
HISTORY OF VA, The American Historical Society, Chica-
go, IL, 1924, volumes 4-6.
__J. W. Campbell, A HISTORY OF VA FROM ITS DISCOVERY TILL
THE YEAR 1781, The Author, Petersburg, VA, 1813.
__T. K. Cartmell, SHENANDOAH VALLEY PIONEERS, THEIR
DESCENDANTS: A HISTORY OF FREDERICK COUNTY, 1738-1908,
VA Book Co., Berryville, VA, 1972 (1908). [9,500
names.]
__R. T. Craighill, VA PEERAGE, Jones, Richmond, VA, 1880.
__EMINENT AND REPRESENTATIVE MEN OF VA AND THE DC IN THE
19TH CENTURY, Brant and Fuller, Madison, WI, 1893.
__M. W. Fishwick, GENTLEMEN OF VA, Dodd, Mead, New York,
NY, 1971.
__W. H. Foote, SKETCHES OF VA, HISTORICAL AND BIOGRAPH-
ICAL, John Knox Press, Richmond, VA, 1956-66 (1850-55),
2 volumes.
__H. B. Handy, THE SOCIAL RECORDER OF VA, The Recorder,
Richmond, VA, 1928.
__H. Howe, HISTORICAL COLLECTIONS OF VA, Genealogical
Publ. Co., Baltimore, MD, 1969 (1845). [About 2,000
names, county-by-county biographies.]
__F. Johnston, MEMORIALS OF OLD VA CLERKS, 1634-PRESENT,
Bell, Lynchburg, VA, 1888. [Old county clerks.]
__J. E. Norris, HISTORY OF THE LOWER SHENANDOAH VALLEY,
VA Book Co., Berryville, VA, 1973 (1890).
__C. B. Polk, SOME OLD COLONIAL FAMILIES OF VA.
__M. V. Smith, VA, 1492-1892, Lowdersilk, Washington, DC,
1893. [Executives of the colony and the state of VA.]
__W. H. T. Squires, THROUGH CENTURIES THREE: A SHORT
HISTORY OF THE PEOPLE OF VA, Printcraft, Portsmouth,
VA, 1929. [Almost all biographies.]

__L. G. Tyler, ENCYCLOPEDIA OF VA BIOGRAPHY, Lewis His-
torical Publ. Co., New York, NY, 1915, 5 volumes.
__L. G. Tyler, editor, MEN OF MARK IN VA, Men of Mark
Publ. Co., Washington, DC, 1906-9, 5 volumes, plus one
further volume, Richmond, VA, 1935.
In VSL&A there is a good-sized collection of unpublished
biographies of prominent Virginians.   There is a card
index to them in the Archives Reading Room.
__CARD INDEX TO S. B. FRENCH 19TH CENTURY BIOGRAPHICAL
SKETCHES, VSL&A, Richmond, VA, Archives Reading Room,
alphabetical.

In addition to the above national, state, and
regional works, there are county and city biographical
volumes which will be indicated under the counties in
Chapter 4. Almost all of the national, state, regional,
county, and city biographical books are available at
VSL&A, VHSL, ALUV, and LOC. Many are at GSU and can be
borrowed through BLGSU. Many are also in RL in VA and
some are available in LGL, particularly those near VA.
The volumes relating to specific counties and cities are
usually available in LL of the corresponding counties and
cities.

4. Birth records

VA State law required births to be registered with
the local commissioners of revenue (tax collectors) for
1853-96. Careful enforcement was not practiced, some
records were not kept during the Civil War, and some were
destroyed in the War. Even so, they are about 65% complete. In 1896, the registration law lapsed and state-
wide record keeping of births ceased until 1912. During
1896-1912, poor or no records were kept in most places,
but fairly good records were kept by several cities and
one county: Roanoke(1896-1912), Norfolk(1896-1912),
Newport News(1896-1912), Richmond(1900-12), Portsmouth
(1900-12), Elizabeth City County(1900-12), Petersburg
(1910-2), and Lynchburg(1910-2). On 04 June 1912, a new
law took effect and state birth registration was once
more required. Again, monitoring of record collection
was not too good in the early years, but by 1917
registration was running over 90% complete. Copies of
registered birth records for 1853-96 and from 1912
forward may be obtained for a fee from:

__Bureau of Vital Statistics, James Madison Bldg., 109
Governor St., Richmond, VA 23219.
Copies of the available birth records between 1896 and
1912 for the seven cities and one county mentioned above
may be obtained for a fee from the City Public Health
Departments in the cities named and in Hampton (which
absorbed Elizabeth City County). When ordering birth
records from either the state or one of the cities, be
sure and give them as many of the following as you can:
full name, sex, race, parents' names, maiden name of
mother, approximate birth date, place, your relationship
to the person, and the reason you want the record (namely, genealogical research).

Since the birth records for the years before 1912
are not complete, those available before 1912 for each of
the 100 VA counties and for the pertinent cities are
listed in Chapter 4. You must remember that some of
these records are severely incomplete and not be surprised to find no listings for some of your ancestors.
The original records for 1853-96 are mostly in VSL&A, and
microfilm copies are available for use there. Microfilm
copies are also at GSU, which makes them obtainable
through BLGSU. Examination of them will provide you with
the information you need to request certified copies of
the records from the Bureau of Vital Statistics. Lists
of many of these microfilms and published volumes which
have been copied from the birth records will be found in:
__J. D. and E. D. Stemmons, THE VITAL RECORDS COMPENDIUM,
Everton Publishers, Logan, UT, 1979.
__M. J. Brown, HANDY INDEX TO THE HOLDINGS OF THE GENEA-
LOGICAL SOCIETY OF UT, Everton Publishers, Logan, UT,
1971.
__J. F. Dorman, editor, THE VA GENEALOGIST, volumes 3
ff., 1959 ff., records of one or more counties in each
issue.

Birth records show some or all of the following:
name, date of birth, county of birth, father's name and
occupation, mother's name, name and relationship of
informant. Prior to the time when VA required birth
registration (1853), during 1896-1912, and when you
suspect that incomplete records have omitted your ancestor, other records may yield dates and places of birth
along with the names of parents: biographical, cemetery,
census, church, death, divorce, marriage, military,

mortuary, newspaper, pension, and published. These are all discussed in other sections of this chapter. The finding of birth record articles in genealogical periodicals is also described separately in this chapter.

5. Cemetery records

If you know or suspect that your ancestor was buried in a certain VA cemetery, the best thing to do is to write to the caretaker of the cemetery, enclose an SASE and $5, and ask if the records show your ancestor. If no luck is had, try writing the local genealogical and/or historical societies (see separate sections in this chapter) inquiring about records for cemeteries in the area.

Should this prove unsuccessful, then the next step is to look into cemetery record collections for your ancestor's county. These collections have been made by the DAR, the state, regional, and local genealogical and historical societies and individuals. Sizable listings of many of the available records will be found in:
__A. M. Hogg and D. A. Tosh, VA CEMETERIES, A GUIDE TO RESOURCES, University Press of VA, Charlottesville, VA, 1986.
__J. D. and E. D. Stemmons, THE CEMETERY RECORD COMPEN-DIUM, Everton Publishers, Logan, UT, 1979.
__M. J. Brown, HANDY INDEX TO THE HOLDINGS OF THE GENEA-LOGICAL SOCIETY OF UT, Everton Publishers, Logan, UT, 1971.
When you consult these books, you will find that the main sources of VA cemetery records are VSL&A, DARL, GSU, BLGSU, and VHSL. In addition, LL in the VA counties often have records of their own cemeteries. RL in VA and LGL outside of VA may also have records. Several of the larger genealogical periodicals published in or about VA contain cemetery listings quite frequently (especially The William and Mary Quarterly, The VA Magazine of History and Biography, Tyler's Quarterly, and The VA Genealogist), and the National Genealogical Society Quarterly also carries listings. In addition, the Daughters of the American Revolution have compiled numerous records, only some of which have been published. Others still are in typed or handwritten form, but most are in the DARL.

In Chapter 4, those counties for which cemetery records exist in printed or microfilmed form are indicated. Instructions regarding locating the above records will be presented in Chapter 3. Instructions regarding the finding of cemetery records in genealogical periodical articles are given in a separate section of this chapter devoted to such periodicals.

6. Census records

Excellent ancestor information is available in nine types of census reports which have been accumulated for VA: some early resident rolls and lists in the period 1623-1789, tax substitutes for lost censuses(T), regular (R), farm and ranch(F), manufactures(M), mortality(D for death), slaveholder(S), the special 1840 Revolutionary War pension census(P), and the special 1890 Civil War veterans' census(C).

The early lists, enumerations, and polls during 1623-1789 are valuable because they provide useful data during the colonial period. Some of these listings resemble censuses, other resemble tax lists. Among the most important are:

__1623 RESIDENTS: J. C. Hotten, THE ORIGINAL LISTS OF PERSONS OF QUALITY, Baker and Co., New York, NY, 1931; also William and Mary Quarterly, volume 24, pp. 124-30.
__1624 RESIDENTS: J. C. Hotten, THE ORIGINAL LISTS OF PERSONS OF QUALITY, Baker and Co., New York, NY, 1931.
__1624 CENSUS: New England Historical and Genealogical Register, volume 31, pages 22, 147, 265, 393.
__1624/5 MUSTER ROLL: DAR of DC, MUSTER OF INHABITANTS IN VA, 1624/5, The Society, Washington, DC, 1948-9.
__1625 RESIDENTS: VA Magazine of History and Biography, volume 16, pp. 9-15.
__1625 SLAVEHOLDERS: New England Historical and Genealogical Register, volume 31, p. 22.
__1626 RESIDENTS: J. C. Hotten, THE ORIGINAL LISTS OF PERSONS OF QUALITY, Baker and Co., New York, NY, 1931.
__1704 QUIT RENTS in A. L. W. Smith, THE QUIT RENTS OF VA, 1704, Genealogical Publishing Co., Baltimore, MD 1980.
__1774-5 RESIDENTS: William and Mary College Quarterly, 1st series, volume 5, pp. 244-55.
__1775-8 PETITIONERS: VA Magazine of History and Biogra-

phy, volume 18, pp. 266-7; CARD INDEX OF PETITIONS,
1775-8, VSL&A, Richmond, VA.
__1779 LIMITED CENSUS: National Genealogical Society
Quarterly, volume 46, pp. 166-210.
__1785 PETITIONERS: William and Mary Quarterly, 1st
series, volume 20, pp. 12-15.
__1787 PENSIONERS: VA Magazine of History and Biography,
volume 50, pp. 162-8.

Tax records have been put together in order to
provide substitute records(T) for the 1790 VA census
records which were destroyed. These records list the
names of land owners along with their counties of resi-
dence plus other information in most cases.
__US Bureau of the Census, HEADS OF FAMILIES AT THE FIRST
CENSUS OF THE US TAKEN IN 1790: RECORDS OF THE STATE
ENUMERATIONS, 1782-5, Genealogical Publishing Co.,
Baltimore, MD, 1970.
__A. B. Fothergill and J. M. Naugle, VA TAX PAYERS, 1782-
7, Genealogical Publ. Co., Baltimore, MD, 1974 (1940).
[34,000 names, supplements US Bureau of Census Report.]
__N. Schreiner-Yantis, THE 1787 CENSUS OF VA, GBIP,
Springfield, VA, 1987.
Census records for 1800 are available for only two
counties (Accomack and Louisa), but a leading VA
genealogical journal is in the process of printing alpha-
betical tax lists for the VA counties in 1800. These
records are to be found in:
__ACCOMACK COUNTY CENSUS, original in Accomack CH at
Accomac, microfilm copy in VSL&A, Richmond, VA.
__1800 LOUISA COUNTY CENSUS, Louisa County Historical
Magazine, volume 4, number 1, 1972, in VSL&A, Richmond,
VA.
__COUNTY TAX LISTS FOR 1800, The VA Genealogist, volume 1
and after, 1957 and after.
Chapter 4 lists the 1790 and 1800 tax-substitute census
records(T) available for each of the VA counties in
existence at these times.

The 1810 regular(R) Federal Census for VA is incomplete with 19 counties missing. Fortunately, tax records
for these 19 counties have been gathered to form a supplement which completes the 1810 census. These records
are available as:
__M. W. Crickard, 1810 CENSUS, The Author, Beverly, WV,
1971 ff, 80 volumes.

_ US National Archives, THIRD CENSUS OF THE US, 1810, VA,
The Archives, Washington, DC, M252, microfilm rolls 66–71.

_ N. Schreiner-Yantis, A SUPPLEMENT TO THE 1810 CENSUS OF
VA, The Author, Springfield, VA, 1971. [Supplement to
regular 1810 census.]

Regular census records(R) are available for all VA
counties in 1820, 1830, 1840, 1850, 1860, 1870, 1880,
1900, and 1910. The 1840 census and all before it listed
the head of the household plus a breakdown of the number
of persons in the household according to age and sex
brackets. Beginning in 1850, the names of all persons
were recorded along with age, sex, real estate, marital,
and other information, including the state of birth. With
the 1880 census and thereafter, the birthplaces of the
mother and father of each person are also shown. Chapter
4 lists the regular census records(R) available for each
of the 100 VA counties.

_ US National Archives, FOURTH CENSUS OF THE US, 1820,
VA, The Archives, Washington, DC, M33, microfilm rolls
139–142.

_ US National Archives, FIFTH CENSUS OF THE US, 1830, VA,
The Archives, Washington, DC, M19, microfilm rolls 189–201.

_ US National Archives, SIXTH CENSUS OF THE US, 1840, VA,
The Archives, Washington, DC, M704, microfilm rolls
549–579.

_ US National Archives, SEVENTH CENSUS OF THE US, 1850,
VA, The Archives, Washington, DC, M432, microfilm rolls
932–982.

_ US National Archives, EIGHTH CENSUS OF THE US, 1860,
VA, The Archives, Washington, DC, M653, microfilm rolls
1330–1385.

_ US National Archives, NINTH CENSUS OF THE US, 1870, VA,
The Archives, Washington, DC, M593, microfilm rolls
1630–1682.

_ US National Archives, TENTH CENSUS OF THE US, 1880, VA,
The Archives, Washington, DC, T9, microfilm rolls 1341–1395.

_ US National Archives, TWELFTH CENSUS OF THE US, 1900,
VA, The Archives, Washington, DC, T623, microfilm rolls
1697–1740.

_ US National Archives, THIRTEENTH CENSUS OF THE US,
1910, The Archives, Washington, DC, T624, microfilm
rolls 1619–1652.

The 1790 census-substitute tax records are indexed in the published volumes mentioned above, and the 1800 census-substitute tax records are indexed county-by-county in the magazine The VA Genealogist, as referenced above. Indexes have been printed for the 1810, 1820, 1830, 1840, and 1850 regular census records, and some counties have been indexed for later years. Chief among these indexes are:

___E. P. Bentley, INDEX TO THE 1810 CENSUS OF VA, Genealogical Publ. Co., Baltimore, MD, 1980.

___M. W. Crickard, INDEX TO THE 1810 VA CENSUS, The Author, Beverly, WV, 1971.

___R. V. Jackson and G. R. Teeples, VA 1810 CENSUS, Accelerated Indexing Systems, Bountiful, UT, 1974.

___J. R. Felldin, INDEX TO THE 1820 CENSUS OF VA, Genealogical Publ. Co., Baltimore, MD, 1976.

___R. V. Jackson, VA 1820 CENSUS INDEX, Accelerated Indexing Systems, Bountiful, UT, 1976.

___R. V. Jackson, G. R. Teeples, and D. Schaefer-Meyer, VA 1830 CENSUS INDEX, Accelerated Indexing Systems, Bountiful, UT, 1976.

___R. V. Jackson and G. R. Teeples, VA 1840 CENSUS INDEX, Accelerated Indexing Systems, Bountiful, UT, 1977.

___R. V. Jackson and G. R. Teeples, VA 1850 CENSUS INDEX, Accelerated Indexing Systems, Bountiful, UT, 1976.

In addition to these bound indexes, there is a microfilm index which contains only families with a child 10 or under in the 1880 censuses. There are also complete microfilm indexes to the 1900 and 1910 census. All three of these indexes are arranged by a sound-related system which librarians or archivists can show you how to use.

___US National Archives, INDEX (SOUNDEX) TO THE 1880 POPULATION SCHEDULES, VA, T776, microfilm rolls 1-82.

___US National Archives, INDEX (SOUNDEX) TO THE 1900 POPULATION SCHEDULES, VA, T1076, microfilm rolls 1-164.

___US National Archives, INDEX (MIRACODE) TO THE 1910 POPULATION SCHEDULES, VA, T1278, microfilm rolls.

Unfortunately, no overall indexes to the VA 1860 and VA 1870 censuses are available.

The above indexes are exceptionally valuable as time-saving devices. However, some of the computer-published volumes have enough errors in them that you need to use them with caution. If you do not find your ancestor in them, do not conclude that he or she is not in the state; this may mean only that your forebear has been accidentally omitted or that the name has been misread. Once you have located an ancestor in the indexes, you can then go directly to the reference in the census microfilms and read the entry. When indexes are not available (chiefly 1860, 1870, and partially 1880), it is necessary for you to go through the census listings entry-by-entry. This can be essentially prohibitive for the entire state, so it is necessary to know the county in order to limit your search. Both the census indexes and the census microfilms are available in VSL&A, ALUV, NA, GSU, BLGSU, and in some LGL, RL, and LL. Other LGL, RL, and LL have the printed indexes but not the microfilmed indexes or censuses. The regional branches of the NA also have the indexes and microfilms of the censuses. They are located in or near Boston, New York, Philadelphia, Chicago, Atlanta, Kansas City, Fort Worth, Denver, San Francisco, Los Angeles, and Seattle. Their exact addresses can be obtained from telephone directories in these cities or from:

__National Archives and Records Service, REGIONAL BRANCHES OF THE NATIONAL ARCHIVES, Leaflet No. 22, The Archives, Washington, DC, 1980.

The NA microfilm indexes and censuses can also be borrowed on interlibrary loan from your local library (through AGLL).

Farm and ranch census records(F), also known as agricultural census records, are available for 1850, 1860, 1870, and 1880 for VA. These records list the name of the owner, size of the farm or ranch, value of the property, and other details. If your ancestor was a farmer (many were), it will be worthwhile to seek him in these records. No indexes are available, so it helps to know the county. Microfilm copies of the records are available at VSL&A and NA.

Manufactures census records(M) are available for 1850, 1860, 1870, and 1880. These records list manufacturing firms which produced articles having an annual value of $500 or more. Given in the records are the name of the firm, the owner, the product(s), the machinery used, and the number of employees. No indexes are available, so a knowledge of the county is helpful. The microfilmed records are available at VSL&A and NA.

Mortality census records(D for death) are available for the periods June 01, 18-9-to-May 31, 1850, 1860, 1870, and 1880. These records give information on persons who died in the year preceding the 1st of June of each of the census dates: 1850, 1860, 1870, 1880. The data contained in the compilations include name, age, sex, occupation, place of birth, and other information. The records or copies of them are located at VSL&A and NA. Indexed forms of the records are scheduled for publication soon:

___VA MORTALITY CENSUS SCHEDULE, 1850 (1860, 1870, 1880), Accelerated Indexing Systems, Salt Lake City, UT, 1986-8.

Slaveholder census records(S) for 1850 and 1860 are available. No indexes have been compiled, so it is important to know the county. The records list the names of slaveholders along with the number of slaves. The microfilmed records are available at VSL&A and NA.

In 1840, a special census of Revolutionary War Pensioners(P) was taken. This compilation was an attempt to list all pension holders, however, there are some omissions and some false entries. The list and an index have been published:

___CENSUS OF PENSIONERS, A GENERAL INDEX FOR REVOLUTIONARY OR MILITARY SERVICE (1840), Genealogical Publ. Co., Baltimore, MD, 1965.

This volume may be found at VSL&A, VHSL, LOC, DARL, GSU, and BLGSU, in many LGL and RL, and in some LL.

In 1890, a special census of Civil War Union Veterans(C) was taken. Please note that only Union veterans were listed, so, as you might expect there are only two microfilm rolls for VA. These records are arranged by county, so a knowledge of your veteran's county will help. However, with only two rolls of microfilm to search through, a long search will not be required. Microfilm copies of the records are available at VSL&A, NA, GSU, and BLGSU, and some RL. These records show the veteran's name, widow (if applicable), rank, company, regiment or ship, and other pertinent military data.

7. Church records

Many early VA families were affiliated with a church, the major denominations being Baptist, Catholic, Christian [Disciples of Christ], Episcopal [the established church until 1786], Friends [Quakers], German Reformed, Huguenot, Jewish, Lutheran, Methodist, Moravian, Presbyterian, and Unitarian-Universalist. The records of these churches often prove very valuable since they frequently contain information on births, christenings, baptisms, marriages, deaths, admissions, dismissals, and reprimands. The data are particularly important for the years before county or state vital records were kept. Some of these church records have been copied into books or microfilmed, some have been sent to denominational or state archives, but many remain in the individual churches. Several major works list sizable numbers of available church records or give sources for them:

__J. D. and E. D. Stemmons, THE VITAL RECORDS COMPENDIUM, Everton Publishers, Logan, UT, 1979.

__E. K. Kirkham, A SURVEY OF AMERICAN CHURCH RECORDS, Everton Publishers, Logan, UT, 1971, 21 volumes, especially pp. 195-206 of volume 1.

__E. I. Binsfield, CHURCH ARCHIVES IN THE US AND CANADA, American Archivist, volume 21, 1958, pp. 311-32.

__M. E. Deutrich, AMERICAN CHURCH ARCHIVES, American Archivist, volume 24, 1961, pp. 387-402.

__Society of American Archivists, A PRELIMINARY GUIDE TO CHURCH RECORD REPOSITORIES, The Society, Washington, DC, 1969.

__M. J. Brown, HANDY INDEX TO THE HOLDINGS OF THE GENEALOGICAL SOCIETY OF UT, Everton Publishers, Logan, UT, 1971.

Especially pertinent to VA are the following volumes:

__J. T. Clark and E. T. Long, A GUIDE TO CHURCH RECORDS IN THE ARCHIVES BRANCH, VSL&A, VA State Library, Richmond, VA, 1981.

__Historical Records Survey of VA, INVENTORY OF CHURCH ARCHIVES OF VA, The Survey, Richmond, VA, 1939.

__BIBLIOGRAPHY OF ORIGINAL BAPTIST CHURCH RECORDS IN THE VA BAPTIST HISTORICAL SOCIETY, UNIVERSITY OF RICHMOND, University of VA Library, Charlottesville, VA, 1937.

__J. S. Rawlings, VA COLONIAL CHURCHES, Barrett and Massie, Richmond, VA, 1963.

Use of the above books and articles will convince you that the major sources of church records are the individual churches, VSL&A, VHSL, ALUV, SCLWM, DARL, GSU, BLGSU, and some other specialized repositories. In addition to these, LL may have some records for their own areas, as is often the case for RL. The card catalogs of the above libraries and archives need to be carefully examined for their church record holdings. And, in some of them, there are special indexes which will lead you to church records. The holdings of VSL&A are listed in the book by Clark and Long mentioned above. At VHSL and ALUV, you should consult the:

__CARD INDEX OF MANUSCRIPT MATERIALS, VHSL, Richmond, VA.
__CARD INDEX TO MANUSCRIPTS, ALUV, Charlottesville, VA, look under church records, denominations, counties, and cities.

Other repositories which could be pertinent are the following. Baptist church records for VA are in the churches and at the VA Baptist Historical Society, University of Richmond, Richmond, VA. A bibliography of the records at the Society was mentioned above. It is considerably out of date, so remember that it is incomplete. Catholic records are usually to be found in the parishes and sometimes in the diocesan offices. The following book contains a bibliography on VA Catholic church history:

__E. R. Vollman, THE CATHOLIC CHURCH IN AMERICA, St. Louis University Press, St. Louis, MO.
Until 1820, VA Catholic churches were under the Diocese of Baltimore, then 1820-2 in the Diocese of Richmond, then 1822-40 back in the Diocese of Baltimore, then since 1840 under a reestablished Diocese of Richmond. Records of Episcopal (Anglican, Church of England) churches, which was the colonial church of VA, were taken over by the state when the church was disestablished (1786), but unfortunately, few have survived. The VSL&A has the registers of only 13 out of over 100 parishes. Many records survive from the period after 1786. The VA Episcopal Historian may be addressed at the Diocese of VA, Mayo Memorial Church House, 110 West Franklin, Richmond, VA 23220. Friends' (Quaker) records for VA have been collected in:

__W. W. Hinshaw and T. W. Marshall, ENCYCLOPEDIA OF AMERICAN QUAKER GENEALOGY, Genealogical Publ. Co., Baltimore, MD, 1973 (1950), volume 6.

There are copies of other records in the Valentine Museum
(Richmond), the Library of Swarthmore College (Swarthmore, PA), and the Library of Haverford College (Haverford, PA). Many German Reformed and Lutheran church
records are in VSL&A. Other Lutheran records are in the
Archives of the Synod of VA at the Church House, 317
Washington Ave., SW, in Roanoke. Records kept by
churches of the Evangelical and Reformed denomination are
held in their Historical Society at Franklin and Marshall
College in Lancaster, PA. Huguenot church data and
history are available in three publications, two books
and several volumes of a periodical:
__R. A. Brock, DOCUMENTS RELATING TO THE HUGUENOT EMIGRA-
TION TO VA, Genealogical Publ. Co., Baltimore, MD, 1973
(1886).
__R. A. Brock, HUGUENOT EMIGRATION TO VA, Genealogical
Publ. Co., Baltimore, MD, 1979 (1886).
__Huguenot Society of the Founders of Manakin in the
Colony of VA, THE HUGUENOT, The Society, Vallejo, CA
and Richmond, VA, 1924-54, 16 volumes.
The early history of the Jewish faith in VA centered
around the Beth Shalom and the Beth Ahabah congregations
in Richmond. The latter ministered to Jews throughout VA
for many years until other congregations called rabbis.
Records were kept by the individual congregations, however, much early data on Jews throughout the state is
found in Bath Ahabah's records. Some Methodist records
are in the Library at Randolph-Macon College in Ashland,
VA, and others in the archives of the United Methodist
Historical Society, 2200 St. Paul St., Baltimore, MD.
Information on Methodist church histories can often be
obtained at the United Methodist VA Conference Bldg.,
4016 West Broad St., Richmond, VA. Moravian records of
quite some extent for VA are incorporated in:
__A. L. Fries and others, RECORDS OF THE MORAVIANS IN NC,
1752-1879, Edwards & Broughton, Raleigh, NC, 11 volumes.
Presbyterian records for many churches have been collected in the Library at Union Theological Seminary in
Richmond.
__RECORDS OF THE SYNOD OF VA ON MICROFILM, The Library,
Union Theological Seminary, Richmond, VA, 1970, 510
reels of microfilm, printed index.
The book by Clark and Long mentioned in the first paragraph, gives capsule histories of denominations in VA,
references to volumes on church history, locations of

colonial parish registers and vestry books, and refers
you to records in other locations.

Should you have the good fortune to know your ancestor's church, you can write directly, enclosing $5 and an
SASE, and requesting a search of the records or information on the location of the records. In Chapter 4,
counties which have church records in published or microfilmed form are indicated. Instructions regarding the
above referenced volumes and locating the records will be
given in a section to follow.

If, as is often the case, you do not know your
ancestor's church, you will need to dig deeper. Knowing
his nationality, his county, and perhaps some other
pertinent details which will permit some good guesses
about his denomination, you should write some letters.
Send an SASE to the LL, the local genealogical society,
and/or the local historical society, and ask them about
churches which your ancestor might have belonged to and
the availability of records. Names and addresses of
these organizations are given under the various counties
in Chapter 4. If these procedures still do not yield
data, then it might be well for you to contact the headquarters of the denomination you think your ancestor may
have belonged to. Remember that English immigrants were
usually Episcopalian, Methodist, or Congregational,
Germans and Swiss were usually Lutheran or Reformed
(although those from southern Germany were often Catholic), the Scotch-Irish were generally Presbyterian or
Friends, the Dutch were Reformed, the Swedes Lutheran,
and the Irish usually Catholic. The denominational
headquarters can usually give you a list of the churches
of their denomination in a given county and the dates of
their origins. Often they can also direct you to collections of church records. A list of denominational headquarters and instructions for writing them will be found
in:
___The Cache Genealogical Library, HANDBOOK FOR GENEALOGI-
   CAL CORRESPONDENCE, Everton Publishers, Logan, UT,
   1974.
Many VA city and county histories contain histories of
individual churches. These city and county histories are
discussed in section 9 of this chapter. Further references to religious groups will be found in:

___ O. K. Miller, MIGRATION, EMIGRATION, IMMIGRATION, Everton Publishers, Logan, UT, 1974, 1981, 2 volumes.

There are also histories of most denominations during the early years of VA. They may be located in VSL&A, VHSL, ALUV, LOC, RL, GSU, BLGSU, LGL, and some LL by looking up the denominational name in the card catalog (or in the case of GSU and BLGSU under the general VA listings in their local index).

8. City directories

During the 19th century many larger cities in the US began publishing city directories. These volumes usually appeared erratically at first, but then began to come out annually a little later on. They list heads of households and workers plus their addresses and occupations. The earliest series of directories in VA were for Norfolk (1801, 1806-7, 1851-2, 1859-60, etc.) and Richmond (1819, 1845-6, 1850-2, 1855-6, 1858-1901). In 1851 there was a Statewide Directory, and in 1852 a VA Business Register contained information on Alexandria, Augusta, Norfolk, Petersburg, Portsmouth, Richmond, Staunton, and Winchester. The 1859-60 Richmond Directory also contains listings for Norfolk, Petersburg, and Portsmouth. In general, the smaller cities and towns of VA did not begin regular publications until late in the 19th century or in the 20th century. Many of these directories are available in VSL&A, VHSL, ALUV, and the LOC. LL may also have collections pertaining to their own cities. Those counties having cities with early city directories are listed in Chapter 4.

The telephone was invented in 1876-7, underwent rapid development, and became widespread fairly quickly. By the late years of the century telephone directories were coming into existence. Older issues can often be found in LL, and as the years go on, they have proved to be ever more valuable genealogical sources.

9. City and county histories

Histories for many VA counties and numerous VA cities have been published. These volumes usually contain biographical data on leading citizens, details about early settlers, histories of organizations, businesses,

trades, and churches, and often list clergymen, lawyers,
physicians, teachers, governmental officials, farmers,
military men, and other groups. Several works which list
many of these histories are:
__M. J. Kaminkow, US LOCAL HISTORIES IN THE LOC, Magna
  Carta, Baltimore, MD, 1975, 4 volumes.
__P. W. Filby, BIBLIOGRAPHY OF AMERICAN COUNTY HISTORIES,
  Genealogical Publ. Co., Baltimore, MD, 1985.
__D. Haynes, editor, VIRGINIANA IN THE PRINTED BOOK COL-
  LECTIONS OF THE VA STATE LIBRARY, VA State Library,
  Richmond, VA, 1975, vol. 2.
__R. O. Hummel, Jr., VA LOCAL HISTORY: A BIBLIOGRAPHY, VA
  State Library, Richmond, VA, 1876 (1971).

    Most of the VA volumes in these bibliographies can
be found in VSL&A, VHSL, ALUV, and LOC, many are available at GSU and thus through BLGSU, and some are usually
in LGL.   RL and LL are likely to have those relating to
their particular areas. In Chapter 4, you will find
listed under the counties various recommended county
histories. Not all are listed, only the better one(s)
for each county. There will also be an indication under
each county which has city histories available.

10. Colonial record compilations

    The colonial period for VA extended from 1607 until
1776, during which time the area was a colony either
sponsored by or directly related to Great Britain.   Many
other sections in this chapter describe specific types of
records relating to colonial VA, particularly sections 3,
4, 5, 7, 9, 11, 13, 15, 16, 17, 18, 22, 23, 24, 25, 32,
34, and 35. This section, therefore, will be made up of
two sub-sections, one dealing with general reference
materials to all the colonies (including VA), a second
dealing with general reference materials to colonial VA.

    Among the important genealogical materials relating
to all the colonies are the following. They should be
consulted as you search for your colonial VA ancestor.
However, some of these volumes must be used with care,
since much of the information is them is not from original sources, and is therefore often inaccurate.
__F. A. Virkus, THE ABRIDGED COMPENDIUM OF AMERICAN
  GENEALOGY, Genealogical Publ. Co., Baltimore, MD, 1968

(1925-42), 7 volumes. [425,000 names of colonial people]

__G. M. MacKenzie and N. O. Rhoades, COLONIAL FAMILIES OF THE USA, Genealogical Publ. Co., Baltimore, MD, 1966 (1907-20), 7 volumes. [125,000 names]

__H. Whittemore, GENEALOGICAL GUIDE TO THE EARLY SETTLERS OF AMERICA, Genealogical Publ. Co., Baltimore, MD, 1967 (1898-1906).

__T. P. Hughes and others, AMERICAN ANCESTRY, Genealogical Publ. Co., Baltimore, MD, 1968 (1887-9), 12 volumes.

__BURKE'S DISTINGUISHED FAMILIES OF AMERICA, Burke's Peerage, London, England, 1948.

__W. M. Clemens, AMERICAN MARRIAGE RECORDS BEFORE 1699, Genealogical Publ. Co., Baltimore, MD, 1967 (1926-30). [10,000 entries]

__C. E. Banks, PLANTERS OF THE COMMONWEALTH, Genealogical Publ. Co., Baltimore, MD, 1972.

__G. R. Crowther, III, SURNAME INDEX TO 65 VOLUMES OF COLONIAL AND REVOLUTIONARY PEDIGREES, National Genealogical Society, Washington, DC, 1964.

__M. B. Colket, Jr., FOUNDERS OF EARLY AMERICAN FAMILIES, Order of Founders and Patriots of America, Cleveland, OH, 1975.

__H. K. Eilers, NSDAC BICENTENNIAL ANCESTOR INDEX, National Society Daughters of American Colonists, Ft. Worth, TX, 1976.

__National Society of Daughters of Founders and Patriots of America, FOUNDERS AND PATRIOTS OF AMERICA INDEX, The Society, Washington, DC, 1975.

__National Society of the Colonial Dames of America, REGISTER OF ANCESTORS, The Society, Richmond, VA, 1979.

__N. Currer-Briggs, COLONIAL SETTLERS AND ENGLISH ADVENTURERS, Genealogical Publ. Co., Baltimore, MD, 1971.

__P. W. Filby and M. K. Meyer, PASSENGER AND IMMIGRATION LIST INDEX, Gale Research Co., Detroit, MI, 1981, 3 volumes. [300 sources, 480,000 names]

__W. A. Crozier, KEY TO SOUTHERN PEDIGREES, Southern Book Co., Baltimore, MD, 1953 (1911). [7,000 listings]

__G. F. T. Sherwood, AMERICAN COLONISTS IN ENGLISH RECORDS, Sherwood, London, England, 1932, 2 volumes.

__P. W. Coldham, ENGLISH ESTATES OF AMERICAN COLONISTS, Genealogical Publ. Co., Baltimore, MD, 1980-1, 3 volumes.

__J. C. Hotten, THE ORIGINAL LISTS OF PERSONS OF QUALITY, Genealogical Publ. Co., Baltimore, MD, 1980 (1874).

__S. P. Hardy, COLONIAL FAMILIES OF THE SOUTHERN STATES OF AMERICA, Genealogical Publ. Co., Baltimore, MD, 1981 (1958).

__National Society Colonial Daughters of the 17th Century, LINEAGE BOOK, The Society, Rotan, TX, 1982 (1979). [2,000 names]

There are also important genealogical compendia relating specifically to colonial VA which you should search. The four sources which are the most important, and therefore should be examined first are:

__N. M. Nugent, CAVALIERS AND PIONEERS: ABSTRACTS OF VA LAND PATENTS AND GRANTS, 1623, 1732, Genealogical Publ. Co., Baltimore, MD, 1977-9 (1934), 3 volumes. [very important, over 80,000 listings]

__G. C. Greer, EARLY VA IMMIGRANTS, 1623-66, Genealogical Publ. Co., Baltimore, MD, 1973 (1912). [25,000 names, important volume]

__E. G. Swem, VA HISTORICAL INDEX, Peter Smith, Northampton, MA, 1965 (1934-6), 4 volumes.

__R. B. True, THE BIOGRAPHICAL DICTIONARY OF EARLY VA, 1607-60, Association for Preservation of VA Antiquities, Jamestown, VA, 1982. [over 120,000 entries]

Among the other significant volumes which may merit your attention as you further the quest for your colonial VA forebears are:

__AMERICAN COLONIAL AND FRONTIER SERIES: EARLY VA, Accelerated Indexing Systems, Salt Lake City, UT, 1982, 2 volumes.

__L. C. Bell, THE OLD FREE STATE: A CONTRIBUTION TO THE HISTORY OF LUNENBURG COUNTY AND SOUTHSIDE VA, Genealogical Publ. Co., Baltimore, MD, 1974 (1927). [20,000 Southside listings, very important for Southside]

__L. C. Bell, SUNLIGHT ON THE SOUTHSIDE: LIST OF TITHES, LUNENBURG COUNTY, 1748-83, Genealogical Publishing Co., Baltimore, MD, 1974 (1931). [10,000 early people between James River and NC]

__J. B. Boddie, COLONIAL SURRY, Genealogical Publ. Co., Baltimore, MD, 1974 (1948). [early Surry covered almost all of southern VA]

__W. F. Boogher, GLEANINGS OF VA HISTORY: AN HISTORICAL AND GENEALOGICAL COLLECTION, Genealogical Publ. Co., Baltimore, MD, 1965 (1903).

__L. J. Cappon and S. F. Duff, VA GAZETTE INDEX, 1736-80, Institute of Early History and Culture, Williamsburg, VA, 1950, 2 volumes.

J. J. Casey, PERSONAL NAMES IN HENING'S STATUTES AND SHEPHERD'S CONTINUATION, Genealogical Publ. Co., Baltimore, MD, 1967 (1896). [22,500 names]

W. A. Crozier, VA COUNTY RECORDS, Genealogical Publ. Co., Baltimore, MD, 1965-73 (1905-13), 11 volumes. [very early records]

N. Currer-Briggs, VA SETTLERS AND ENGLISH ADVENTURERS: ABSTRACTS OF WILLS, 1484-1798, AND LEGAL PROCEEDINGS: 1566-1700, Genealogical Publ. Co., Baltimore, MD, 1970. [12,000 names, 400 families]

L. O. Duvall, VA COLONIAL ABSTRACTS, Series 1 and 2.

L. des Cognets, Jr., ENGLISH DUPLICATES OF LOST VA RECORDS, The Author, Princeton, NJ, 1960. [pioneer VA records, 17th and early 18th centuries]

B. Fleet, VA COLONIAL ABSTRACTS, Genealogical Publ. Co., Baltimore, MD, 1961-71 (1973-49), 34 volumes. [early records of 13 counties, very important]

L. P. Foley, EARLY VA FAMILIES ALONG THE JAMES RIVER, The Author, Richmond, VA, 1974. [Henrico and Goochland Counties]

J. H. Gwathney, TWELVE VA COUNTIES WHERE THE WESTERN MIGRATION BEGAN, Genealogical Publ. Co., Baltimore, MD, 1981 (1937). [Albemarle, Augusta, Caroline, Essex, Gloucester, Goochland, Hanover, King William, King and Queen, Louisa, New Kent, Orange]

R. V. Jackson, A. Polson, S. P. Zachrison, and L. V. Jackson, EARLY AMERICAN SERIES, EARLY VA, 1600-1789, AIS, Bountiful, UT, 1980, 2 volumes.

A. L. Jester with M. W. Hiden, ADVENTURES OF PURSE AND PERSON, VA, 1607-25, Order of the First Families of VA, Richmond, VA, 1964. [very early VA families]

F. B. Kegley, KEGLEY'S VA FRONTIER, 1740-83, The Author, Roanoke, VA, 1967. [early Botetourt, Washington, Fincastle, Montgomery, and Wythe Counties]

S. M. Kingsbury, VA COMPANY OF LONDON RECORDS, Government Printing Office, Washington, DC, 1906-35, 4 volumes, plus introductory volume. [covers 1619-24]

E. Lawrence-Dow, VA RENT ROLLS, 1704, The Author, Richmond, VA, 1976. [5,544 land owners]

J. N. Meredith, GENEALOGICAL RESOURCES FOR 18TH CENTURY RESEARCH FOUND IN THE LIBRARY OF CONGRESS, Virginia Tidewater Genealogy, 1975, volume 6, number 4, pp. 121-6.

H. R. McIlwaine, editor, MINUTES OF THE COUNCIL AND GENERAL COURT OF COLONIAL VA, 1622-32, 1670-6, The

Colonial Press, Richmond, VA, 1924. [extensive surname index]
__Order of the First Families of VA, LIST OF MEMBERSHIP, 1912-71, The Order, Washington, DC, 1972.
__Public Record Office of Great Britain, HISTORY, DE-SCRIPTION, RECORD GROUPS, FINDING AIDS, AND MATERIALS FOR AMERICAN HISTORY WITH SPECIAL REFERENCE TO VA, VA State Library, Richmond, VA, 1960.
__PUBLISHED COLONIAL RECORDS OF THE AMERICAN COLONIES, VA: ROLLS OF MICROFILM-CR62 (W. W. Hening, editor, THE STATUTES AT LARGE, 1619-1792), CR63 (S. M. Kingsbury, editor, RECORDS OF THE VA COMPANY OF LONDON), CR64 (H. R. McIlwaine and W. L. Hall, editor, EXECUTIVE JOURNALS OF THE COUNCIL OF COLONIAL VA, 1680-1775), CR65 (H. R. McIlwaine, editor, JOURNALS OF THE COUNCIL OF THE STATE OF VA, 1776-81), CR66 (J. P. Kennedy and H. R. McIl-waine, editors, JOURNALS OF THE HOUSE OF BURGESSES OF VA, 1619-1776), CR67 (H. R. McIlwaine, editor, LEGISLA-TIVE JOURNALS OF THE COUNCIL OF COLONIAL VA), CR68 (H. R. McIlwaine, MINUTES OF THE COUNCIL AND GENERAL COURT OF COLONIAL VA, 1622-32, 1670-6), CR69 (B. Fleet, editor, VA COLONIAL ABSTRACTS, 1652-1820), CR70 (T. H. Wynne and W. S. Gilman, editors, COLONIAL RECORDS OF VA, 1619-80), most of these records available also in printed form. [Genealogical content varies widely, as does indexing]
__H. G. Somerby, PASSENGERS FOR VA, 1635, New England Historical and Genealogical Register (1848-61), volumes 2-15.
__W. G. Stanard, SOME EMIGRANTS TO VA, Genealogical Publ. Co., Baltimore, MD, 1972 (1915). [several hundred emigrants]
__W. G. and M. N. Stanard, THE COLONIAL VA REGISTER, 1607-1776, Genealogical Publ. Co., Baltimore, Me, 1965 (1902). [lists of governmental officials]
__C. Torrence, A TRIAL BIBLIOGRAPHY OF COLONIAL VA, 1608-1776, VA State Library, Richmond, VA, 1908, 1910, 2 volumes.
__VA Committee on Colonial Records, CALENDAR OF VA State Papers, 1652-1869, Kraus Reprint Corp., New York, NY, 1967 (1875-93), 11 volumes. [much genealogical data]
__VA State Library, JUSTICES OF THE PEACE IN COLONIAL VA, 1757-77, Bottom, VA, 1922.
__W. K. Winfree, THE LAWS OF VA: A SUPPLEMENT TO HENING, 1700-50, VA State Library, Richmond, VA, 1971. [limi-ted genealogical information]

L. Withington, VA GLEANINGS IN ENGLAND, Genealogical Publ. Co., Baltimore, MD, 1980 (1903-29). [15,000 colonists]

This is quite a long list of possible sources, but you need to remember that VA was the first among the colonies, and therefore, it has the longest colonial period. The amount of genealogical data in these materials varies widely, so some brief notes have been appended to them to alert you to their pertinence and their value.

Most of the works mentioned in the two preceding paragraphs will be found in VSL&A and LOC, many of them in VHSL, ALUV, and GSU (the latter's holdings being available through BLGSU), and some in LGL, RL, and LL.

11. Court records

Among the most unexplored genealogical source materials are certain types of court records of the VA counties and cities. They are often exceptionally valuable, giving information that often is obtainable nowhere else. It is therefore of great importance that you carefully examine all available court documents. There are two minor difficulties that need to be recognized if you are not to miss data. The first is that there were several types of courts, some no longer exist, some replaced others, some had their names changed, often their jurisdictions overlapped, and further, the exact court situation varies from county to county. All this is complicated more since there are also independent city courts whose jurisdictions sometimes overlap and/or interlock with the counties. You are likely to run into records of the Governor and Council acting as the judiciary (until 1619), the Governor, Council, and Burgesses acting as the judiciary (after 1619), monthly courts (after 1623), county courts replacing monthly courts (after 1642), quarter courts, the Assembly acting as the state supreme court, the orphans courts, the district courts (after 1792), the supreme court, the circuit courts (replacing district courts after 1809), hustings courts, courts of law and chancery, chancery courts, corporation courts, and perhaps others. The second difficulty is that the records of the different courts appear in record books, file cabinets, and filing boxes with various titles and labels. These titles and labels do not always describe everything contained, and records of various types may be mixed up or they may all appear in a single set of books. This is especially true in the earlier years. Fortunately, there is a simple rule that avoids all these difficulties: look for your ancestor in all available court records, regardless of the labellings on the books, cabinets, files, and boxes.

In certain kinds of court matters (such as trials), the record books will refer to folders which contain detailed documents concerning the matters. These folders are usually filed in the court house (CH) and must not be overlooked because they are often gold mines of information. In the county and/or city of your interest, you will find records dealing with the proceedings of the various courts (records, minutes, dockets, enrollments, registers, orders), with land (deeds, entries, grants, mortgages, trust deeds, ranges, surveys, plats, roads), with probate matters (wills, estates, administrators, executors, inventories, settlements, sales, guardians, orphans, insolvent estates, bastardy, apprentices, insanity), with vital records (birth, death, marriage, divorce), with taxation (taxes, bonds, appropriations, delinquent taxes), and with trials, suits, criminal and civil actions, and judgments. In most cases, there will not be records with all these titles, but several of these items are likely to appear in one type of book, cabinet, file, or box. If all of this seems complicated, do not worry. All you need to do is to remember the rules: examine all court records, be on the lookout for references to folders, ask about them, and then examine them also.

Most of the original record books before 1865 have been deposited in VSL&A, although a few counties have retained some or all of them in the CH. The original record books after 1865 are usually in the CH, as are practically all of the surviving cabinets, files, and boxes of records. Microfilm copies of many of the books and some of the loose documents before 1865 have been made, but only a few of the numerous boxes, files, and folders have been copied. Even though most of the land, marriage, birth, death, tax, will, and probate records are indexed, the court order, docket, and minute books (records of all matters brought before the courts) are usually not. They often contain much genealogical information, but when they have no indexes, they must be gone

through page-by-page. Many of the microfilmed and transcribed records are available at VSL&A. Many are in GSU
and thus available through BLGSU. Some of the transcribed records are to be found in RL and LGL, but only a
few or none of microfilms. LL may have transcribed
and/or microfilmed copies for their local areas. Listings of many of the microfilms available at VSL&A, GSU,
and BLGSU are shown in:

__M. L. Brown, HANDY INDEX TO THE HOLDINGS OF THE GENEA-
LOGICAL SOCIETY OF UT, Everton Publishers, Logan, UT,
1971.

__J. D. and E. D. Stemmons, VITAL RECORD COMPENDIUM,
Everton Publishers, Logan, UT, 1979.

__J. F. Dorman, editor, VA GENEALOGIST, 1959 ff., Volumes
3 ff., one or more listings of county records in each
volume.

Chapter 3 discusses the process of obtaining these records, and Chapter 4 lists those available for each of the
100 VA counties and the independent cities.

12. DAR records

The Daughters of the American Revolution (DAR), in
their quests for the family lines linking them to their
Revolutionary War ancestors, have gathered and published
many volumes of records of genealogical pertinence. The
VA chapters of the organization have provided a number of
volumes of county records (chiefly court, deed, marriage,
probate, tax, will), Bible records, cemetery records, and
family records. Copies of all the books are available in
DARL, and many will be found in VSL&A, GSU, and through
BLGSU. Copies of some are in RL and LGL, and materials
of local interest will often be found in LL. Chapter 3
tells you how to locate these records, and in Chapter 4,
these records are included in the listings for the various VA counties.

13. Death records

VA State law required deaths to be registered with
the local commissioners of revenue (tax assessors) for
1853-96. Careful enforcement was not practiced, some
records were not kept during the Civil War, and some were
destroyed in the War. Even so, they are about 65% complete. In 1896, the registration law lapsed, and state-
wide record keeping of deaths ceased until 1912. During

1896-1912, poor or no records were kept in most places, but fairly good records were kept by several cities and one county: Roanoke(1896-1912), Norfolk(1896-1912), Newport News(1896-1912), Richmond(1900-12), Portsmouth (1896-1912), Elizabeth City County(1900-12), Petersburg (1900-12), and Lynchburg(1910-2). On 04 June 1912, a new law took effect and state death registration was once more required. By the end of 1913, registration had reached a 90% level. Copies of registered death records for 1853-96 and from 1912 forward may be obtained for a fee from:

  Bureau of Vital Statistics, James Madison Bldg., 109 Governor St., Richmond, VA 23219.

Copies of the available death records between 1896 and 1912 for the seven cities and one county mentioned above may be obtained for a fee from the City Public Health Department in the cities named and in Hampton (which absorbed Elizabeth City County). When ordering death records from either the state or one of the cities, be sure to give them as many of the following as you can: full name, sex, race, parents' names, maiden name of mother, approximate death date, place, your relationship to the person, and the reason you want the record (namely, genealogical research).

Since the death records for the years before 1912 are not complete, the records available before 1912 for each of the 100 VA counties and for the pertinent cities are listed in Chapter 4. You must remember that some of these records are markedly incomplete and not be surprised to find no listings for some of your ancestors. The original records for 1853-96 are mostly in VSL&A, and microfilm copies are available for use there. Microfilm copies are also at GSU which makes them obtainable from BLGSU. Examination of them will provide you with the information you need to request certified copies of the records from the Bureau of Vital Statistics. Lists of many of these microfilms and published volumes which have been copied from the records will be found in:

  J. D. and E. D. Stemmons, THE VITAL RECORDS COMPENDIUM, Everton Publishers, Logan, UT, 1979.

  M. J. Brown, HANDY INDEX TO THE HOLDINGS OF THE GENEALOGICAL SOCIETY OF UT, Everton Publishers, Logan, UT, 1971.

  J. F. Dorman, editor, VA GENEALOGIST, volumes 3 ff.,

1959 ff., records of one or more counties in each issue.

Death records show some or all of the following: name, county of death, cause of death, age at death, names of parents, birthplace, occupation, name of spouse, name and relationship of informant. Prior to the time when VA required death reports (1853), during 1896-1912, and when you suspect that incomplete records have omitted your ancestor, other records may yield dates and places of death: biographical, cemetery, census, church, military, mortuary, newspaper, pension, and published. These are all discussed in other sections of this chapter. The locating of death record articles in genealogical periodicals is also described separately in this chapter. Another source of death data is in card indexes of obituaries:
___CARD INDEX TO OBITUARIES IN THE RICHMOND INQUIRER, alphabetical, VSL&A, Richmond, VA.
___CARD INDEX TO VA MARRIAGES AND OBITUARIES FROM VA NEWSPAPERS, 1736-1820, alphabetical, incomplete but being completed, VHSL, Richmond, VA.
___CARD INDEX TO VA MARRIAGES AND OBITUARIES FROM VA NEWSPAPERS, 1820-, alphabetical, incomplete but being completed, VHSL, Richmond, VA.
Some obituaries have also been collected and published:
___H. R. McIlwaine, INDEX TO OBITUARY NOTICES IN THE RICHMOND INQUIRER, 1804-28, AND THE RICHMOND WHIG, 1924-38, Genealogical Publ. Co., Baltimore, MD, 1974 (1921).
___Historical Records Survey, INDEX TO OBITUARY NOTICES IN THE RELIGIOUS HERALD, 1828-1938, The Survey, Richmond, VA, 1941, 2 volumes.

14. Divorce records

Since 1918, divorce records for VA have been filed in Richmond on a state-wide basis. For a copy of a given record, send to the following address:
___Bureau of Vital Statistics, James Madison Bldg., 109 Governor St., Richmond, VA 23219.
Divorce records can be very valuable since they usually contain family information. Items often included are names of parties involved, their marriage date and place, their ages or dates of birth, their states or counties of birth, and the date and grounds of the divorce. If the couple had children, their names are usually given in the

records. Prior to 1918, divorce records were kept by the
courts in the various counties and cities, and copies of
the records should be requested from the Clerk of the
Circuit Court. The cost is usually small.

15. Emigration and immigration

Since VA was the earliest colony to be settled, and
since many persons continued to enter North America in
VA, this colony was a center for immigration from over-
seas and for emigration north, south, and west.   Available for searching out ancestors who were immigrants to
VA is a large multi-volumed set of indexes to hundreds of
sources of passenger lists. Each of the over one million
listings gives the full name, the names of accompanying
relatives, ages, the date and port of arrival, and the
source of the information. These volumes are:
__P. W. Filby, PASSENGERS AND IMMIGRATION LISTS INDEX,
  Gale Research Co., Detroit, MI, 1981, plus annual
  SUPPLEMENTS.
Also of importance for locating passenger lists is:
__H. Lancour, R. J. Wolfe, and P. W. Filby, BIBLIOGRAPHY
  OF SHIP PASSENGER LISTS, 1538-1900, Gale Research Co.,
  Detroit, MI, 1981.
This book will lead you to many published lists of early
immigrants. Several other books of lists of ship passen-
gers are:
__J. C. Hotten, ORIGINAL LISTS OF PERSONS OF QUALITY,
  Genealogical Printing Co., Baltimore, MD, 1974.
__C. Boyer, SHIP PASSENGER LISTS: NATIONAL AND NEW ENG-
  LAND, 1600-1825, The Author, Newhall, CA, 1980. [with
  bibliography of other lists]
__C. Boyer, SHIP PASSENGER LISTS: THE SOUTH, 1538-1825,
  The Author, Newhall, CA, 1980.   [with bibliography of
  other lists]
__J. C. Brandow, OMITTED CHAPTERS FROM HOTTEN'S ORIGINAL
  LISTS, Genealogical Publ. Co., Baltimore, MD, 1982.
__The Staff of the National Archives, GUIDE TO GENEA-
  LOGICAL RESEARCH IN THE NATIONAL ARCHIVES, The Arch-
  ives, Washington, DC, 1982. [passenger lists for ships
  arriving at VA ports: Alexandria (1820-52), East River
  (1830), Hampton (1821), Norfolk and Portsmouth (1820-
  57), Petersburg (1819-22), Richmond (1820-44)]
__R. A. Brock, DOCUMENTS RELATING TO THE HUGUENOT EMIGRA-
  TION TO VA, Genealogical Publ. Co., Baltimore, MD, 1973
  (1886).

L. des Cognets, Jr., ENGLISH DUPLICATES OF LOST VA RECORDS, The Author, Princeton, NJ, 1960. [pioneer VA records, 17th and early 18th centuries]

G. C. Greer, EARLY VA IMMIGRANTS, 1623-66, Genealogical Publ. Co., Baltimore, MD, 1973 (1912). [25,000 names, important volume]

B. C. Holtzclaw, ANCESTRY AND DESCENDANTS OF THE NASSAU-SIEGEN IMMIGRANTS TO VA, 1714-50, Memorial Foundation of the Germanna Colonies, Harrisonburg, VA, 1964.

A. L. Jester and M. W. Hiden, ADVENTURES OF PURSE AND PERSON, VA, 1607-25, Order of First Families of VA, Richmond, VA, 1964. [very early VA families]

W. G. Stanard, SOME EMIGRANTS TO VA, Bell, Richmond, VA, 1953.

H. G. Somerby, PASSENGERS FOR VA, 1635, New England Historical and Genealogical Register, Volumes 2-15, 1848-61.

In addition to works on immigrants, there are also several volumes on emigrants, that is, people who migrated out of VA to settle areas to the north, west, and south. Among those that might be helpful to you in your search for a migratory ancestor are:

A. M. Coppage, III and D. F. Wulfeck, VA SETTLERS IN MD, Nangatuck, CT, no date.

K. B. Elliott, EMIGRATION TO OTHER STATES FROM SOUTH-SIDE VA, The Author, South Hill, VA, 1966, 2 volumes.

T. M. Green, HISTORIC FAMILIES OF KY...DERIVED FROM THE VALLEY OF VA, Clarke & Co., Cincinnati, OH, 1889.

G. C. Greer, EARLY VA IMMIGRANTS, 1623-66, Genealogical Publ. Co., Baltimore, MD, 1973 (1912). [25,000 names, important volume]

C. H. Hamlin, VA ANCESTORS AND ADVENTURERS, Genealogical Publ. Co., Baltimore, MD, 1975 (1967-73).

C. H. Hamlin, THEY WENT THATAWAY, Genealogical Publ. Co., Baltimore, MD, 1974 (1964-7).

C. H. Robertson, KS TERRITORIAL SETTLERS OF 1860 WHO WERE BORN IN TN, VA, NC, AND SC, Genealogical Publ. Co., Baltimore, MD, 1976.

For further references to VA immigrants and emigrants, see:

O. K. Miller, MIGRATION, EMIGRATION, IMMIGRATION, Everton Publishers, Logan, UT, 1974, 1981, 2 volumes.

The above books may be located in VSL&A, VHSL, ALUV, LOC,

and in some RL, LGL, and LL. Many of them are in GSU, and thus obtainable through BLGSU.

16. Ethnic records

In addition to the English settlers, many other ethnic groups were involved quite early in the settlement of VA. Since most of these groups adhered to a particular religious affiliation, some of the publications of importance to this section were listed in Section 7 on Church records. Two of the largest ethnic groups were the German-Swiss and the Scotch-Irish. Some books relating to them and a couple treating the Irish are:

__ M. J. O'Brien, many articles on the Irish in the Journal of the American-Irish Historical Association, volumes 1912-30.

__ M. J. O'Brien, THE IRISH IN AMERICA, Genealogical Publ. Co., Baltimore, MD, 1974. [almost 1,000 VA immigrants]

__ L. Chalkley, CHRONICLES OF THE SCOTCH-IRISH SETTLEMENT IN VA, EXTRACTED FROM THE ORIGINAL COURT RECORDS OF AUGUSTA COUNTY, 1745-1800, Genealogical Publ. Co., Baltimore, MD, 1974 (1912), 3 volumes.

__ B. C. Holtzclaw, ANCESTRY AND DESCENDANTS OF THE NASSAU-SIEGEN GERMAN IMMIGRANTS TO VA, 1714-50, Memorial Foundation of the Germanna Colonies in VA, Harrisonburg, VA, 1964.

__ U. S. A. Heavener, THE GERMAN NEW RIVER SETTLEMENT, Genealogical Publ. Co., Baltimore, Md, 1981 (1929).

__ E. Meynen, A BIBLIOGRAPHY OF GERMAN SETTLEMENTS IN COLONIAL NORTH AMERICA, Gale Research Co., Detroit, MI, 1966 (1937).

__ H. Schuricht, HISTORY OF THE GERMAN ELEMENT IN VA, Genealogical Publ. Co., Baltimore, Md, 1977 (1898-1900).

__ J. W. Wayland, THE GERMAN ELEMENT OF THE SHENANDOAH VALLEY OF VA, Carrier Co., Bridgewater, VA, 1964 (1907).

__ K. G. Wust, THE VA GERMANS, University Press of VA, Charlottesville, VA, 1969.

These volumes may be found in VSL&A, VHSL, ALUV, LOC, in many RL and in some LGL. Some of the works are in GSU, and therefore are available through BLGSU. Some are also in LL.

17. Gazetteers, atlases, and maps

A gazetteer is a volume which lists geographical names (towns, settlements, rivers, streams, hills, mountains, valleys, crossroads, villages, districts), locates them and sometimes gives a few details concerning them. Several such volumes and some related publications on place names which could be of help to you include:

__J. Martin, A NEW AND COMPREHENSIVE GAZETTEER OF VA AND THE DC, Martin, Charlottesville, VA, 1835.

__H. Gannett, A GAZETTEER OF VA, US Geological Survey, Washington, DC, 1904. [12,000 place names]

__R. McD. Hanson, VA PLACE NAMES, DERIVATIONS, HISTORICAL USES, McClure Press, White Marsh, VA, 1969.

__R. O. Hummel, Jr., A LIST OF PLACES INCLUDED IN 19TH CENTURY VA DIRECTORIES, VA State Library, Richmond, VA, 1960.

__D. W. Tanner, PLACE NAME RESEARCH IN VA: A HANDBOOK, University of VA Library, Charlottesville, VA, 1976.

__M. Topping and others, APPROVED PLACE NAMES IN VA, US Board on Geographic Names, Columbia Historical Society, Washington, DC, 1971.

__THE VA LOCATOR, Ye Olde Genealogie Shoppe, Indianapolis, IN, 1982.

__VA Place Name Society, VA PLACE NAME SOCIETY NEWSLETTER, University of VA Library, Charlottesville, VA, 1973-, numbers 1-.

__VA Place Name Society, VA PLACE NAME SOCIETY OCCASIONAL PAPERS, University of VA Library, Charlottesville, VA, 1961-, numbers 1-.

There are also some important volumes dealing with early parish lines, county boundaries, and roads:

__E. M. Sanchez-Saavedra, DESCRIPTION OF THE COUNTRY, VA'S CARTOGRAPHERS AND THEIR MAPS, VSL&A, Richmond, VA, 1975.

__C. F. Cocke, PARISH LINES: DIOCESE OF SOUTHERN VA, DIOCESE OF VA, DIOCESE OF SOUTHWESTERN VA, VA State Library, Richmond, VA, 1960, 1964, 1967, 3 volumes.

__M. W. Hiden, HOW JUSTICE GREW: VA COUNTIES, AN ABSTRACT OF THEIR FORMATION, University Press of VA, Charlottesville, VA, 1957.

__M. P. Robinson, VA COUNTIES: THOSE RESULTING FROM VA LEGISLATION, VA State Library, Richmond, VA, 1916.

__N. M. Pawlett, A BRIEF HISTORY OF THE ROADS OF VA,

1607-1840, VA Highway and Transportation Council, Charlottesville, VA, 1979.

A number of atlases are available for VA, for its counties, and for some of its larger cities. Many of these are listed in:
__C. E. LeGear, US ATLASES, Library of Congress, Washington, DC, 1950-3, 2 volumes.
Those counties and cities for which atlases before 1900 are available are indicated in Chapter 4. A very useful set of maps showing VA boundaries every ten years for the period 1790-1920 is available:
__W. Thorndale and W. Dollarhide, MAP GUIDE TO THE US FEDERAL CENSUS OF VA, 1790-1920, Dollarhide Systems, Bellingham, WA, 1984.

Good to excellent map collections are in VSL&A (over 55,000 maps), VHSL (16,000 items), ALUV, and LOC. The special indexes in each of these places should be consulted as should the regular card catalogs (look under VA-ATLASES and VA-MAPS). These collections contain numerous state maps, county maps, many city maps, and some for towns. A volume listing many VA maps is:
__J. W. Sames, III, and L. C. Woods, Jr., INDEX TO KY AND VA MAPS, 1562-1900, KY Historical Society, Frankfort, KY, 1976.
Especially useful are landowner maps. These are maps which show the lands of a county with the names of the owners written on them. Most of these maps date between 1860 and 1900 and are available for over 70 VA counties. Such maps are listed in the following volume, which also gives instructions for obtaining them:
__R. W. Stephenson, LAND OWNERSHIP MAPS, Library of Congress, Washington, DC, 1967.
Counties having such maps are indicated in Chapter 4.

Very good detail maps of VA are available at reasonable prices from the US Geological Survey. Each of these maps shows only a portion of a county and therefore a great deal of detail can be shown. Write to the address below and request the Index to Topographic Maps of VA. Then order the maps pertaining to your ancestor's area. These maps show roads, streams, cemeteries, settlements, railroads, and churches. Such maps will aid you greatly if your ancestor lived in a rural area and you desire to visit the property and the surrounding region.

_Branch of Distribution, Eastern Region, US Geological Survey, 1200 South Eads St., Arlington, VA 22202 [or if you live west of the MS River], Central Region, Box 25286, Denver, CO 80225.

Another source of detailed county and city maps is the VA Highways and Transportation Department. They can provide you with individual maps of VA counties and cities showing roads, streets, streams, railroads, and other features. Order them from:

_VA Highways and Transportation Dept., 1401 East Broad St., Richmond, VA 23219.

They also sell a county map atlas containing all the county maps and a city and town map atlas containing all the city and town maps:

_VA Highways and Transportation Dept., COUNTY ROAD MAP ATLAS, COMMONWEALTH OF VA, The Department, Richmond, VA, 1981.

_VA Highways and Transportation Dept., CITY AND TOWN MAP ATLAS, COMMONWEALTH OF VA, The Dept., Richmond, VA, 1980.

Most of the gazetteers and atlases mentioned in this section will be found in VSL&A and LOC, many in VHSL, ALUV, and GSU (BLGSU), and some in RL, LGL, and LL.

18. Genealogical indexes & compilations for VA

There are sizable numbers of genealogical indexes and compilations for the colony and state of VA. These are of considerable utility because they save you from going through many small volumes as you search for your VA forebears. Most notable among the indexes is the utterly indispensable 4-volume work by Swem:

__E. G. Swem, VA HISTORICAL INDEX, Peter Smith, Northampton, MA, 1965 (1934-6), 4 volumes.

These books index names from eight genealogically-laden sets of publications: (1) Lower Norfolk County Antiquary, 1895-1906, (2) Tyler's Quarterly Historical and Genealogical Register, 1919-29, (3) VA Historical Register, 1848-53), (4) The VA Magazine of History and Biography, 1893-1930), (5) William and Mary Quarterly, 1st Series, 1892-1919, (6) William and Mary Quarterly, 2nd Series, 1921-30, (7) Calendar of VA State Papers and Other Manuscripts, 1632-1869, and (8) Hening's Statutes at Large, Being a Collection of all the Laws of VA, 1809-23. The dates written after these publications are not the dates of the records; they are the dates during which the items were published. Early in any VA research you should take a thorough look for your ancestor in Swem. This has a good chance of saving you considerable time by locating reference materials which are already published. There are several other indexes which can often yield fruitful results for you:

  S. E. Brown, Jr., VA GENEALOGIES: A TRIAL LIST OF PRINTED BOOKS AND PAMPHLETS, VA Book Co., Berryville, VA, 1967, 1980, 2 volumes. [over 4500 families]

  J. J. Casey, PERSONAL NAMES IN HENING'S STATUTES AND SHEPHERD'S CONTINUATION, Genealogical Publ. Co., Baltimore, MD, 1967 (1896). [22,500 names]

  R. A. Stewart, INDEX TO PRINTED VA GENEALOGIES, Genealogical Publ. Co., Baltimore, MD, 1970 (1930). [750 books, 6,000 family names, 18,000 references]

  E. G. Swem, BIBLIOGRAPHY OF VA, VA State Library Bulletin 8, Richmond, VA, 1916.

  CARD CATALOGS at VSL&A (Library Section), VHSL, ALUV, LOC, GSU, and BLGSU.

In addition to these valuable indexes, there are also some very helpful _compilations_ of genealogies. Among those which you should examine are:

  L. P. du Bellet, SOME PROMINENT VA FAMILIES, Genealogical Publ. Co., Baltimore, MD, 1976 (1907), 2 volumes. [hundreds of genealogies]

  J. B. Boddie, SOUTHSIDE VA FAMILIES, Genealogical Publ. Co., Baltimore, MD, 1966 (1955-6), 2 volumes. [over 100 families]

  J. B. Boddie, VA HISTORICAL GENEALOGIES, Genealogical Publ. Co., Baltimore, MD, 1965 (1954). [4,000 people, 50 families]

  W. F. Boogher, GLEANINGS OF VA HISTORY: AN HISTORICAL AND GENEALOGICAL COLLECTION, Genealogical Publ. Co., Baltimore, MD, 1965 (1903).

  R. L. Brown and R. E. Brown, GENEALOGICAL NOTES, PRINCIPALLY OF SC AND VA, Wist, Greenville, SC, 1937.

  A. W. Burns, VA GENEALOGIES AND COUNTY RECORDS, The Author, Washington, DC, 1941-4, 11 volumes. [pension abstracts of Revolutionary War, War of 1812, Indian Wars]

  T. K. Cartmell, SHENANDOAH VALLEY PIONEERS AND THEIR DESCENDANTS: A HISTORY OF FREDERICK COUNTY, 1738-1908, VA Book Co., Berryville, VA, 1972 (1908). [9,500 names]

__N. Currer-Briggs, VA SETTLERS AND ENGLISH ADVENTURERS: ABSTRACTS OF WILLS, 1484-1798, AND LEGAL PROCEEDINGS, 1566-1700, Genealogical Publ. Co., Baltimore, MD, 1970. [12,000 names, 400 families]

__C. L. Edwards, III, A GUIDE TO THE BUSINESS RECORDS IN THE ARCHIVES BRANCH, VA STATE LIBRARY, VA State Library, Richmond, VA, 1983.

__GENEALOGIES OF VA FAMILIES FROM TYLER'S QUARTERLY, Genealogical Publ. Co., Baltimore, MD, 1981, 4 volumes.

__GENEALOGIES OF VA FAMILIES FROM THE VA MAGAZINE OF HISTORY AND BIOGRAPHY, Genealogical Publ. Co., Baltimore, MD, 1981, 5 volumes. [10,000 names]

__GENEALOGIES OF VA FAMILIES FROM THE WILLIAM AND MARY QUARTERLY, Genealogical Publ. Co., Baltimore, MD, 1982, 5 volumes.

__S. P. Hardy, COLONIAL FAMILIES OF THE SOUTHERN STATES OF AMERICA, Genealogical Publ. Co., Baltimore, MD, 1981 (1958)

__L. H. Hart, III, GUIDE TO GENEALOGICAL NOTES AND CHARTS, VA State Library, Richmond, VA, 1983.

__H. E. Hayden, VA GENEALOGIES, Genealogical Publ. Co., Baltimore, MD, 1979 (1891).

__W. W. Hening, THE STATUTES AT LARGE, 1606-1807, University Press of VA, Charlottesville, VA, 1969 (1819-23), 13 volumes.

__W. W. Hening, THE STATUTES AT LARGE: SUPPLEMENT, by S. Shepherd, AMS Press, New York, NY, 1967 (1823), 3 volumes.

__H. H. Howe, HISTORICAL COLLECTIONS OF VA, Genealogical Publ. Co., Baltimore, MD, 1969 (1845). [about 2,000 names, county-by-county biographies]

__E. E. Lantz and A. H. Keller, GENEALOGICAL AND HERALDIC ARTICLES PUBLISHED IN THE BALTIMORE SUN, 1905-8, available at MD Historical Society, Baltimore, MD, with a typescript index.

__W. Meade, OLD CHURCHES, MINISTERS, AND FAMILIES OF VA, Genealogical Publ. Co., Baltimore, MD, 1978 (1857), 2 volumes. [6,900 names]

__H. M. McIlhany, SOME VA FAMILIES, Genealogical Publ. Co., Baltimore, MD, 1962 (1903).

__J. E. Norris, HISTORY OF THE LOWER SHENANDOAH VALLEY, VA Book Co., Berryville, VA, 1973 (1890). [Berkeley, Clarke, Frederick, Jefferson Counties]

__C. Torrence, editor, THE VALENTINE PAPERS, Genealogical Publ. Co., Baltimore, MD, 1979 (1927), 4 volumes.

___B. F. Van Meter, GENEALOGIES AND SKETCHES OF SOME OLD
FAMILIES IN THE DEVELOPMENT OF VA AND KY, Morton & Co.,
Louisville, KY, 1901.
___VA LAND, MARRIAGE, MILITARY, TAX, VITAL, AND WILL
RECORDS FROM VA MAGAZINES, Genealogical Publ. Co.,
Baltimore, MD, 1982-3, 6 volumes.
___P. G. Wardell, TIMESAVING AID TO VA AND WV ANCESTORS,
Iberian Publishing Co., Athens, GA, 1986.
___D. F. Wulfeck, GENEALOGY NOTES ON VA FAMILIES, The Au-
thor, Naugatuck, CT, several dates, several volumes.
___D. F. Wulfeck, THE VA GAZETTE GENEALOGY, The Author,
Naugatuck, CT, 1960-5, 4 volumes.
Most of the above books, both indexes and compilations,
will be found in VSL&A, VHSL, ALUV, LOC, and GSU. This
makes them also available through BLGSU. Many of the
volumes are in RL and LGL, and some are located in LL.
Further reference works on published genealogies will be
given in section 32 of this chapter.

19. Genealogical periodicals

Several genealogical periodicals and history periodicals carrying some genealogy have been or are being
published in VA. These journals or newsletters contain
genealogies, local histories, genealogical records,
family queries and answers, book reviews, and other
pertinent local information. If you had a VA ancestor,
you will find it of great value to subscribe to one or
more of the state-wide periodicals, as well as to any
periodicals published in the region or county where
he/she lived. Among the more important previous or
present VA periodicals are:
___PAPERS OF THE ALBEMARLE COUNTY HISTORICAL SOCIETY,
continued as THE ALBEMARLE COUNTY HISTORY, The Society,
Charlottesville, VA.
___ARLINGTON HISTORY MAGAZINE, Arlington Historical Soci-
ety, Arlington, VA.
___AUGUSTA HISTORICAL BULLETIN, Augusta County Historical
Society, Staunton, VA.
___BLUE RIDGE GENEALOGICAL SOCIETY JOURNAL, The Society,
Wise, VA.
___BULLETIN OF THE VA-NC PIEDMONT GENEALOGICAL SOCIETY,
The Society, Danville, VA.
___COUNTY COURT NOTEBOOK, edited by M. Ljungstedt, Be-
thesda, MD, 1922-31. [abstracts of court records prior
to 1800]

__CUMBERLAND EMPIRE, edited by J. T. Adams, Big Laurel, VA, 1932.

__GENEALOGY HARVEST, Seven Fountains, VA.

__HARRISONBURG ROCKINGHAM HISTORICAL SOCIETY NEWSLETTER, The Society, Harrisonburg, VA.

__GOOCHLAND COUNTY HISTORICAL SOCIETY MAGAZINE, The Society, Goochland, VA.

__JOURNAL OF THE ROANOKE VALLEY HISTORICAL SOCIETY, The Society, Roanoke, VA.

__KENMORE NEWS NOTES, Kenmore Association, Fredericksburg, VA.

__LOUDON COUNTY HISTORICAL SOCIETY BULLETIN, The Society, Leesburg, VA, 1958-.

__LOUISA COUNTY HISTORICAL MAGAZINE, Louisa, VA, 1969-.

__LOWER NORFOLK COUNTY ANTIQUARIAN, edited by E. W. James, Peter Smith, New York, NY, 1895-1906. [indexed in Swem]

__MAGAZINE OF ALBEMARLE COUNTY HISTORY, Albemarle County Historical Society, Charlottesville, VA.

__NORTHERN NECK OF VA HISTORICAL MAGAZINE, Northern Neck Historical Society, Montross, VA, 1951-.

__THE RESEARCHER, A MAGAZINE OF HISTORY AND GENEALOGICAL EXCHANGE, edited by R. A. Stewart, Richmond, VA, 1926-8.

__SOUTHWEST VIRGINIAN, JOURNAL OF GENEALOGY AND HISTORY THIS SIDE OF THE BLUE RIDGE, Norton, VA.

__TYLER'S QUARTERLY HISTORICAL AND GENEALOGICAL MAGAZINE, Richmond, VA, and Nashville, TN, 1919-52. [1919-29 volumes indexed in Swem]

__VA APPALACHIAN NOTES, Southwestern VA Genealogical Society, Roanoke, VA.

__VA GENEALOGIST, edited by J. F. Dorman, Box 4883, Washington, DC 20008, 1957-. [The most important journal for the VA researcher. Subscribe.]

__VA GENEALOGICAL SOCIETY QUARTERLY, VA Genealogical Society, Richmond, VA, 1961-. [excellent]

__VA HISTORICAL REGISTER, edited by W. Maxwell, Reprint Co., Spartanburg, SC, 1848-53. [indexed in Swem]

__VA MAGAZINE OF HISTORY AND BIOGRAPHY, VA Historical Society, Richmond, VA, 1894-. [1894-1930 volumes indexed in Swem, not much genealogy after 1945]

__VA PHOENIX, VA History Federation, Norfolk, VA 1969-.

__VA TIDEWATER GENEALOGY, Genealogical Society of Tidewater VA, Hampton, VA, 1970-.

__WILLIAM AND MARY COLLEGE QUARTERLY, The College, Wil-

liamsburg, VA, 1892-. [1892-1930 indexed in Swem,
little genealogy after 1943]
__WYTHE COUNTY HISTORICAL REVIEW, Wythe County Historical
Society, Wytheville, VA.
Most of these periodicals will be found in VSL&A and
VHSL, some in ALUV, LOC, and GSU (and thus through
BLGSU), some in LGL and RL, and those pertaining to the
surrounding areas in LL.

    Not only do articles pertaining to VA genealogy
appear in the above publications, they are also printed
in other genealogical periodicals. Fortunately, indexes
to major genealogical periodicals are available.
__For periodicals published 1858-1952, consult D. L.
Jacobus, INDEX TO GENEALOGICAL PERIODICALS, Genealogical Publ. Co., Baltimore, MD, 1973.
__For periodicals published 1957-62, consult the annual
volumes by I. Waldenmaier, ANNUAL INDEX TO GENEALOGICAL
PERIODICALS AND FAMILY HISTORIES, The Author, Washington, DC, 1957-8-9-60-1-2.
__For periodicals published 1962-9 and 1974-85, consult
the annual volumes by various editors, E. S. Rogers, G.
E. Russell, L. C. Towle, and C. M. Mayhew, GENEALOGICAL
PERIODICAL ANNUAL INDEX, various publishers, most re-
cently Heritage Books, Bowie, MD, 1962-3-4-5-6-7-8-9,
1974-5-6-7-8-9-80-1-2-3-4-5.
These index volumes will be found in VSL&A, LOC, and GSU
(available through BLGSU), most LGL, some RL, and a few
LL. In them, you should consult all general VA listings,
then all listings under the counties which concern you,
as well as listings under family names (if included).

20. Genealogical societies

    In the Commonwealth of VA various societies for the
study of genealogy, the accumulation of data, and the
publication of the materials have been organized. The
state and regional societies include:
__VA Genealogical Society, PO Box 1397, Richmond, VA
23211.
__Blue Ridge Genealogical Society, Wise, VA 24293.
__Central VA Genealogical Association, Route 5, Box 258,
Charlottesville, VA 22901.
__Genealogical Society of Tidewater VA, PO Box 9407,
Hampton, VA 23670.

__Lower Del-Mar-VA Genealogical Society, Wicomico County Library, Salisbury, MD 21801.
__Southwestern VA Genealogical Society, 301 Houston Ave., Roanoke, VA 24012.
__VA-NC Piedmont Genealogical Society, PO Box 2272, Danville, VA 24541.

There are also genealogical societies whose interests are more local, most usually county-wide. These societies are listed in Chapter 4 under the names of the VA counties. Some of the state, regional, and local societies publish regular journals containing data they have gathered, queries from their members, book reviews, and items of general interest. The members of regional and local societies are generally well informed about the genealogical resources of their regions, and often can offer considerable help to non-residents who had ancestors in the area. It is thus advisable for you to join the societies in your ancestor's county and region as well as the VA Genealogical Society. All correspondence with such societies should be accompanied by an SASE.

21. Historical societies

In addition to the VA Historical Society, there are many city, county, and regional historical societies in VA. These organizations along with their addresses are listed under the counties in chapter 4. Some of these societies deal with genealogical interests in addition to their historical pursuits. Even if they do not carry out much genealogical work as such, their efforts will be of considerable interest to you, since they deal with the historical circumstances through which your ancestor lived. It is often well for you to dispatch an SASE and an inquiry to one or more asking about membership, genealogical interests if any, and publication.

22. Land records

One of the most important types of genealogical records are those which deal with land. This is because VA throughout much of its earlier history was predominantly an agricultural area with its population largely rural. In addition, land up until the present century was widely available and quite inexpensive. This meant that the majority of Virginians owned land and therefore their names appear in land records in VA. (1) The first kind involves the transactions by which the government originally transferred the land to its first private owner. These transactions made use of documents and records called certificates, grants, patents, plats, surveys, vouchers, and warrants. (2) The second kind of land records are those by which one private owner trans- ferred the land to another private owner. These trans- actions were evidenced by documents and records called deeds, mortgages, and surveys.

The first category of land records (transfers from the colonial or state government to the first private owner) dates from 1621 forward. These are probably the most valuable and comprehensive colonial records avail- able (1623-1775). They are also very useful for the post-revolutionary period (after 1775). The term certif- icate refers to a document issued by some government agency or officer certifying that a person is entitled to land. A grant or a patent is a document which conveys land from the government to the individual. A plat or a survey is a map of a tract of land giving its location and measurements. A voucher is a certificate indicating that payment has been made for a tract of land.   A war- rant is a document which authorized a professional surveyor to lay off and map a tract of land for a person who had bought it or had been granted it. The VSL&A has the large collection of land records kept by the VA Land Office from 1623 forward. All of these are noted and briefly described in
    D. S. Gentry and J. S. Salmon, VA LAND OFFICE INVENT- ORY, VA State Library, Richmond, VA, 1981.
Chief among the genealogically-important records are Northern Neck grants, surveys, plats, and certificates (1690-1874), patents and grants (1623-1774, 1779-1980) and surveys (1779-1963) for the entire state, and land bounty documents for lands awarded to veterans of the French and Indian War (1779-83) and of the Revolutionary War (1782-1876).   The following indexes in VSL&A (some also in GSU) will lead you to the original records or microfilms of them:
    INDEX TO LAND SURVEYS, 1779-1924, VSL&A, Richmond, VA, microfilms 366-7 in Archives Division, 5 volumes, each indexed separately, each alphabetical by surname initial.

__INDEX TO LAND PATENTS AND GRANTS, 1623-1774, 1779-1980,
VSL&A, Richmond, VA, card file in Reading room, Arch-
ives Division, alphabetical.
__INDEX TO LAND BOUNTY CERTIFICATES, FRENCH AND INDIAN
WAR, 1774, 1779-80, VSL&A, Richmond, VA, Reading Room,
Archives Division, alphabetical.
__INDEX TO LAND BOUNTY BOOKS, FRENCH AND INDIAN WARS,
1779-83, VSL&A, Richmond, VA, microfilm 360 in Archives
Division, alphabetical by surname initial.
__INDEX TO MILITARY CERTIFICATES, REVOLUTIONARY WAR,
1782-1876, VSL&A, Richmond, VA, card index in Reading
Room, Archives Division, alphabetical.
__INDEX TO LAND OFFICE MILITARY CERTIFICATES, REVOLUTION-
ARY WAR, 1782-1876, VSL&A, Richmond, VA, microfilm 347a
in Archives Division, alphabetical.
__INDEX TO NORTHERN NECK LAND GRANTS, SURVEYS, PLATS, AND
CERTIFICATES, 1690-1874, VSL&A, Richmond, VA, card file
in Reading Room, Archives Division, alphabetical.
The book by Gentry and Salmon lists several other indexes
and sets of records relating to VA land matters of the
type being here described.

In addition to the above indexes in VSL&A (some in
GSU), there are available some published volumes setting
forth and indexing some of the records. Notable among
them is Nugent's multi-volume set which gives practically
all of the genealogical information contained in the
first 14 patent books (1632-1732). This set of volumes
probably constitutes the most important and most compre-
hensive record compilation for colonial VA. The work is
thoroughly indexed and can save you much searching in
VSL&A indexes.
__N. M. Nugent, CAVALIERS AND PIONEERS: ABSTRACTS OF VA
LAND PATENTS AND GRANTS, 1623-1732, Genealogical Publ.
Co., Baltimore, MD, 1977-9 (1934), 3 volumes, plus
Supplements. [very important, over 80,000 listings]
Other volumes of early land records which you must not
fail to examine are:
__P. C. Kaylor and G. W. Chapplear, ABSTRACT OF LAND
GRANT SURVEYS, 1761-91, Shenandoah Press, Dayton, VA,
1938.
__B. W. Gahn, ORIGINAL PATENTEES OF LAND AT WASHINGTON
PRIOR TO 1700, Genealogical Publ. Co., Baltimore, MD,
1969.
__G. C. Greer, EARLY VA IMMIGRANTS, 1623-66, Genealogical

Publ. Co., Baltimore, MD, 1973 (1912). [25,000 persons who were not original patentees of land]
___R. W. Stitt, Jr., MOTHER EARTH LAND GRANTS IN VA, 1607-99, VA 350th Anniversary Celebration Corporation, Williamsburg, VA, 1957.

Lands awarded for service in the French and Indian War (fought 1754-63, awards made 1779-83) were located in western VA and what is now WV. No awards were made prior to 1779. Bounty lands given for service in the Revolutionary War (fought 1775-83, awards made 1779-1878) were situated in what is now KY and in the Military District of OH. Revolutionary War bounty land was not awarded to all VA militia, but all Virginians who served in the Continental Army were eligible. The VSL&A French and Indian War bounty land records are not complete because of losses of records.

As indicated above, the records of the issuance of Revolutionary War bounty land warrants are in the VSL&A (some in GSU), but you must remember that these warrants were redeemed for land in KY and the Military District of OH. The warrants were transferable, so the original warrant receiver was not always the person who obtained the land. The records showing who took up the land for the various warrant numbers are in:
___Land Office, KY Secretary of State, Room 148, Capitol Bldg., Frankfort, KY 40601, or
___OH Land Grant Office, OH State Auditor, 4th Floor, 88 East Broad St., Columbus, OH 43215.
There are also some helpful volumes which contain data on bounty land warrant redemptions:
___W. K. Jillson, THE KY LAND GRANTS, Standard Printing Co., Louisville, KY, 1925.
___W. R. Jillson, OLD KY ENTRIES AND DEEDS, Standard Printing Co., Louisville, KY, 1926.
___P. F. Taylor, A CALENDAR OF THE WARRANTS FOR LAND IN KY FOR SERVICE IN THE FRENCH AND INDIAN WAR, Genealogical Publ. Co., Baltimore, MD, 1967.
___S. M. Wilson, CATALOGUE OF REVOLUTIONARY SOLDIERS AND SAILORS TO WHOM LAND BOUNTY WARRANTS WERE GRANTED BY VA, Genealogical Publ. Co., Baltimore, MD, 1967.
___J. Brookes-Smith, MASTER INDEX TO VA SURVEYS AND GRANTS, 1774-91, KY Historical Society, Frankfort, KY, 1976.

  __J. Brookes-Smith, INDEX FOR OLD KY SURVEYS AND GRANTS,
KY Historical Society, Frankfort, KY, 1975.
  __C. N. Smith, A CALENDAR OF ARCHIVAL MATERIALS ON THE
LAND PATENTS ISSUED BY THE US, VOLUME 4, PARTS 1 AND 2:
GRANTS IN THE VA MILITARY DISTRICT OF OH, American
Library Association, Chicago, IL, 1982, 1984.

Most books mentioned here and in the previous paragraphs
are to be found in VSL&A, VHSL, ALUV, and LOC. Many are
in DARL and in GSU (thus being available through BLGSU).
LGL, RL, and LL are likely to have some of them.

The second category of land records (transfers
between individual private persons or groups) consists of
deeds, land suits, mortgages, entries, surveys, and tax
records. These records were kept by the VA counties.
They are indicated under the counties in Chapter 4 along
with the dates for which they are available. In most
cases, the originals before 1866 are in the court houses
(CH), in some, they are in VSL&A. Almost all after 1865
are in the CH. Microfilm or photostatic copies of those
before 1866 are in VSL&A and GSU, those in the latter
being available through BLGSU. Some of the records have
been transcribed and published. These are available in
VSL&A and LOC, and some are in DARL, GSU (BLGSU), RL, and
LGL. Microfilm copies and/or published transcript copies
are sometimes available in LL for their own counties.

23. Manuscripts

The most valuable sources of manuscripts relating to
the state of VA are VSL&A, VHSL, ALUV, The Swem Library
of the College of William and Mary in Williamsburg, VA
(SLCWM), and the LOC. Others of importance are listed
in:
  __P. M. Hamer, editor, A GUIDE TO ARCHIVES AND MANU-
SCRIPTS IN THE US, Yale University Press, New Haven,
CT, 1961.
  __National Historical Publications and Records Commis-
sion, DIRECTORY OF ARCHIVES AND MANUSCRIPT REPOSITORIES
IN THE US, The Commission, Washington, DC, 1978.
  __US Library of Congress, NATIONAL UNION CATALOG OF
MANUSCRIPT COLLECTIONS, Shoe String Press, Hamden, CT,
1959-. [numerous volumes, index of names, places, and
historical periods in each volume]

__J. B. Howell, SPECIAL COLLECTIONS IN LIBRARIES OF THE SOUTHEAST, Southeastern Library Association, Jackson, MS, 1978.

__Task Force on Library Resources, A DIRECTORY OF VA LIBRARY RESOURCES, VA Council of Higher Education, Richmond, VA, 1976.

The contents of the manuscript collections mentioned above consist of records of religious, educational, patriotic, business, social, civil, professional, governmental, and political organizations; documents, letters, memoirs, notes, and papers of early settlers, politicians, ministers, business men, educators, physicians, dentists, lawyers, judges, and farmers; records of churches, cemeteries, mortuaries, schools, corporations, and industries; works of artists, musicians, writers, sculptors, photographers, and architects; and records, papers, letters, and reminiscences of participants in the various wars, as well as records of military organizations and campaigns.

The reference books mentioned in the first paragraph are available in VSL&A, ALUV, LOC, and in many large libraries, including LGL. If you find in these books materials which you suspect may relate to your ancestor, write to the appropriate library asking for details. Don't forget to send an SASE and to ask them for the names of researchers if you cannot go in person. In VSL&A, VHSL, ALUV, SLCWM, and LOC, there are special manuscript indexes (alphabetically by name or title or location or organization) that facilitate the process of finding materials. In most cases there are several indexes, not just one, so you need to be careful to examine all of them. In VSL&A, they are in the Archives Reading Room, in VHSL the main index is a large card catalog (of over 3.6 million items), in ALUV the indexes are located in the Manuscripts Division, and in LOC you will find the indexes in Room 3005 of the Annex, which is the Manuscripts Division.

24. Marriage records

Microfilm copies of marriage records for the period 1853-1935 and arranged by county are in VSL&A. These are copies of the state records and if you want photocopies or certified copies of them, they may be obtained from:

__Bureau of Vital Statistics, James Madison Bldg., 109
Governor St., Richmond, VA 23219.
It is best to use the records at VSL&A to locate your
ancestor's marriage and then to write to the Bureau if
you want an official copy. When ordering, be sure and
give the Bureau as many of the following data as you can:
full names of bride and groom, date and county of marriage, your relationship to the couple, and the reason
you want the record (namely, genealogical research). This
need to supply the Bureau with data is why you should
first use the records at VSL&A. The marriage registers
there generally list the bride and groom, their birthplaces, their parents' names, their counties of residence, the groom's occupation, the date, and the
officiating minister.

     Prior to 1853, marriage records were largely kept by
the individual counties. In many instances, they were
begun when the counties were created, but because of
losses and ineffective enforcement of registration, very
few marriage records before 1715 exist. The records of
most counties are quite incomplete until after the Revolutionary War. The early marriage records include
several types, the major ones being banns records (three
notices of the marriage given by a church), bonds (given
to County Court as security), licenses, consents (given
by parents for underage persons), returns (ministers'
lists of marriages performed), and church records. In
Chapter 4, you will find listed under each county the
dates for which marriage records are available. Some of
the originals are in the CH, others are in VSL&A. Both
VSL&A and GSU have extensive microfilm copies of county
marriage records, most of those indicated in Chapter 4
being in these collections. Those at GSU are available
through BLGSU. The VHSL has compiled two incomplete, but
nonetheless very valuable, card indexes containing references to VA marriages:
__CARD INDEX TO VA MARRIAGES AND OBITUARIES FROM VA
NEWSPAPERS, 1736-1820, VHSL, Richmond, VA, alphabetical, incomplete, but being completed.
__CARD INDEX TO VA MARRIAGES AND OBITUARIES FROM VA
NEWSPAPERS, AFTER 1820, VHSL, Richmond, VA, alphabetical, incomplete, but being added to continually.
There is an excellent finding aid to marriage records in
the VSL&A:

___J. Vogt and T. W. Kethley, Jr., MARRIAGE RECORDS IN THE VSL, A RESEARCHERS' GUIDE, Iberian Press, Athens, GA, 1985.

The VSL&A also has a card index which frequently leads to sought-after marriage information:

___CARD INDEX TO MARRIAGES IN THE RICHMOND ENQUIRER, VSL&A, Richmond, VA, Library Reading Room, alphabetical.

Another important aid to early marriage searches is:

___I. Waldenmaier, A FINDING LIST OF VA MARRIAGE RECORDS BEFORE 1853, The Author, Washington, DC, 1956-7, 2 volumes.

Transcriptions of a number of county marriage records have been made; some have been published, some remain in typewritten or handwritten form. These may be sought in VSL&A, VHSL, LOC, DARL, and in some RL and LGL. Those pertaining to individual counties are likely to be in their LL.

There are also some state-wide and regional compilations of marriages which are likely to prove useful. Among them are:

___B. M. Ashby, SHENANDOAH VALLEY MARRIAGE BONDS, 1772-1850, VA Book Co., Berryville, VA, 1967. [large index]

___L. H. M. Baber, L. A. Blunt, and M. A. L. Collins, MARRIAGES AND DEATHS FROM LYNCHBURG, VA NEWSPAPERS, 1794-1836, Genealogical Publ. Co., Baltimore, MD, 1980. [6,000 names]

___W. A. Crozier, EARLY VA MARRIAGES, Genealogical Publ. Co., Baltimore, MD, 1973 (1907).

___W. Douglas, THE DOUGLAS REGISTER, Genealogical Publ. Co., Baltimore, MD, 1973 (1928).

___Historical Records Survey, INDEX TO THE MARRIAGE NOTICES IN THE RELIGIOUS HERALD, 1828-1938, The Survey, Richmond, VA, 1941.

___Historical Records Survey, INDEX TO MARRIAGE NOTICES IN THE SOUTHERN CHURCHMAN, 1835-1941, The Survey, Richmond, VA, 1942, 2 volumes.

___C. L. Knorr, MARRIAGE LISTS OF VA COUNTIES, The Author, Pine Bluff, AR, several volumes.

___C. D. McDonald, SOME VA MARRIAGES, 1700-99, The Author, Seattle, WA, 1973-, volumes 1-.

___C. D. McDonald, SOME VA MARRIAGES, 1800-25, The Author, Seattle, WA, 1973-, volumes 1-.

___VA Genealogical Society, SOME MARRIAGES IN THE BURNED RECORD COUNTIES OF VA, The Society, Richmond, VA, 1972.

__D. F. Wulfeck, MARRIAGES OF SOME VA RESIDENTS, 1607–
1800, The Author, Naugatuck, CT, 1961-7, 7 volumes.

Other records which often yield marriage dates and
places include Bible, biographical, cemetery, church,
mortuary, newspaper, obituary, pension, and published
records. All of these are discussed in other sections of
this chapter. In addition, the location of marriage data
in genealogical periodicals has been described in section
19.

25. Military records: Colonial

The colonial period of VA (1607-1776) was a time in
which each county maintained a military unit of its own
called the county militia. In times of war, these
militia combined their efforts under colony leadership.
Very few data, such as rolls or lists of militia members,
are available prior to 1754. More data are available for
the time after 1754 during which the French and Indian
War (1754-63) and Dunmore's War (1774) were fought. This
last of the colonial wars may be viewed as a bridge to
the Revolutionary War in colonial VA, since it was a
rebellion against British authority. Unfortunately, all
the records do is give lists of participants. This often
lets you know the location of a soldier, but little
additional genealogical data are given.

Most of the extant military records (largely pay-
rolls and muster lists) are available in or referenced by
several major works and one card index:
__W. A. Crozier, VA COLONIAL MILITIA, Genealogical Publ.
Co., Baltimore, MD, 1973 (1905).
__H. J. Eckenrode, LIST OF THE COLONIAL SOLDIERS OF VA,
VA State Library, Richmond, VA, 1916-7.
__M. J. Clark, COLONIAL SOLDIERS OF THE SOUTH, 1732-74,
Genealogical Publ. Co., Baltimore, MD, 1983.
__VA MILITARY RECORDS, Genealogical Publ. Co., Baltimore,
MD, 1983.
__VA Historical Society, VA MAGAZINE OF HISTORY AND BIO-
GRAPHY, The Society, Richmond, VA, 1893-, volumes 1,
indexed in E. G. Swem, VA HISTORICAL INDEX, Peter
Smith, Northampton, MA, 1965 (1934-6), 4 volumes.
__US Library of Congress, WASHINGTON MANUSCRIPTS, The
Library, Washington, DC, copy in VSL&A along with typed
index.

__CARD INDEX TO PARTICIPANTS IN DUNMORE'S WAR, 1774, VSL&A, Richmond, VA Archives Reading Room, alphabetical, leads to microfilmed records.

In addition to the above-referenced materials, there are some other volumes or indexes which it may pay you to employ:
__J. D. Neville, BACON'S REBELLION, ABSTRACTS FROM MATERIALS IN THE COLONIAL RECORDS PROJECT, The Jamestown Foundation, Jamestown, VA, 1976.
__VA State Library, LORD DUNMORE'S WAR, The Library, Richmond, VA. [military and civilian claims from Augusta, Bedford, Botetourt, and Fincastle Counties, with index]
__VA State Library, THE ROMNEY, WINCHESTER, AND PITTSBURGH PAYROLLS OF 1775, The Library, Richmond, VA. [indexed in Gwathmey (see next section), but many of the soldiers became Loyalists in the Revolution]
__P. F. Taylor, A CALENDAR OF WARRANTS FOR LAND IN KY GRANTED FOR SERVICE IN THE FRENCH AND INDIAN WAR, Genealogical Publ. Co., Baltimore, MD, 1967.
__R. G. Thwaites and L. P. Kellogg, DOCUMENTARY HISTORY OF DUNMORE'S WAR, The Draper Manuscripts, 1974 (1905).
Other references to colonial military service may be found in court orders, land records, and executive journals of the Colonial Council. None of these, however, contains lists or rosters of soldiers. The abovementioned materials are available in VSL&A. Some of them will be found in VHSL, ALUV, LOC, DARL, GSU, (BLGSU), RL, and LGL. LL in the VA counties and cities may also have some of them.

26. Military records: Revolutionary War

As mentioned in Chapter 1, VA was heavily involved in the American War for Independence, particularly in the latter half of the conflict. About 27,000 Virginians were members of the Continental Army, and over 4,000 did militia service. Quite a number of records, which you should try to find, are available for this War: national service records, national pension records, national bounty land records, state service records, state pension records, state bounty land records, and state civilian service records. The _first_ step you should take in searching for your VA ancestor who served in this War (or gave public service supporting the War) is to employ the

following <u>national</u> record sources and look for him in
them.

__National Archives, GENERAL INDEX TO COMPILED SERVICE
RECORDS OF REVOLUTIONARY WAR SOLDIERS, The Archives,
Washington, DC, Microfilm Publication M860, 58 rolls.
[copies in VSL&A, NA, GSU]

__National Archives, INDEX TO COMPILED SERVICE RECORDS OF
AMERICAN NAVAL PERSONNEL DURING THE REVOLUTIONARY WAR,
The Archives, Washington, DC, Microfilm PUblication
M879, 1 roll. [also includes Marines, copies in VSL&A,
NA, GSU]

__National Genealogical Society, INDEX OF REVOLUTIONARY
WAR PENSION APPLICATIONS IN THE NATIONAL ARCHIVES, The
Society, Washington, DC, 1976. [also includes bounty
land records]

__National DAR, DAR PATRIOT INDEX, The Society, Washing-
ton, DC, 1979, 2 volumes.

__US Pay Department, War Department, REGISTER OF CERTIFI-
CATES ISSUED BY JOHN PIERCE TO OFFICERS AND SOLDIERS OF
THE CONTINENTAL ARMY, Genealogical Publ. Co., Balti-
more, MD, 1973.

If you locate your ancestor in these reference sources,
write the following address and ask for 3 copies of Form
NATF-80.

__Military Service Records (NNCC), National Archives,
Washington, DC 20408.

Upon receipt, fill them out, check the box on one asking
for Military Service Records, and if you found pension or
bounty land references, check on others the boxes
labelled Pension Records and/or Bounty Land Records.
Then mail the forms back. The Archives staff is very
busy, and the filling of your request may be slow. If
you want faster service you can go to the NA in person or
you can hire a researcher in Washington, DC to do the
work for you. Addresses of researchers will be found in:

__V. N. Chambers, editor, THE GENEALOGICAL HELPER, Ever-
ton Publishers, Logan, UT, latest September-October
issue.

There is another very useful possibility for obtaining
some of these microfilms. The indexes (M860, M879) and
the records to which they refer (M881), as well as the
microfilmed pension and bounty land applications can be
borrowed on interlibrary loan by your local library from
AGLL (PO Box 244, Bountiful, UT 84010).

The __second__ step that you should take, especially if you failed to find your ancestor in the first step, is to look into __state__ sources. State sources attempt to list both militia and Continental Army soldiers, whereas the national records list mainly the Continental Army soldiers. The best printed state record compilations dealing with VA War participants are:

__ H. J. Eckenrode, LIST OF REVOLUTIONARY SOLDIERS OF VA, VA State Library, Richmond, VA, 1912, and SUPPLEMENT, 1913.

__ J. H. Gwathmey, HISTORICAL REGISTER OF VIRGINIANS IN THE REVOLUTION, 1775-83, Genealogical Publ. Co., Baltimore, MD, 1973 (1938).

__ M. and L. Gardner, VA REVOLUTIONARY WAR STATE PENSIONS, VA Genealogical Society, Richmond, VA, 1980.

__ VA MILITARY RECORDS, Genealogical Publ. Co., Baltimore, MD, 1983.

The first two volumes deal chiefly with __service records__. The third volume lists __state pensions__ which were awarded to about 600 persons by the VA State Legislature. There are two indexes in VSL&A which also deal with __pension claims__:

__ CARD INDEX TO THE REVOLUTIONARY WAR PENSIONS GRANTED BY VA, VSL&A, Richmond, VA, Archives Reading Room, alphabetical.

__ INDEX TO REVOLUTIONARY WAR REJECTED PENSION CLAIMS, VSL&A, Richmond, VA, Archives Reading Room, typescript, alphabetical.

In addition to pensions, a great number of __bounty land awards__ were made to VA Revolutionary veterans. These have been discussed in section 22, where instructions for obtaining the records have been given. During the War, many civilians gave goods, supplies, and services for support of American troops. Indexes of those who made __claims__ for payment after the War are in VSL&A:

__ CARD INDEX TO REVOLUTIONARY WAR PUBLIC SERVICE CLAIMS, VSL&A, Richmond, VA, Archives Reading Room, alphabetical, leads to public service claim records and microfilm copies of records.

__ CARD INDEX TO REJECTED REVOLUTIONARY WAR CLAIMS, VSL&A, Richmond, VA, Archives Reading Room, alphabetical.

Other works which should be looked at as you seek further information include:

__ G. M. Brumbaugh, REVOLUTIONARY WAR RECORDS, Genealogical Publ. Co., Baltimore, MD, 1967 (1936). [VA bounty land warrants, Military District of OH]

__L. A. Burgess, VA SOLDIERS OF 1776, Reprint Co., Spartanburg, SC, 1973 (1927-9), 3 volumes.

__A. W. Burns, VA GENEALOGIES AND COUNTY RECORDS, The Author, Washington, DC, 1941-4, 11 volumes. [pension abstracts of Revolutionary War, War of 1812, Indian Wars]

__J. T. Cannon, INDEX TO MILITARY CERTIFICATES, 1787, Register of KY State Historical Society 22 (1924).

__DAR of NC, BIOGRAPHICAL SKETCHES OF SOLDIERS AND PATRIOTS IN THE BATTLE OF GUILFORD COURT HOUSE, The Society, Greensboro, NC, 1958, 9 volumes.

__DAR of VA, ROSTER, 1890-1958, SUPPLEMENT, 1959-62, The Society, Pulaski, VA, 1959, 1963.

__J. F. Dorman, VA REVOLUTIONARY PENSION APPLICATIONS ABSTRACTED, The Author, Washington, DC, 1958-, volumes 1-.

__W. H. English, CONQUEST OF THE COUNTRY NORTHWEST OF THE RIVER OHIO, 1778-83, (1896). [men who served in this campaign, land allotments to them]

__A. Latham and B. G. Leonard, A ROLL OF THE OFFICERS IN THE VA LINE OF THE REVOLUTIONARY ARMY WHO HAVE RECEIVED LAND BOUNTY IN OH AND KY, Chillicothe, OH, 1966 (1822).

__LIST OF NON-COMMISSIONED OFFICERS AND SOLDIERS WHO HAVE NOT RECEIVED BOUNTY LAND, Ye Olde Genealogie Shoppe, Indianapolis, IN, 1979 (1835).

__J. T. McAllister, VA MILITIA IN THE REVOLUTIONARY WAR, The Author, Hot Springs, VA, 1913.

__L. K. McGhee, VA PENSION ABSTRACTS OF THE WARS OF THE REVOLUTION, 1812, AND INDIAN WARS, The Author, Washington, DC, 1953-66, 35 volumes.

__W. T. R. Saffell, RECORDS OF THE REVOLUTIONARY WAR, Genealogical Publ. Co., Baltimore, MD, 1969 (1894).

__E. M. Sanchez-Saavedra, A GUIDE TO VA MILITARY ORGANIZATIONS IN THE AMERICAN REVOLUTION, 1774-87, VA State Library, Richmond, VA, 1978.

__Sons of the Revolution of VA, SONS OF THE REVOLUTION IN THE STATE OF VA, The Sons, Richmond, VA, 1922-32, volumes 1-10; also GENEALOGY OF MEMBERS, Mitchell & Hotchkiss, Richmond, VA, 1939.

__R. A. Stewart, THE HISTORY OF VA'S NAVY OF THE REVOLUTION, Mitchell & Hotchkiss, Richmond, VA, 1934.

__R. G. Thwaites, editor, FRONTIER DEFENSE ON THE UPPER OHIO, 1777-8, WI Historical Society, Madison, WI, 1912.

__C. Torrence, GENEALOGY OF MEMBERS OF THE SOCIETY OF THE
SONS OF THE AMERICAN REVOLUTION, The Society, Richmond,
VA, 1939.

__S. M. Wilson, CATALOGUE OF REVOLUTIONARY SOLDIERS AND
SAILORS OF VA TO WHOM LAND BOUNTY WARRANTS WERE GRANTED
BY VA, Genealogical Publ. Co., Baltimore, MD, 1967
(1913).

One further index in VSL&A might be of use

__CARD INDEX TO REVOLUTIONARY WAR PARTICIPANTS MENTIONED
IN THE J. K. MARTIN PAPERS, VSL&A, Richmond, VA, Archives Reading Room, alphabetical.

For considerably more detail on tracing your Revolutionary War ancestor, you may consult a book devoted entirely
to this topic:

__Geo. K. Schweitzer, REVOLUTIONARY WAR GENEALOGY, The
Author, 407 Regent Court, Knoxville, TN 37923 ($7
postpaid).

27. Military records: 1812-1860

Numerous soldiers from VA saw active service in the
War of 1812, which was fought 1812-5. As was the case
with the Revolutionary War, three types of records should
be sought: military service, pension, and bounty land.
The NA has original service records, pension records, and
bounty land records, plus indexes to all three. Hence,
you should write the following and request 3 copies of
NATF Form 80.

__Military Service Records (NNCC), National Archives,
Washington, DC 20408.

Upon receipt, fill them out, giving your ancestor's name
and state (VA), as much other pertinent data as you can,
check one request box on each (military service, pension,
bounty land), attach a note asking for all records, and
then mail back. Because of their backlog, the Archives
is often slow. If you want faster service, hire a
researcher in Washington, DC, to search the records for
you. Such researchers may be located in:

__V. N. Chambers, editor, THE GENEALOGICAL HELPER, Ever-
ton Publishers, Logan, UT, latest September-October
issue.

These procedures should procure for you the service
records, the pension records, and the bounty land application file (containing a bounty land warrant number). If
you get the number, you may then write the following
office for copies of the bounty land warrant file:

__General Archives Division, National Archives, Washington, DC, 20409.

Microfilm copies of the indexes to service records and pension applications are at NA and GSU (available through BLGSU), and are available at many LGL.

__National Archives, INDEX TO COMPILED SERVICE RECORDS OF VOLUNTEER SOLDIERS WHO SERVED DURING THE WAR OF 1812, Microfilm Publication M602, The Archives, Washington, DC, 234 rolls.

__National Archives, INDEX TO WAR OF 1812 PENSION APPLICATION FILES, Microfilm Publication M313, The Archives, Washington, DC, 102 rolls.

These microfilms (M602, M313), as well as those on bounty land warrants (M848) can be borrowed on interlibrary loan by your local library from AGLL (PO Box 244, Bountiful, UT 84010).

Among published national sources for War of 1812 information are these:

__F. I. Ordway, Jr., REGISTER OF THE GENERAL SOCIETY OF THE WAR OF 1812, The Society, Washington, DC, 1972.

__E. S. Galvin, 1812 ANCESTOR INDEX, National Society of US Daughters of 1812, Washington, DC, 1970.

__C. S. Peterson, KNOWN MILITARY DEAD DURING THE WAR OF 1812, The Author, Baltimore, MD, 1955.

In addition, there are several source materials relating specifically to the state of VA:

__CARD INDEX TO WAR OF 1812 PARTICIPANTS MENTIONED IN THE J. K. MARTIN PAPERS, VSL&A Richmond, VA, Archives Reading Room, alphabetical.

__CARD INDEX TO VA WAR OF 1812 SOLDIERS PAID BY VA PRIOR TO FEDERAL PAYMENT, VSL&A, Richmond, VA, Archives Reading Room, alphabetical.

__VA WAR OF 1812 MUSTER AND PAY ROLLS, VSL&A, Richmond, VA, Archives Division, 26 volumes.

__L. K. McGhee, VA PENSION ABSTRACTS OF THE WARS OF THE REVOLUTION, 1812, AND INDIAN WARS, The Author, Washington, DC, 1953-66, 35 volumes.

__A. W. Burns, VA GENEALOGIES AND COUNTY RECORDS, The Author, Washington, DC, 1941-4, 11 volumes. [pension abstracts of Revolutionary War, War of 1812, Indian Wars]

Of great value are two published volumes which have been compiled by the state of VA from official state records:

__VA Auditor's Office, MUSTER ROLLS OF THE VA MILITIA IN THE WAR OF 1812, The Office, Richmond, VA, 1852.

__VA Auditor's Office, PAY ROLLS OF MILITIA ENTITLED TO
LAND BOUNTY UNDER THE ACT OF CONGRESS OF SEP. 28, 1850,
The Office, Richmond, VA, 1851.
VSL&A, VHSL, ALUV, LOC, and GSU have most of these books
(both the national and the VA), and those held by GSU can
be borrowed through BLGSU. The nationally-oriented books
are likely to be found in many LGL, and some of the
national and VA volumes will be found in RL.

During the Indian Wars period (1817-98), some VA
personnel were involved in several conflicts. NA again
has military records, pension records, and bounty land
records, plus indexes to all three. NATF Form 80 should
be obtained and used in accordance with the above instructions to obtain records. The books by McGhee and
Burns (mentioned above) should also be consulted. The NA
indexes to the Indian Wars service records and pension
files are available on microfilm and may be found in NA,
as well as GSU (BLGSU) and some other LGL.
__National Archives, INDEX TO COMPILED SERVICE RECORDS OF
VOLUNTEER SOLDIERS WHO SERVED DURING INDIAN WARS,
Microfilm Publication M629, The Archives, Washington,
DC, 42 rolls.
__National Archives, INDEX TO INDIAN WARS PENSION FILES,
Microfilm Publication T318, The Archives, Washington,
DC, 12 rolls.

The Mexican War was fought 1846-8. As before, NATF
Form 80 should be obtained and employed to request military service, pension, and bounty land records from the
NA. Please recall that there are two types of bounty
land records (applications and warrants) and that they
must be sought in two different divisions of the NA. An
exceptionally valuable publication is a complete roster
of both regular and volunteer troops in the Mexican War:
__W. H. Roberts, MEXICAN WAR VETERANS, 1846-8, Washing-
ton, DC, 1887.
Other helpful sources include:
__C. S. Peterson, KNOWN MILITARY DEAD DURING THE MEXICAN
WAR, The Author, Baltimore, MD, 1957.
__CARD INDEX TO VA MEXICAN WAR SOLDIERS, VSL&A, Richmond,
VA, Archives Reading Room, alphabetical.
The volumes of MUSTER ROLLS by the VA Auditor's Office,
which were listed under the material on the War of 1812,
also contain muster rolls for the Mexican War. Microfilm
indexes to Mexican War service records and pension files

are available in NA, as well as GSU (BLGSU) and some other LGL.

__National Archives, INDEX TO THE COMPILED SERVICE REC-ORDS OF VOLUNTEER SOLDIERS DURING THE MEXICAN WAR, Microfilm Publication M616, The Archives, Washington, DC, 41 rolls.

__National Archives, INDEX TO MEXICAN WAR PENSION FILES, Microfilm Publication T317, The Archives, Washington, DC, 14 rolls.

The two books mentioned above (Roberts and Peterson) are in VSL&A, LOC, and GSU (BLGSU), and in some LGL and RL.

28. Military records: Civil War

There are several major keys to service records of Civil War veterans, both Confederate and Union, who fought from the state of VA:

__National Archives, INDEX TO THE COMPILED SERVICE REC-ORDS OF VOLUNTEER UNION SOLDIERS WHO SERVED IN ORGANI-ZATIONS FROM THE STATE OF VA, Microfilm Publication M394, The Archives, Washington, DC, 1 roll.

__National Archives, INDEX TO THE COMPILED SERVICE REC-ORDS OF CONFEDERATE SOLDIERS WHO SERVED IN ORGANIZA-TIONS FROM THE STATE OF VA, Microfilm Publication M382, The Archives, Washington, DC, 62 rolls.

__CARD INDEX TO VA CONFEDERATE SOLDIERS, VSL&A, Richmond, VA, Archives Reading Room, alphabetical, leads to many Confederate Roster Volumes filed in the Reading Room.

__CARD INDEX TO VA CONFEDERATE NAVAL PARTICIPANTS, VSL&A, Richmond, VA, Archives Reading Room, alphabetical.

All four of these sources are available in VSL&A, and the microfilms are to be found in many places including NA, GSU (BLGSU), and some LGL and RL. The two microfilm indexes lead to the compiled service records which are in NA. The NA has microfilmed these records making them available in VSL&A, GSU (BLGSU), and some LGL and RL.

__National Archives, COMPILED SERVICE RECORDS OF VOLUN-TEER UNION SOLDIERS WHO SERVED IN ORGANIZATIONS FROM VA, Microfilm Publication M398, The Archives, Washington, DC, 7 rolls.

__National Archives, COMPILED SERVICE RECORDS OF CONFED-ERATE SOLDIERS WHO SERVED IN ORGANIZATIONS FROM VA, Microfilm Publication M324, The Archives, Washington, DC, 1075 rolls.

The service records may be viewed on the microfilms, but if you want copies of them, they should be ordered from

NA using NATF Form 80 (see section 26 for instructions), or by having a researcher in Washington, DC, obtain them. The two card indexes in VSL&A will lead you to VA state records which are also in VSL&A.

There were no bounty land awards made by either VA or the US for service in the 1861-5 conflict. The US did award pensions to Union veterans, widows, and heirs, but obviously not to Confederates. These pension records for Union participants can be obtained from NA though the use of NATF Form 80, or you can hire a researcher in Washington, DC, to do it (see previous section 26, end of 1st paragraph for instructions). In 1888 VA passed an act providing pensions to disabled Confederate veterans and to widows of those killed in action. Coverage was broadened in succeeding acts to veterans, widows, daughters, and sisters. All the VA pension applications are in VSL&A, and an index is provided:
__CARD INDEX TO CONFEDERATE PENSION APPLICATIONS BY PARTICIPANTS AND WIDOWS, VSL&A, Richmond, VA, Archives Branch, ask for index at desk, alphabetical, leads to applications.
In order to locate pension applications by sisters and daughters (possible after 1915), VSL&A needs to have the full name of the applicant, the county, and the application date. The various pension applications contain differing amounts of genealogical information, early ones limited amounts (veteran's or widow's name, husband's name, residence, military unit, date and place of enlistment, veteran's military death place and date or disability, age), later ones more.

A number of other volumes and sources relating to VA and its participants in the War Between the States are given below. Some of them may be helpful to you in your ancestor search:
__CARD INDEX TO VA CONFEDERATE UNITS AND LOCALITIES IN WHICH THEY WERE RAISED, VSL&A, Richmond, VA, Archives Reading Room, alphabetical according to county and name of unit.
__NAME INDEX TO THE CONFEDERATE VETERAN MAGAZINE, VSL&A, Richmond, VA, Library Reading Room, alphabetical. [40 volumes of Confederate information and memories]
__J. I. Robertson, Jr., AN INDEX-GUIDE TO THE SOUTHERN HISTORICAL SOCIETY PAPERS, Kraus International PUblica-

tions, Millwood, NY, 1980, 2 volumes. [indexes 52 volumes of Confederate historical information]
__R. A. Brock, THE APPOMATTOX ROSTER: A LIST OF PAROLEES OF THE ARMY OF NORTHERN VA, Antiquarian Press, New York, NY, 1962.
__D. A. Lilley, OBITUARY INDEX TO THE CONFEDERATE VETER-AN, Morningside Bookshop, Dayton, OH, 1978.
__R. P. Riggs, REGISTER OF REBEL DESERTERS, VA Genealo-gist (1973-), volumes 17-.
__J. I. Robertson, Jr., PROCEEDINGS OF THE ADVISORY COUNCIL OF VA, April 21-June 19, 1861, VA State Libra-ry, Richmond, VA, 1977. [100s of VA officers]
__L. A. Wallace, Jr., A GUIDE TO VA MILITARY ORGANIZA-TIONS, 1861-5, VA Book Co., Berryville, VA, 1964. [every company involved is named, 48 page index of names]
__R. W. Watkins, CONFEDERATE BURIALS IN VA CEMETERIES.
These books are available at VSL&A; some of them are in VHSL, ALUV, LOC, and GSU (BLGSU). Some are also to be found in LGL and RL.

If you care to go into detail in researching your VA Civil War ancestor, the following book will be of consid-erable help:
__Geo. K. Schweitzer, CIVIL WAR GENEALOGY, The Author, 407 Regent Court, Knoxville, TN 37923 ($7 postpaid).
This work treats local, state, and national records, service and pension records, regimental and naval histor-ies, enlistment rosters, hospital records, court-martial reports, burial registers, national cemeteries, grave-stone allotments, amnesties, pardons, state militias, discharge papers, officer biographies, prisons, prison-ers, battle sites, maps, relics, weapons, museums, monu-ments, memorials, deserters, black soldiers, Indian soldiers, and many other topics.

There is in the NA an index to service records of the Spanish-American War. Again a properly filled out and submitted NATF Form 80 (see section 26 for instruc-tions) will bring you both military service and pension records. Or, you may choose to hire a researcher in Washington, DC, to obtain the copies for you. As you will recall, researchers may be located in:
__V. N. Chambers, editor, THE GENEALOGICAL HELPER, Ever-ton Publishers, Logan, UT, latest September-October issue.

Records for <u>World</u> <u>War</u> <u>I</u> and subsequent wars may be
obtained from:
__National Personnel Records Center, GSA (Military
   Records), 9700 Page Blvd., St. Louis, MO 63132.

29. <u>Mortuary</u> <u>records</u>

   Very few VA mortuary records have been transcribed
or microfilmed. This means that you must write directly
to the mortuaries which you know or suspect were involved
in burying your ancestor. Sometimes a death certificate
will name the mortuary; sometimes it is the only one
nearby; sometimes only one existed in the area where your
ancestor died; sometimes you will have to write several
to ascertain which one might have done the funeral ar-
rangements. Mortuaries for VA with their addresses are
listed in the following volume:
__C. O. Kates, editor, THE AMERICAN BLUE BOOK OF FUNERAL
   DIRECTORS, Kates-Boyleston Publications, New York, NY,
   latest issue.
This reference book will usually be found in the offices
of most mortuaries. In all correspondence with mortuaries be sure to enclose an SASE.

30. <u>Naturalization</u> <u>records</u>

   In the early colonial period (1607-1700), the major
immigrants to the territory that later became the US were
English. This was especially true for VA. By the end of
the century (1699/1700), when large groups of other
nationalities were beginning to arrive, English tradi-
tions, customs, and language had become firmly established. In spite of the English dominance, many early
foreign settlers simply did not bother to change their
citizenship. This was particularly the case in frontier
areas and when foreigners set up a separate community of
their own as many did. However, those who chose to do so
could swear loyalty to the British Sovereign and thereby
become citizens. In 1671, VA passed a statute permitting
a foreigner to petition the Grand Assembly for citizenship and then to take an oath of allegiance to the King.
In 1680, another statute appointed the Governor as an
officer who could accept an oath of loyalty and grant
naturalization. This provision was broadened in 1705 to
the authorization of the VA Commander in Chief as a
naturalization officer. These laws were a part of the

action of the colonial government, as time went on, to insist more strongly that foreigners change their citizenship if they intended to be permanent residents. In 1740, the English Parliament passed a law which set requirements for naturalization: seven years residence in one colony, and then the taking of an oath of allegiance to the Crown. This oath was generally certified by a court.

In 1779, VA declared that all white people born in VA, living there two years, or all who came in later would become citizens. However, in 1783, a new law required all aliens to come before a court of record, declare their intention to live in the state, and swear allegiance to the Commonwealth of VA. In 1790, the US Congress enacted a federal naturalization act. This law required one year's residence in a state, two year's residence in the US, and the taking of an oath of loyalty in a court. In 1795, a five year residence came to be required, then in 1798, a fourteen year residence and the filing of a declaration of intention (to become a citizen) five years before the taking of the oath. In 1802, a revised law required residence in a state for one year and in the US for five years, and the filing of the declaration of intent three years before the taking of the oath. The declaration of intention and the final oath taking could be done in any circuit or district court of the US or any court of record of a state. Wives and children of naturalized males usually became citizens automatically. When the US took over new areas of land (LA Purchase, FL, TX, CA, NV, UT, etc.), the inhabitants automatically received citizenship. Persons who gave military service to the US and received an honorable discharge also received citizenship.

In 1906, a federal law created the Bureau of Immigration and Naturalization, and this agency has kept records on all naturalizations since then. Thus, if you suspect that your ancestor was naturalized after June 1906, write to the following address for a Form 6641 which you can use to request records:
 __Immigration and Naturalization Service, 415 I St., Washington, DC 20536.
For naturalization records before June 1906, you need to recall that the process could have taken place in any US, state, or local court. This often makes locating the

records a difficult process. What it usually means is
that all possible court records must be gone through. And
since few indexes have been made, this is generally a
page-by-page endeavor using court records for the time
period you think is proper. The US Court at Norfolk has
records and indexes for 1851 and later; the records of
the US Court at Roanoke for 1855, 1864-8, and 1867-96 are
in the Federal Records Center at Suitland, MD, along with
indexes; and the VSL&A has indexes and records for
various US Courts in VA during 1790-1861. A few cities
and counties have indexed some of their naturalization
records: Nansemond(1866-1904), Norfolk(1870-), Nottoway
(1865-1900), Pittsylvania(1767-1904). But, in most
cities and counties, the records are included in court
order books, the majority of which are not indexed. For
further information on naturalization records, you may
consult:

__J. C. and L. L. Neagles, LOCATING YOUR IMMIGRANT ANCES-
   TOR: A GUIDE TO NATURALIZATION RECORDS, Everton Pub-
   lishers, Logan, UT, 1987.
__National Archives, PRE-1840 FEDERAL DISTRICT AND CIR-
   CUIT COURT RECORDS, Special List No. 31, The Archives,
   Washington, DC, 1970.

31. Newspaper records

A number of original and microfilmed newspapers are
available for towns, cities, and counties of VA. Some of
them have been indexed, but the number is not large.
These newspapers are likely to contain information on
births, deaths, marriages, anniversaries, divorces,
family reunions, land sales, legal notices, ads of pro-
fessionals and businesses, and local news. The largest
VA collections are to be found in VSL&A, VHSL, and ALUV.
There are special indexes to newspapers in each of these
places:

__REVOLVING INDEX TO VA NEWSPAPERS ON MICROFILM, VSL&A,
   Richmond, VA, Library Reading Room, at desk, alphabeti-
   cal.
__CARD INDEX TO NEWSPAPER ARTICLES, VSL&A, Richmond, VA,
   Library Reading room, look under county, city, town,
   event, and also under the heading Biography — then per-
   son's name.
__CARD INDEX TO NEWSPAPERS, VHSL, Richmond, VA, Reading
   Room, by year, then alphabetical.

__CARD INDEX TO NEWSPAPERS, ALUV, Charlottesville, VA,
Rare Book Department, look under VA, then under city or
town.

General listings of VA newspapers and their loca-
tions will be found in:
__C. S. Brigham, HISTORY AND BIBLIOGRAPHY OF AMERICAN
NEWSPAPERS, 1690-1820, American Antiquarian Society,
Worcester, MA, 1947, 1961, 2 volumes.
__W. Gregory, AMERICAN NEWSPAPERS, 1821-1936, H. W.
Wilson Co., New York, NY, 1937.
__Library of Congress, NEWSPAPERS IN MICROFILM, US
Library of Congress, Washington, DC, 1973; Supplements,
1978, 1979.
GSU, BLGSU, and RL have some VA newspapers. Some of the
VA newspapers which have been indexed are listed in the
following volumes along with the index locations:
__A. C. Milner, NEWSPAPER INDEXES, Scarecrow Press,
Metuchen, NJ, 1977, 1980, 1981, 3 volumes.
Not to be overlooked is a published index to VA's colo-
nial newspaper:
__L. J. Cappon and S. F. Duff, VA GAZETTE INDEX, 1736-80,
Institute of History and Culture, Williamsburg, VA,
1950, 2 volumes.
And of great value is a publication of the VA Historical
Society:
__VA Historical Society, MARRIAGES AND DEATHS FROM RICH-
MOND NEWSPAPERS, 1780-1820, The Society, Richmond, VA,
1983.
A few LL have newspapers and/or newspaper indexes which
are not listed in the above works, so it is always
important to inquire.

32. Published genealogies for the US

There are a large number of published indexes,
microfilm indexes, and card indexes which list published
genealogies at the national level. The most important
indexes and compilations dealing exclusively with VA were
listed in section 18. These listings included the Card
Catalogs in VSL&A (Library Section), VHSL, ALUV, LOC,
GSU, and BLGSU. This section sets out indexes to genealogies all over the US. They contain many references to
Virginians and therefore you must not fail to look into
them. Among the larger ones are
__SURNAME INDEX, GSU and BLGSU.

__CARD CATALOG, LOC, Washington, DC.
__F. Rider, AMERICAN GENEALOGICAL INDEX, Godfrey Memorial
Library, Middletown, CT, 1942-52, 48 volumes. [mil-
lions of references]
__F. Rider, AMERICAN GENEALOGICAL & BIOGRAPHICAL INDEX,
Godfrey Memorial Library, Middletown, CT, 1952-79, over
110 volumes. [millions of references]
__The Newberry Library, THE GENEALOGICAL INDEX OF THE
NEWBERRY LIBRARY, G. K. Hall, Boston, MA, 1960, 4
volumes. [500,000 names]
__The New York Public Library, DICTIONARY CATALOG OF THE
LOCAL HISTORY & GENEALOGY DIVISION OF THE NEW YORK
PUBLIC LIBRARY, G. K. Hall, Boston, MA, 1974, 20 vol-
umes. [318,000 entries]
__M. J. Kaminkow, GENEALOGIES IN THE LIBRARY OF CONGRESS,
Magna Carta, Baltimore, MD, 1972. [25,000 references]
__J. Munsell's Sons, INDEX TO AMERICAN GENEALOGIES, 1711-
1908, reprint, Genealogical Publ. Co., Baltimore, MD,
1967. [60,000 references]
__M. J. Kaminkow, A COMPLEMENT TO GENEALOGIES IN THE
LIBRARY OF CONGRESS, Magna Carta Book Co., Baltimore,
MD, 1981.
The first index is obviously available at GSU and all
BLGSU. The third item and those following are available
at VSL&A, other LGL, GSU (BLGSU), and LOC. Many are
available at VHSL and ALUV, and some may be found in RL.

Also available at VSL&A, VHSL, ALUV, LOC, GSU
(BLGSU), and in some RL and LL are several regional
volumes which can lead you to genealogical information on
VA families:
__Z. Armstrong, NOTABLE SOUTHERN FAMILIES, Lookout Pub-
lishing Co., Chattanooga, TN, 1918-33, 6 volumes.
__J. B. Boddie, HISTORICAL SOUTHERN FAMILIES, Pacific
Coast Publishers, Redwood City, CA, 1957-, 15 volumes,
others in process. [CARD INDEX in VSL&A, Library
Section]
__E. K. Kirkham, INDEX TO SOME OF THE FAMILY RECORDS OF
THE SOUTHERN STATES, Everton Publishers, Logan, UT,
1979.

33. Regional records

In addition to state publications and local publications, there are a sizable number of valuable regional
publications which should not be overlooked by a VA

researcher. These publications apply to specific regions which are made up of a few or many VA counties. Quite a few volumes relating to the Shenandoah Valley are of considerable value. Among them are:

__B. M. Ashby, SHENANDOAH VALLEY MARRIAGE BONDS, 1772–1850, VA Book Co., Berryville, VA, 1967. [large index]

__J. Braun, SHENANDOAH VALLEY FAMILY DATA, 1799–1813, The Author.

__T. K. Cartmell, SHENANDOAH VALLEY PIONEERS AND THEIR DESCENDANTS: A HISTORY OF FREDERICK COUNTY, 1738–1908, VA Book Co., Berryville, VA, 1972 (1908). [9,500 names]

__F. H. Hart, THE VALLEY OF VA IN THE REVOLUTION, 1763–89, Russell & Russell, New York, NY, 1971 (1942).

__S. Kercheval, A HISTORY OF THE VALLEY OF VA, VA Book Co., Berryville, VA, 1973 (1925).

__J. E. Norris, HISTORY OF THE LOWER SHENANDOAH VALLEY, VA Book Co., Berryville, VA, 1973 (1890). [Berkeley, Clarke, Frederick, Jefferson Counties]

__J. W. Wayland, TWENTY-FIVE CHAPTERS ON THE SHENANDOAH VALLEY, Carrier Co., Bridgewater, VA, 1976 (1957).

__J. W. Wayland, VA VALLEY RECORDS, Genealogical Publ. Co., Baltimore, MD, 1973 (1930).

__H. McK. Wilson, THE LEXINGTON PRESBYTERY HERITAGE, McClure Press, Verona, VA, 1971.

The Southside is also represented by useful books of the regional type, including:

__L. C. Bell, THE OLD FREE STATE: A CONTRIBUTION TO THE HISTORY OF LUNENBURG COUNTY AND SOUTHSIDE VA, Genealog-ical Publ. Co., Baltimore, MD, 1974 (1927). [20,000 Southside listings, very important for Southside]

__L. C. Bell, SUNLIGHT ON THE SOUTHSIDE: LIST OF TITHES, LUNENBURG COUNTY, 1748–83, Genealogical Publ. Co., Baltimore, MD, 1974 (1931). [10,000 early people between James River and NC]

__J. B. Boddie, COLONIAL SURRY, Genealogical Publ. Co., Baltimore, MD, 1974 (1948). [early Surry covered almost all of southern VA]

__J. B. Boddie, SEVENTEENTH CENTURY ISLE OF WIGHT COUNTY, Genealogical Publ. Co., Baltimore, MD, 1973 (1938).

__J. B. Boddie, SOUTHSIDE VA FAMILIES, Genealogical Publ. Co., Baltimore MD, 1966 (1955-6), 2 volumes. [over 100 families]

__W. A. Watson, NOTES ON SOUTHSIDE VA, Genealogical Publ. Co., Baltimore, MD, 1977 (1925).

Below are some very helpful __books__ dealing with the Southwestern area of VA:

___L. H. M. Baber, L. A. Blunt, and M. A. L. Collins,
MARRIAGES AND DEATHS FROM LYNCHBURG, VA NEWSPAPERS,
1794-1836, Genealogical Publ. Co., Baltimore, MD, 1980.
[6,000 names]

___N. Schreiner-Yantis, MONTGOMERY COUNTY-CIRCA 1790, The
Author, Springfield, VA, 1973.   [in 1790 Montgomery
County covered area of 22 later counties]

___L. P. Summers, ANNALS OF SOUTHWEST VA, 1769-1800,
Genealogical Publ. Co., Baltimore, MD, 1970 (1929).
[Botetourt, Fincastle, Montgomery, Washington, Wythe
Counties]

___L. P. Summers, HISTORY OF SOUTHWEST VA, Genealogical
Publ. Co., Baltimore, MD, 1971 (1903). [territory now
occupied by 19 VA counties]

___A. L. Worrell, OVER THE MOUNTAIN MEN: THEIR EARLY COURT
RECORDS IN SOUTHWEST VA, Genealogical Publ. Co., Baltimore, MD, 1979 (1934). [9,000 persons in 9 counties,
late 18th-early 19th centuries]

In the region of __Northwest VA__ __and__ __Southwest PA__, these
works should be utilized:

___B. Crumrine, VA COURT RECORDS IN SOUTHWESTERN PA,
Genealogical Publ. Co., Baltimore, MD, 1974 (1902-5).
[time period 1775-80]

___L. V. McWhorter, THE BORDER SETTLERS OF NORTHWESTERN
VA, Genealogical Publ. Co., Baltimore, MD, 1975 (1915).

___I. Waldenmaier, INDEX TO THE MINUTE BOOKS OF THE VA
COURTS HELD WITHIN THE LIMITS OF SOUTHWESTERN PA,
Washington, DC, 1957. [time period 1775-80]

For the __Eastern__ __Shore__, three of the better reference
volumes are:

___H. C. Forman, THE VA EASTERN SHORE AND ITS BRITISH
ORIGINS, Eastern Shore Publ. Asso., Easton, MD, 1975.

___M. M. Turman, THE EASTERN SHORE OF VA, 1603-1964,
Eastern Shore News, Onancock, VA, 1964.

___R. T. Whitelaw, VA'S EASTERN SHORE, A HISTORY OF NORTH-
AMPTON AND ACCOMACK COUNTIES, Peter Smith, Magnolia,
MA, 1968 (1951), 2 volumes.

The advancing __VA__ __Frontier__ has given rise to several
volumes, two of the most serviceable being:

___J. H. Gwathmey, TWELVE VA COUNTIES WHERE THE WESTERN
MIGRATION BEGAN, Genealogical Publ. Co., Baltimore, MD,
1981 (1937).   [Albemarle, Augusta, Caroline, Essex,
Gloucester, Goochland, Hanover, King William, King and
Queen, Louisa, New Kent, Orange Counties]

__F. B. Kegley, KEGLEY'S VA FRONTIER, 1740-83, The Author, Roanoke, VA, 1967. [early Botetourt, Washington, Fincastle, Montgomery, and Wythe Counties]

Finally, two other important books need to be called to your attention, one treating the Northern Neck and another the Lower Tidewater region:

__B. Mitchell, BEGINNING AT A WHITE OAK-PATENTS AND NORTHERN NECK GRANTS, Fairfax County Publ., Fairfax, VA, 1977.

__R. D. Whichard, THE HISTORY OF LOWER TIDEWATER, VA, Lewis Historical Publ. Co., New York, NY, 1959, 3 volumes, the third on family history.

Almost all of these volumes will be found in VSL&A, VHSL, and LOC. Most are in ALUV, and many may be located in LGL and GSU (BLGSU), and those dealing with specific regions will be in the corresponding RL.

34. Tax lists

Tax lists of various sorts (assessments, land, personal property, delinquent) are exceptionally valuable records for establishing · the year-to-year locations of ancestors. Unfortunately, very few such lists survive for the colonial years (1607-1776). Some volumes of collected records for limited portions of this time period are available:

__E. Lawrence-Dow, VA RENT ROLLS, 1704, The Author, Richmond, VA, 1976. [5,544 land owners]

__A. L. W. Smith, THE QUIT RENTS OF VA, Genealogical Publ. Co., Baltimore, MD, 1980 (1957). [rolls of the Northern Neck for 1704 plus rent rolls of the 14 VA counties which paid rent to the King]

__R. F. and I. B. Woodson, VA TITHABLES FROM BURNED RECORD COUNTIES, The Authors, Richmond, VA, 1970. [counties of Buckingham 1773-4, Gloucester 1770-1, 1774-5, Hanover 1763 and 1770, James City 1768-9, Stafford 1768-73]

__VA TAX RECORDS, Genealogical Publ. Co., Baltimore, MD, 1983.

The VSL&A also has a check list of all known records including tithable (taxable person) lists, rental lists, and poll lists (names of persons who voted for legislature candidates).

__TYPESCRIPT INDEX TO LISTS OF TITHABLES, RENT ROLLS, AND POLLS, VSL&A, Richmond, VA, Archives Reading Room, by

counties, then chronologically, leads to original
records, published volumes, and microfilmed record
copies, ask at desk.
The four books mentioned above may be found in VSL&A,
VHSL, ALUV, LOC, and GSU (BLGSU), and one or more of them
may be in LGL and RL.

Starting in 1782, there are two types of tax lists
for all VA counties. These are land tax lists and personal property tax lists. The originals are held by
VSL&A and a few copies may be found in CH. The year 1808
is missing in all these records because the VA Legislature appropriated no money to finance the data collection
in 1808. The land tax lists show the taxpayer's name,
the amount of land in acres, the value, and the amount of
tax. About 1810, a general location of the land is
added, this usually referring only to the river or stream
on which the land was located or to the neighboring
property owners. Dates of death can sometimes be spotted
in the records of land being listed as an estate or in
the widow's name. About 1820, the property location is
given in miles and direction from the county CH. The
personal property tax lists include the taxpayer's name
and the number of white taxable persons (tithes) in the
household over the age of 16. Sometimes this age is
considered to be 21. In some lists, in earlier years,
the number of slaves over and under 16 is given. Sometimes items of property were also taxed and thus listed:
cattle, horses, carriages, clocks, and some pieces of
furniture. Be on the lookout for marginal notes which
the enumerator may have added. These records exist from
1782 to now and thus constitute a year-by-year enumera-
tion of adult males in VA.

The tax records are available in microfilm copy form
in VSL&A and for 1782-1863 in GSU, the latter making them
available through BLGSU. The tax lists available for
each of the 100 VA counties are listed in Chapter 4.
Inventories of these tax lists are also provided in:
___ J. F. Dorman, editor, THE VA GENEALOGIST, 1959 ff.,
    volumes 3 ff., one or more counties listed in each
    issue.

35. <u>Wills</u> <u>and</u> <u>probate</u> <u>records</u>

When a person died leaving any property (the estate), it was necessary for the authorities in the county of residence to see that his property was properly distributed according to law. If a will had been written, its wishes were carried out in so far as these wishes were in accord with the law; if no will was left (intestate), the law indicated to whom distribution had to be made. The records involved in these operations are generally referred to as will and/or probate records. In the early days, when a county's population was small, all these proceedings might be set down in a single court record book called the Record Book. Sometimes, they were recorded in the Deed Books. Later, there came to be Will Books which contained wills, inventories, and sometimes estate accounts. Other records which you may find include administrator, appraisal, and executor, but these are more rare than the will, inventory, and estate account records. There is only rarely any record of the distribution of the legacies of a will. And there will generally be no probate records for wives who died before their husbands or for persons who died and had no estate.

Prior to 1776 in VA, law limited the inheritance of property to a specified line of heirs, so that it could not be left to anyone else (called entail). And prior to 1786, if there was a will, the law held that the widow received one-third (called her dower) for her lifetime with the remaining two-thirds going to the oldest son, unless specified differently in the will. Upon the widow's death, the oldest son received her one-third. If there was no will, the oldest son received everything. [If the oldest son was dead, the oldest grandson became the heir. If a man was unmarried, his heir was his oldest brother. If a man was married, but childless, his widow kept the land for her lifetime, but if she wanted control, she had to petition for and pay for a new patent to the land.]

Originals of VA will and probate records are in the CH, but VSL&A and GSU (BLGSU) have microfilm copies of those before 1865. The dates for which will and probate records are available for the 100 VA counties (and cities which kept them before 1900) are shown under the county names in Chapter 4. VA wills before 1800 are indexed in a very useful book:

__C. Torrence, VA WILLS AND ADMINISTRATIONS, 1632-1800, Genealogical Publ. Co., Baltimore, MD, 1981 (1931). [over 50,000 names]

This is an exceptionally good volume, but there are some omissions and a few errors. The VSL&A has a card file which contains supplementary listings and corrections:

__CARD INDEX TO WILLS AND ADMINISTRATIONS FROM 1623-1800, VSL&A, Richmond, VA, Archives Reading Room, alphabetical.

Another card file index which should not be overlooked at VSL&A is:

__CARD INDEX TO WILLS FROM LOST WILL BOOKS, VSL&A, Richmond, VA, Archives Reading Room, alphabetical.

In addition to these sources, there are also some published will records which could be helpful to you:

__W. M. Clemens, VA WILLS BEFORE 1799, Genealogical Publ. Co., Baltimore, MD, 1973 (1924). [3,000 names]

__P. W. Coldham, ENGLISH ESTATES OF AMERICAN SETTLERS, 1610-1858, Genealogical Publ. Co., Baltimore, MD, 1980-1, 3 volumes.

__N. Currer-Briggs, ENGLISH WILLS OF COLONIAL FAMILIES, Polyanthos, New Orleans, LA, 1972.

__N. Currer-Briggs, VA SETTLERS AND ENGLISH ADVENTURERS: ABSTRACTS OF WILLS, 1484-1798, AND LEGAL PROCEEDINGS; 1566-1700, Genealogical Publ. Co., Baltimore, MD, 1970. [12,000 names, 400 families]

__DAR OF FL, ORIGINAL BIBLE RECORDS AND WILLS, The Society, Tampa, FL, 1957-8.

__DAR OF VA, BIBLE RECORDS OF VA, The Society, Washington, DC, 1972.

__G. H. S. King, COPIES OF EXTANT VA WILLS FROM COUNTIES WHOSE RECORDS HAVE BEEN DESTROYED, Tyler's Quarterly Magazine 20-33 (1939-52).

__P. Walne, ENGLISH WILLS: PROBATE RECORDS IN ENGLAND AND WALES, VA State Library, Richmond, VA, 1981.

__H. F. G. Waters, GENEALOGICAL GLEANINGS IN ENGLAND, Genealogical Publ. Co., Baltimore, MD, 1969 (1901), 2 volumes.

These books are available in VSL&A, VHSL, and LOC. Some will be found in ALUV, DARL, GSU (BLGSU), and LGL. Those pertaining to their own local areas are likely to be in RL and LL.

Abbreviations

ALUV	Alderman Library, University of VA
AMS	Anne M. Smalley
BLGSU	Branch Library(ies), Genealogical Society of UT
CH	Court House(s)
DARL	Daughters of American Revolution Library, Washington
GKS	Geo. K. Schweitzer or Genealogy Kinship Sources
GSU	Genealogical Society of UT, Salt Lake City
LL	Local Library(ies)
LGL	Large Genealogical Library(ies)
LOC	Library of Congress, Washington
RL	Regional Library(ies)
SLCWM	Swem Library, College of William & Mary Williamsburg
VHSL	VA Historical Society Library, Richmond
VSL&A	VA State Library and Archives, Richmond

Chapter 3

RECORD LOCATIONS

1. Court houses (CH)

Most of the original county records and city records referred to in Chapter 2 and listed under the counties in Chapter 4 are stored in the CH. Some of these originals have been transferred to the VSL&A. The court houses are located in the county seats and in independent cities and are listed along with their zip codes in Chapter 4. The original records usually consist of variously-labelled books (usually handwritten), files with file folders in them, and boxes with large envelopes or file folders in them. The records are generally stored in the offices of various county and city officials or in the case of older records, they may be found in special storage vaults. In many instances, they are readily accessible. In a few cases, they are put away so that they are very difficult to get out and use. The records which will most likely be found in the county and city court houses include civil records (road, merchant, license, physician, etc.), court records (county, city, chancery, circuit, common law, district, law & chancery, levy, superior, hustings, etc.), land records (deed, mortgage, survey, tax, etc.), probate records (inventory, will, administrator, guardian, orphan, etc.), and vital records (birth, marriage, divorce, death).

Once you have located the county in which your ancestor lived, it is usually not a good idea to go there first. It is best to explore the microfilmed, transcribed, and published copies of the records at some central repository such as VSL&A-VHSL, GSU, or BLGSU. (VSL&A-VHSL are hyphenated to remind you that both may be visited together since both are in Richmond, VA.) This is because it is the business of these repositories to make the records available to you, whereas the primary task of the county and city officials and employees at the court houses is to conduct the record-keeping task as an aid to regulating the society and keeping the law. Therefore, it is best not to encroach upon their time and good graces until you have done as much work elsewhere as possible. Most of the major county and city record books prior to 1865 have been microfilmed or transcribed so that you can go through them at VSL&A, GSU, or BLGSU. Or you can hire a researcher to do the investigating for you if a trip is not workable or would be too expensive. Most of the contents of files and boxes, however, have not been copied. Hence, after doing work at VSL&A, GSU, or BLGSU, you then need to make a trip to the city and county CH or hire a researcher to do so for you. In general, you need to remember that the major city and county records are probate, will, deed, some marriage, court, guardian, and survey. For those before 1865, go to the VSL&A, GSU, or BLGSU; for those after 1865, go to the CH. Then, remember, in general, that the major state and federal records are tax, military, census, land, birth, death, and marriage. For these records during all years go to VSL&A, GSU, or BLGSU. Please note that there are both state and county-city marriage records, VSL&A having practically all of them. Also, you need to recall that the major non-governmental records are church, manuscript, Bible, biographical, cemetery, directory, historical, DAR, genealogical compilations, genealogical periodicals, mortuary, and newspaper. For all of these, go to VSL&A-VHSL, LOC-DARL, LGL, GSU, and/or BLGSU. You will find the people in the local CH very helpful and cooperative, and often they will make photocopies for you or will give you access to a copying machine. At the same time you visit the CH, you can also pay visits to the LL in the county seat and/or city and the nearest RL.

Researchers who are near VSL&A-VHSL, LOC-DARL, LGL, GSU, and the CH in the various counties and cities will be listed in:
  V. N. Chambers, editor, GENEALOGICAL HELPER, Everton Publishers, Logan, UT, latest September-October issue.
In addition staff members at VSL&A, VHSL, ALUV, DARL, GSU, LGL, RL, and LL will often send you a list of re-searchers if you will dispatch them a request and an SASE. Do not write the officials in the CH for research-er recommendations since they usually deem this a matter to be handled by the LL and therefore many are unable to meet your request.

2. The major facilities

The best overall place in the world to do VA genea-logical research is in Richmond, VA. This city contains the two most heavily-stocked VA genealogical collections

in existence: the VA State Library and Archives (VSL&A)
and the VA Historical Society Library (VHSL). Within 105
miles of Richmond, there are four other important facilities: in Washington, DC, the National Archives (NA), the
Library of Congress (LOC), and the Daughters of the
American Revolution Library (DARL); in Charlottesville,
VA, the Alderman Library of the University of VA (ALUV).

In the western United States is the largest genealogical library in the world, the library of the Genealogical Society of UT (GSU). This facility has microfilm
copies of much of the contents of the VSL&A. This
library has over 250 branch libraries located all over
the US. The vast microfilm holdings of GSU can be borrowed by its branches so that you can use the records at
the branch nearest you.

3. The VA State Library and Archives (VSL&A)

The VA State Library and Archives (VSL&A) is located
at 11th and Capitol Sts., Richmond, VA 23219, directly
across the street which runs along the north side of
Capitol Square. Capitol Square is the site of the VA
State Capitol which is located in the downtown area of
Richmond. Parking is not readily available except on
Saturdays, and therefore it is recommended that you ride
the easily-available buses to the VSL&A and back to your
hotel/motel. There are a number of good places to eat in
the downtown area near the VSL&A. At this writing the
hours are 8:15 am–5:00 pm, Monday through Saturday except
for legal holidays (but times change, so be sure and
check!). The telephone number is 1-804-786-2306. The
five places closest to VSL&A for lodgings are the Holiday
Inn-Downtown [301 West Franklin St., Richmond, VA 23220,
reservation and information telephone number 1-804-644-
9871], the Ramada Renaissance Hotel [555 E. Canal St.,
Richmond, VA 23219, reservation and information telephone
number 1-804-228-9898], Quality Inn Commonwealth [515
West Franklin St., Richmond, VA 23220, information and
reservation telephone number 1-804-643-2831], the Day's
Inn Downtown [7th at Marshall, Richmond, VA 23240,
reservation and information telephone number 1-800-325-
2525], and the Richmond Marriott [5th and E. Broad Sts.,
Richmond, VA 23219, information and reservation telephone
number 1-804-643-3400]. The two hotels listed last are
within walking distance of VSL&A.

The <u>Archives</u> <u>Branch</u> of the VSL&A is located in the west wing of the main floor of the building. Upon entering the main door, go up to the half-flight of steps into the lobby, then turn to your left and enter the Archives area. Upon entrance, you will find yourself at the desk, where you should sign the register, complete a registration card, and present proper identification to the archivist. Ask for a copy of the rules and regulations leaflet, place your brief case, outdoor clothing, and other non-essential items in the designated area, retain only note paper and research materials, find yourself a seat, and read the leaflet. You will discover that materials are to be handled with extreme care; removal or mutilation of records is a crime; only pencils may be used; food, drink, and smoking are not permitted; records are to be requested by filling out a stack service slip; loose paper records must be used in the special Manuscript Reading room; and microfilm readers in the adjacent Microfilm Reading area must be requested from the microfilm assistant.

The central room in which you will be seated is the Archives Reading Room. On the south and west walls, you will find original volumes, published transcripts, and handwritten transcripts of VA county records arranged alphabetically by county. On the north wall you will find a large number of card indexes to records in the Archives. Along the north wall are tables with all sorts of published and typescript indexes and major reference volumes. In the center of the east wall is the Archives Desk, in the southeast corner the microfilm registration desk, microfilm cabinets, and the Microfilm Reading Area, and in the northeast corner the entrance to the Manuscript Reading Room. The major genealogical holdings of the Archives consist of original, microfilmed, published, and transcribed federal, state, county, city, public, organizational, and personal records along with indexes to them and finding aids for them.

The major <u>federal</u> records pertaining to VA which the Archives holds are census records and indexes, postcolonial military records and indexes, US Geological Survey maps, and military records. The major <u>state</u> records are birth (1853-96), colonial, death (1853-96), divorce, land, marriage (1853-1935), military, and tax. The major <u>county</u> records are court, deed, marriage, and

probate (will), but these are available usually <u>only up
to 1865</u>. Major records of the <u>other categories</u> include
Bible, biography, cemetery, church, DAR, emigration and
immigration, maps, manuscripts, and mortuary. Following
are the major indexes, finding aids, and record categor-
ies located in the Archives Branch of VSL&A. <u>Typescript
indexes</u> include:

__Typescript Index to VA County Records (original, micro-
filmed, published, transcribed), by county, then alphabetical by record type, then chronological.

__Typescript and Published Indexes to Bible Records,
several volumes, alphabetical by name.

__Typescript and Published Indexes to Genealogical Notes
and Charts, several volumes, alphabetical by name.

__Typescript Index to Lists of Tithables, Rent Rolls, and
Polls, by counties, then chronologically, leads to
original, published, and microfilmed records.

__Typescript Listing of Colonial Paper References to
Individuals, not alphabetical, page-by-page examination
required.

__Typescript List of Published Indexes to VA Census and
Tax Lists, chronologically.

__Finding Aid for Personal Papers Collection, ask at
desk.

__Finding Aid for Business Papers Collection, ask at
desk.

    <u>Card Indexes</u> in the Archives Branch, most along the
north wall except when noted otherwise, include:

__Card Index to Wills and Administrations, before 1800,
by county, then alphabetical, incomplete.

__Card Index to Wills and Administrations, 1623-1800,
alphabetical, lists ones not included in Torrence's
book.

__Card Index to Wills from Lost Will Book, alphabetical.

__Card Index to Brock Collection, chronological, then
alphabetical under year, originals in Huntingdon
Library, San Marino, CA.

__Card Index to French's 19th Century Biographical
Sketches of Prominent Virginians, alphabetical.

__Card Index to Revolutionary War Participants Mentioned
in the Martin Papers, alphabetical.

__Card Index to War of 1812 Participants Mentioned in the
Martin Papers, alphabetical.

__Card Index to Participants in Dunmore's War (1774),
alphabetical, leads to microfilmed records.

__Card Index to Revolutionary War Bounty Land Warrants, alphabetical.

__Card Index to Revolutionary War Land Office Military Certificates, alphabetical.

__Card Index to Rejected Revolutionary War Claims, alphabetical.

__Card Index to Public Service Claims, alphabetical, leads to volumes and microfilmed records of those who gave patriotic public service during the Revolutionary War.

__Card Index to Revolutionary War Pensions Granted by VA, alphabetical.

__Card Index to Northern Neck Grants and Surveys, alphabetical.

__Card Index to Land Office Patents and Grants, alphabetical.

__Card Index to VA Mexican War Soldiers, alphabetical.

__Card Index to Confederate Units and Localities in Which They Were Raised, alphabetical according to county and name of unit.

__Card Index to VA Confederate Soldiers, alphabetical, leads to Confederate roster volumes on west wall of Archives Reading Room.

__Card Index to VA Confederate Naval Participants, alphabetical.

__Card Index to Confederate Pension Applications by Participants and Widows, alphabetical, leads to applications index kept in Archives Work Room, ask at desk.

__Card Index to VA War of 1812 Soldiers Paid by VA Prior to Federal Payment, alphabetical.

__Card Index to Map Collection, arranged by counties, then chronologically, ask at desk.

Among the major holdings in the hundreds of cabinet drawers containing thousands of **microfilm reels** are the following:

__VA County Records, by county, then by type of record, then chronologically, up to 1865.

__VA Census Records, by census year, then by county; indexes available for 1782-7, 1800, 1810, 1820, 1830, 1840, 1850, 1880 (partial), 1900.

__VA Land Taxes, some early records then 1782-present, by county.

__VA Personal Taxes, some early records, then 1782-present, by county.

__VA Vital Statistics, births and deaths (1853-96), marriages (1853-1935).
__VA Rejected Revolutionary War Claims, alphabetical.
__VA Revolutionary War Pension Applications, alphabetical.
__VA Revolutionary War Bounty Land Warrants, alphabetical.
__VA Revolutionary War Commissioners Book for Public Service Claims, by county, then alphabetical.
__VA Revolutionary War Service Record Index, alphabetical.
__VA Confederate Service Records Index, alphabetical.
__VA Confederate Records, by military unit, then alphabetical.
__VA Confederate Pension Index, alphabetical.
__VA Manuscript Microfilms, many reels, numerous collections.

Attention should also be called to two map collections other than the maps included in the Card Index to Map Collections:
__Collections of Detailed VA Maps by the US Geological Survey, by counties, then by USGS district name.
__Collection of Sanborn Insurance Maps for VA Cities, by city.

Most of the card indexes, typescript indexes, published county records, and many of the original county record volumes are on the shelves in the Archives Reading Room. These may be used freely. A few indexes must be asked for at the desk as noted above. Once you have signed up for a microfilm reader, you are free to obtain the reels you desire from the cabinets. However, when you finish with a reel, do not replace it in the drawer. Put it on top of the cabinet above the drawer from which you took it. When indexes or finding aids refer you to records which are not on the Archives Reading Room shelves or in the microfilm cabinets, fill out a request form, being sure to give reference numbers and the name of the records you desire. Then take the form to the desk. You will in some cases be asked to use the records in the Manuscript Reading Room. Don't overlook discussing your research with an archivist to make sure that you do not miss relevant materials.

The Library Branch of the VSL&A is located in the east wing of the main floor of the building. Upon enter-

ing the main door, go up the half-flight of steps into
the lobby, then turn to your right and enter the Library
area. Upon entrance, the service desk will be on your
immediate right, in front of you and beyond the service
desk will be the Library Reading Area, and to your left
will be the large card catalog. Go in, find yourself a
seat, review the general rules in the leaflet you obtained from the Archives Branch (careful handling of all
materials, removal or defacing materials is a crime, only
pencils, no food or drink or smoking).

Then, proceed into the area containing the card
catalog, and begin to look for materials of interest to
your research by remembering the word SLANT. S stands
for subject, so look under various subject headings. The
titles of the sections in Chapter 2 will give you a good
idea of the sort of things you need to search, but you
will not find them all. Other subject headings that you
must not overlook are: Registers of births, etc., (vital
records will be found under it), Epitaphs, Genealogy,
Obituaries, and Probate Records. L stands for locality,
therefore examine all cards under the heading Virginia,
then all under the name of the county, then all under the
names of cities and/or towns in the county which might be
pertinent. A stands for author, thus examine the author
listings for any books mentioned in Chapters 2 and 4
which you might want to find. N stands for name, which
reminds you to look under all the surnames which you are
searching for to see if there are books which might be
relevant. T stands for title, and hence your final step
is to look under the titles of books, periodicals, and
agencies (such as Daughters of the American Revolution,
United Daughters of the American Revolution, United
Daughters of the Confederacy, Works Progress Administration, US National Archives) which sponsored publications.
The word SLANT is simply a memory device, and does not
indicate the best order to look for things in. To
shorten your research time, it is recommended that you do
L (locality) first [county first, then state], then N
(name), then S (subject), then A (author), and finally T
(title). This procedure will give you good coverage of
the library holdings which are indexed in the card catalog. Among them you will find almost all of the published materials mentioned in Chapters 2 and 4.

When you run across pertinent materials, write the
call numbers down (upper left corner of the card). If
the abbreviation Ref. appears as part of the call number,
this means you will find the volume on the open shelves
in the Library Reading Area. If Ref. does not appear,
fill out one of the request forms provided at the card
catalog, and present it to the librarian at the desk. The
volume will be brought from the storage stacks for you.
Practically all of the genealogical books which are out
on the open shelves will be found in the southwest corner
and the neighboring west wall.

Your next step is to look into several special
indexes which are in the Library Reading Area. Among the
more important ones are:
___Revolving Index to VA Newspapers on Microfilm, alpha-
betical.
___Card Index to Families in Boddie's HISTORICAL SOUTHERN
FAMILIES, alphabetical.
___Card Index to Newspaper Articles, look under county,
city, town, and event, also under the heading Biography
(then person's name).
___Card Indexes to Marriages in the Enquirer, alphabet-
ical.
___Card Indexes to Obituaries in the Enquirer, alphabet-
ical.
___Card Indexes to Names in the Confederate Veteran Mag-
azine, alphabetical.
Do not fail to talk to the librarian about your search
and be sure to ask about any other special indexes which
might help you.

The staff of VSL&A cannot do genealogical research
for you by mail. They are kept busy serving the State
and the patrons who come to them in person. They will
provide you with a list of researchers if you cannot make
a personal visit. Dispatch them a request and an SASE.
They will provide for you the answer to one or two very
specific questions which can be answered by taking a
brief look at an index. You must include the following
in your request: (1) full name of person, (2) name of
county, (3) specific document desired, and (4) approximate date. For example, a specific question might be:
Is a Thomas W. KEEN(1) mentioned in the Pittsylvania
County(2) marriage records(3) about 1855(4)? Questions

less specific than this will require a personal visit or a hired genealogical researcher.

4. The VA Historical Society Library (VHSL)

The VA Historical Society Library (VHSL) is located at 428 North Blvd., Richmond, VA 23221. It is easily reached by buses from the lodgings mentioned at the beginning of section 3 or you will usually find parking on the north side of the large block which VHSL occupies. At this writing, the library is open 9:00 am–5:00 pm, Monday through Saturday, except legal holidays (but times change, so be sure and check!). The telephone number is 1-804-358-4901. The purposes of the VHSL are the collection and preservation of research materials on VA history and the making of them available to students and scholars. The extensive holdings of the Library include VA manuscripts, Bible records, colonial material, Confederate history, family and personal papers, reference works, biographical data, maps, newspapers, and published books.

Upon entering, you will find yourself in an entrance hall with a reception desk and a check room. You should remove paper and a pencil from your briefcase and leave it along with outer garments in the check room. Then you will be asked to fill out a registration form and give identification. Following this, you may proceed straight ahead into the Library Reading room. On your left will be the service desk, the reading area, and the south wall which is filled by shelves of major reference works. On your right will be two large card catalogs plus a number of smaller card indexes. You need to recall the general library rules as you set about beginning your work: work quietly, extreme care with materials, only pencils, no food or drink or smoking.

Your first move should be to walk over to the south wall and scan the reference works there. Then, you should proceed to the main card catalog. Using the memory word SLANT, and doing your card catalog search in the order L-N-S-A-T, follow the general instructions given in the previous section (9th paragraph, section 3). When you come across materials you think you can use, write the call numbers (upper left corner) on a request form. Hand this form to the librarian, and an attendant will bring you the book. Most of the books mentioned in Chapters 2 and 4 will be found in this excellent library.

Next, you may shift your focus to the very large card catalog index of manuscript materials which VHSL has. There are well over 3.6 million items in the collection. The card catalog is arranged by name of person, so you need to carefully look up the name of every ancestor you think may have been in VA or even connected with the state. Again, copy the numbers, designation, and name of the materials you need on a request form and give it to the librarian. After this, look into a number of other exceedingly valuable card indexes which hold great promise for all VA ancestor searchers:
__Card Index to VA Marriages and Obituaries from VA Newspapers, 1730-1820, alphabetical, incomplete, more material being added continually.
__Card Index to VA Marriages and Obituaries from VA Newspapers, after 1820, alphabetical, incomplete, more material being added continually.
__Card Index to Bible Records, alphabetical.
__Card Index to Newspapers, by year, then alphabetical.
__Card Index to Maps, by VA or county or city or town, over 16,000 items.
__Card Index to Maps, by date, then alphabetical, over 16,000 items.
Please don't fail to talk with the librarian about your search so that you do not overlook important research approaches.

The staff at VHSL are kept busy collecting, cataloging, doing research for the Society, and serving the needs of members of the Society. Thus, they have very little time for helping you by mail. They will send you a list of searchers if you will dispatch them an SASE and a request. The Society welcomes you as a member, so if you are interested in supporting their very valuable efforts, write them, enclose an SASE, ask for a membership application.

5. The Alderman Library of the University of VA (ALUV)

The Alderman Library of the University of VA (ALUV) is located on the campus of the University of VA in Charlottesville, VA 22901. There are several special visitor parking lots around the campus, directions to them being given by numerous signs. The hours for the general areas of the library are 8:00 am–10:00 pm Friday, 9:00 am–6:00 pm Saturday, and 12:00 noon to midnight on Sunday. However, two very important genealogically-oriented departments (The Rare Book Department and the Manuscripts Department) are open only 9:00 am–5:00 pm Monday through Friday, and 9:00 am–1:00 pm Saturday. The Copy Center is open only 8:00 am–5:00 pm Monday through Friday. The library is closed on legal holidays, and hours are curtailed during University vacations, so check before you go! There are four motels within walking distance of the Library: Best Western Cavalier Inn [105 Emmet St., Charlottesville, VA 22901, information and reservations telephone 1–804–296–8111], EconoLodge [400 Emmet Street, Charlottesville, VA 22906, information and reservations telephone 1–804–296–2104], Howard Johnson [13th & West Main, Charlottesville, VA 22906, information and reservations telephone 1–804–296–8121], and University Lodge [Rt. 29 North, Charlottesville, VA 22901, information and reservations telephone 1–804–293–5141].

In the ALUV there are four major areas which have genealogical relevance: the main Card Catalog, the Reference Department, the Manuscripts Department, and the Rare Book Department. The Library had made available a very good reference book to assist persons who are interested in their genealogical resources:

L. A. Bullock, P. Potter, and R. A. English, A GUIDE TO GENEALOGICAL SOURCES IN THE UNIVERSITY OF VA LIBRARY, Reference Dept, University of VA Library, Charlottesville, VA, 1986.

The major genealogical strengths of ALUV are their holdings in VA historical publications, manuscripts, family papers, business records, biographies, church records, maps, and newspapers. When you enter the ALUV through the main entrance, you will find yourself on the fourth floor. Go directly to the main Card Catalog which is on this floor and look for materials relating to your ancestor(s) using the SLANT procedure as described in the 9th paragraph, section 3. However, your search will differ somewhat from those described previously because the main Card Catalog is subdivided into an author-title catalog (A and T), a subject catalog (S, L, and N), and a newspaper catalog. Be sure to examine all three. When you locate a book you want, record the call number and any special location symbol (Rare Book Coll., Mss., or Ref.).

If no special location symbol is given, determine the stack floor on which the call number is found, and go directly to that place, and locate the book. If the book is missing, check at the circulation desk on the 4th floor. You will find that many of the published volumes mentioned in Chapters 2 and 4 are in VSL&A.

The Reference Department, which is on the 4th floor, has on its shelves many major genealogical reference sourcebooks. They are listed in the main Card Catalog with a special symbol indicating their location (Ref.). It would be of help to you if you would scan the shelves in the Reference Department for books beginning with CS, CT, E176-through-E360, F140-through-F235, the Z1300s, the Z5300s, and the Z7100s. Next, you should visit the Manuscripts Department on the 2nd floor, where you will find several useful indexes and finding aids:

__Card Index to Names and Locations and Subject topics of Manuscripts, Bible Records, Biographies, Church Records, and Military Records, alphabetical.
__Card Index to Manuscript Materials on Microfilm, alphabetical.
__Card Index to Names in Several Large Manuscript Collections, alphabetical.
__Several Shelves of Typescript Finding Aids and Indexes Listing Contents and Giving Descriptions of Major Manuscript Collections.
__B. P. O'Brien, BIBLE RECORDS IN THE MANUSCRIPTS DIVISION, ALUV, The VA Genealogist, volume 15, pp. 206-11, 1971.
Finally, a trip down the hall to the Rare Books Department to examine two further indexes should be made:
__Card Index to Maps, look under VA, then the county, city, and/or town.
__Card Index to Newspapers, look under VA, then the city or town.
When you find materials in either of these 2nd floor departments that you want to examine, fill out a request form using the proper location numbers, hand the form to the archivist, take a seat at one of the provided tables, and the documents will be brought to you. The staff at ALUV has as its top priority service to the University teaching and research function. This means that they are unable to do genealogical research for people who might write in. They welcome you or your hired researcher, and

they are always glad to assist those who use the library in person.

6. The National Archives (NA)

The National Archives (NA) is located on Pennsylvania Ave. between 7th and 9th Sts., NW, in Washington, DC 20408. The telephone number is 1-202-523-3232. The major rooms in the Archives in which VA-related records may be found are the Central Research Room (Room 203, 2nd floor), and the Microfilm Research Room (Room 400, 4th floor). These areas are open 8:45 am-9:45 pm Monday through Friday and 8:45 am-4:45 pm Saturday; they are closed on Sundays and federal holidays. The Snack Bar, which is located in the basement is open only Monday through Friday 9:20 am-4:30 pm. Among nearby lodgings are the Hyatt Regency Hotel [400 New Jersey Ave., NW, Zip 20001, Phone: 1-800-228-9000], Loew's L'Enfant Plaza Hotel [480 L'Enfant Plaza East, SW, Zip 20024, Phone: 1-202-484-1000], the Quality Inn Capitol Hill [415 New Jersey Avenue, NW, Zip 20001, Phone: 1-800-228-5151], the Holiday Inn Capitol [550 C St. SW, Zip 20024, Phone: 1-202-479-4000], and the Hotel Washington [15th St. and Pennsylvania Ave., NW, Zip 20004, Phone: 1-202-638-5900]. Two very valuable guides to the resources of the NA are the following volumes:
__C. S. Neal, LEST WE FORGET: A GUIDE TO GENEALOGICAL RESEARCH IN THE NATION'S CAPITAL, Annandale Stake of CJCLDS, Annandale, VA, 1982.
__National Archives, GUIDE TO GENEALOGICAL RESEARCH IN THE NATIONAL ARCHIVES, The Archives, Washington, DC, 1982.

Among the most important VA records in the NA are microfilm copies of the 1810-1910 censuses, indexes to the 1810-50 and 1880-1910 censuses, a copy of the 1782-7 tax substitute for the lost 1790 VA census, passenger arrival lists for several VA cities [Alexandria 1820-52, East River 1830, Hampton 1821, Petersburg 1819-22, Richmond 1820-44], military service records (1775-1912) and indexes to them, military pension application records and indexes (1774-1934), military pension payment records and indexes (1774-1934), military bounty land warrant application records and indexes (for service 1774-1855), records and indexes of the southern Branch National Home for Disabled Volunteer Soldiers in Kecoughtan, VA (1870-

1934), Confederate military service records and indexes (for service 1861-5), Confederate amnesty and pardon records (1863-7), records of VA Revolutionary War warrants surrendered for land in the VA Military District of OH, records of Revolutionary War warrants for land in KY and OH for service in the VA State Line and the VA Continental Line, and passport applications.

Many of these microfilm records are also in the Field Branches of the National Archives and as time goes on more are being deposited in them. In addition, these Branches also are depositories for regional records pertaining to their own regions. Research rooms, a basic reference library, microfilm readers, and copying machines are available in each of the Branches. The locations, addresses, and telephone numbers of the Branches are as follows. For each, they should be addressed as Archives Branch, Federal Archives and Records Center, then the detailed address:

   In the Boston area, 380 Trapelo Rd., Waltham, MA 02154. Phone: 617-223-2657.
   In the New York area, Bldg. 22-MOT Bayonne, Bayonne, NJ 07002. Phone: 201-858-7251.
   In the Philadelphia area, 5000 Wissahickon Ave., Philadelphia, PA 19144. Phone: 215-951-5591.
   In the Chicago area, 7358 South Pulaski Rd., Chicago, IL 60629. Phone: 312-353-0161.
   In the Atlanta area, 1557 St. Joseph Ave., East Point, GA 30344. Phone: 404-763-7477.
   In the Kansas City area, 2306 East Bannister Rd., Kansas City, MO 64131. Phone: 816-929-7271.
   In the Fort Worth area, 4900 Hemphill St., Ft. Worth, TX 76115. Phone: 817-334-5525.
   In the Denver area, Bldg. 48, Denver Federal Center, Denver, CO 80225. Phone: 303-234-5271.
   In the San Francisco area, 1000 Commodore Dr., San Bruno, CA 94066. Phone: 415-876-9009.
   In the Los Angeles area, 24000 Avila Rd., Laguna Niguel, CA 92677. Phone: 714-831-4220.
   In the Seattle area, 6125 Sand Point Way, NE, Seattle, WA 98115. Phone: 206-442-4502.

Before you visit any of these Branches, be sure and check their hours. In general, all are open 8:30 am-3:50 pm Monday through Friday, but some have early hours and some have later hours in addition.

7. <u>The</u> <u>Library</u> <u>of</u> <u>Congress</u> (<u>LOC</u>)

The Library of Congress (LOC) consists of the Jefferson (Main) Building at First St., SE, between East Capitol St. and Independence Ave., the Adams Bldg. (Annex) just behind it at Second St., SE, between East Capitol St. and Independence Ave., and the Madison Bldg., Independence Ave, between 1st and 2nd Sts., all three in Washington, DC 20540. The telephone number is 1-202-287-5000. The majority of VA-related genealogical materials are located in the Jefferson Building in the Local History and Genealogy Room (Room 244). Opening times are 8:30 am-9:30 pm Mondays through Saturdays, and 1:00 pm-5:00 pm Sundays. The cafeteria and snack bar, which is located in the basement of the Jefferson Building, is open 8:30 am-3:30 pm Mondays through Fridays. The lodgings mentioned in section 6 (NA) have been selected so that you can reach the NA, the LOC, and the DARL fairly easily from them. A very useful guide to the LOC is:
__ C. S. Neal, LEST WE FORGET: A GUIDE TO GENEALOGICAL RESEARCH IN THE NATION'S CAPITAL, Annandale Stake of CJCLDS, Annandale, VA, 1982.

A large majority of the volumes and periodicals which have been printed in the colonies and in the US and volumes printed elsewhere which are concerned with the US are in the LOC. Practically every volume and periodical mentioned in this book is in the LOC. In the Microform Reading Room (Room 140B, Jefferson Bldg.) will be found Microfilms of Early State Records with indexes, British Manuscripts Project Records and finding aids, index of US Newspapers on Microform, telephone directories, city directories, and an index to the Collection of Genealogical Materials of the National Society of Daughters of Founders and Patriots of America. In the Local History and Genealogy Room (Room 244, Jefferson Bldg.) will be found eleven important sets of indexes: (1, 2, 3) Family Name Indexes by Surname, (4) US Biographical Index, no VA material, (5) Rider's American Genealogical Biographical Index by Surname, and General Index to Newberry Library, and Dictionary Catalog to Local History and Genealogy Division of NY City Public Library, (6) Jacobus' Index to Genealogical Periodicals and Crowther's Surname Index to 65 Volumes of Colonial and Revolutionary Pedigrees, and the Genealogical Periodical Annual Indexes from 1962 forward, (7) Durrie's Index to American Genealogies which is mostly related to New England, (8) Heraldic Indexes, (9) Siebmacher's German Coats-of-Arms Index, 2 drawers of Land Grants Index, 3 drawers of Register of Births Index, and 2 drawers of Wills Index, (10) US Local History Index by Places [city, county, region, state], (11) Author Index to Genealogy and US Local History. These indexes will lead you to the many volumes on the open shelves and in the stacks. You may serve yourself from the open shelves, but to obtain books in the stacks, you need to present a properly filled-out call slip at the Issue Desk in the large adjacent Annex Reading Room. In using the indexes, do not fail to read the instructions on the sides of the files. In the Manuscript Division (Room 3005, Annex), you will find manuscripts along with in-dexes and other finding aids. In the Newspaper and Current Periodical Room (Room G102D, Annex), both current and old newspapers will be found along with finding aids. Current periodicals and finding aids for them are also there. For older bound and microfilmed periodicals, the Serial (Periodical) Section of the Main Catalog needs to be used to locate the periodicals. The Main Catalog is located in the Main Reading Room (Jefferson Bldg.). For addresses, maps, gazetteers, postal indexes, and finding aids to them, go to the Geography and Map Division of the LOC which is located in Room B02 of the James Madison Bldg., 101 Independence Ave., SE, Washington, DC 20540. It is now open 8:30 am–5:00 pm Mondays through Fridays and 8:30 am–12:30 pm Saturdays (Times change, so check!).

8. The Daughters of the American Revolution Library (DARL)

The Daughters of the American Revolution Library (DARL) is located at 1776 D St., NW, Washington, DC 20006. The telephone number is 1-202-628-4980. Hours are 9:00 am–4:00 pm Mondays through Fridays, but they are closed Saturdays and Sundays, and during the entire month of April, only members can use the facilities. There is a small fee charged for the use of the library. The lodgings mentioned in section 6 (NA) have been selected so that you can reach the DARL, the NA, and the LOC fairly easily from them. A very useful guide to the DARL is:

C. S. Neal, LEST WE FORGET: A GUIDE TO GENEALOGICAL RESEARCH IN THE NATION'S CAPITAL, Annandale Stake of the CJCLDS, Annandale, VA, 1982.

The DAR is an organization that has done extensive tracing of their ancestries back to a Revolutionary War patriot. In the process, they have accumulated a massive amount of information, most of which is collected here at DARL. The library consists of a large reading room surrounded by a card catalog and stacks of shelved books. The stacks continue on a balcony, and down the hall a bit is the Microfilm Center. Materials in the stacks may be located by using the card catalog according to the previous procedure symbolized by SLANT. When using the card index for location references, be sure to look under both STATE-COUNTY and COUNTY-STATE. Especially notable in the DARL collection are the county and city records which they have typed up, the card index to Revolutionary War pensions abstracts, and the abstracts themselves, the church and cemetery records, city and county histories, the DAR Patriot Index and the DAR Lineage Books and Indexes, the many genealogical periodicals, and the 1850-60-70-80 Mortality Census Schedules.

9. Genealogical Society of UT Library (GSU) & Its Branches (BLGSU)

The largest genealogical library in the world is the Library of the Genealogical Society of UT (GSU). This library, which holds well over a million rolls of microfilm plus a vast number of books, is located at 50 East North Temple St., Salt Lake City, UT 84150. The basic key to the library is composed of three indexes: the International Genealogical Index, the Surname Index, and the Locality Index. In addition to the main library, the Society maintains a large number of Branches (BLGSU) all over the US. Each of these Branches has a microfiche copy of the international genealogical index, a microfiche copy of the surname index, a microfiche copy of the locality index, and a set of microfiche integrated census indexes which cover the entire US (1790/1800/10, 1820, 1830, 1840) or cover the US in three regions (1850NE, 1850S, 1850 Rest). In addition, each Branch has a supply of forms for borrowing microfilm copies of the records at the main library. This means that the astonishingly large holdings of the GSU are available through each of its numerous BLGSU.

The BLGSU in VA are as follows:

The Annandale Stake BLGSU, 3900 Howard St., Annandale, VA 22003. Phone: 1-703-256-5518.

The Charlottesville Stake BLGSU, Hydraulic Rd., Charlottesville, VA 22906. Phone: 1-804-973-9856.

The Fairfax Stake BLGSU, Ravensworth, PO Box 1447, Springfield, VA 22151.

The Oakton Stake BLGSU, 2719 Hunter Hill Rd., Oakton, VA 22124. Phone: 1-703-281-1836.

The Richmond Stake BLGSU, 5600 Monument Ave., Richmond, VA 23226. Phone: 1-804-288-9570.

The Roanoke Stake BLGSU, 6311 Wayburn Dr., Salem, VA 24153. Phone: 1-703-366-6727.

The Norfolk Stake BLGSU, 4760 Princess Anne Rd., Virginia Beach, VA 23462. Phone: 1-804-467-9855.

Other BLGSU are to be found in the cities listed below. They may be located by looking in the local telephone directory under the listing CHURCH OF JESUS CHRIST OF LATTER-DAY SAINTS-GENEALOGY LIBRARY or in the Yellow Pages under CHURCHES-LATTER-DAY SAINTS.

In AL: Birmingham, Huntsville, in AR: Little Rock, in AK: Anchorage, Fairbanks, in AZ: Cottonwood, Flagstaff, Globe, Holbrook, Mesa, Phoenix, Prescott, St. David, Safford, St. Johns, Show Low, Snowflake, Tucson, Winslow, Yuma, in CA: Alhambra, Anaheim, Bakersfield, Barstow, Canyon Country, Carmichael, Chico, East Pasadena, Escondido, Eureka, Fairfield, Fresno, Garden Grove, Glendale, Goleta, Gridley, Hemet, La Canada, Lancaster, Long Beach, Los Angeles, Menlo Park, Mission Viejo, Modesto, Needles, Norwalk, Oakland, Palmdale, Redding, Ridgecrest, Riverside, San Bernardino, San Diego, San Jose, San Luis Obispo, Santa Ana, Santa Clara, Santa Fe Springs, Santa Maria, Santa Rosa, Seaside, Simi Valley, Stockton, Turlock, Upland, Ventura, West Covina, Whittier,

In CO: Arvada, Boulder, Colorado Springs, Denver, Durango, Ft. Collins, Glenwood Springs, Grand Junction, LaJara, Littleton, Montrose, Northglenn, in CT: Hartford, in FL: Alachua, Boca Raton, Cocoa, Fern Park, Hialeah, Jacksonville, Marianna, Miami, Orlando, Pensacola, St. Petersburg, Tallahassee, Tampa, in GA: Atlanta, Macon, in HI: Hilo, Honolulu, Kaneohe, Laie, in ID: Arco, Blackfoot, Boise, Burley, Caldwell, Driggs, Firth, Idaho Falls, Lewiston, Malad, Montpelier, Moreland, Nampa, Pocatello, Post Falls, Rexburg, Salmon, Shelley, Twin Falls, Ucon, in IL: Champaign, Lossmoor, Naperville, Wilmette, in IN: Ft. Wayne, Indianapolis,

In IA: Cedar Rapids, Des Moines, in KS: Shawnee Mission, Topeka, Wichita, in KY: Lexington, Louisville, in LA: Baton Rouge, Shreveport, in ME: Brunswick, in MD: Silver Spring, in MA: Sudbury, in MI: Bloomfield, East Lansing, Grand Blanc, Grand Rapids, Midland, Westland, in MN: Richfield, St. Paul, in MS: Petal, in MO: Berkeley, Columbia, Kansas City, Springfield, in MT: Billings, Butte, Great Falls, Helena, Kalispell, Missoula, in NE: Boys Town, in NV: Elko, Ely, Fallon, Las Vegas, Logandale, Reno, Sparks, in NH: Nashua, in NJ: Chatham, East Brunswick, in NM: Albuquerque, Farmington, Gallup, Las Cruces, Los Alamos, Roswell, in NY: East Rochester, Loudonville, Massapequa, New York, Stamford, Syracuse, Vestal, Williamsville,

In NC: Charlotte, Fayetteville, Hampstead, Hickory, Kinston, Raleigh, in ND: Fargo, in OH: Cincinnati, Fairborn, North Elmstead, Reynoldsburg, in OK: Norman, Oklahoma City, Tulsa, in OR: Beaverton Bend, Coos Bay, Corvallis, Eugene, Fairview, Klamath Falls, LaGrande, Medford, Ontario, Oregon City, Portland, Roseburg, Salem, The Dalles, in PA: Broomwall, Pittsburg, Reading, State College, York, in SC: Greenville, Hanahan, Hopkins, in SD: Rapid City, in TN: Bearden, Chattanooga, Kingsport, Madison, Memphis, in TX: Bellaire, Corpus Christi, Dallas, El Paso, Houston, Hurst, LaMarque, Longview, Lubbock, Nederland, Odessa, Richardson, San Antonio,

In UT: Beaver, Blanding, Bountiful, Brigham City, Cedar City, Delta, Duchesne, Fillmore, Heber City, Hurricane, Kanab, Loa, Logan, Moroni, Mt. Pleasant, Nephi, Ogden, Orangeville, Price, Provo, Richfield, Riverton, Roosevelt, Salt Lake City, Sandy, Santaquin, St. George, Springville, Vernal, in VT: Montpelier, in WA: Bellevue, Bremerton, East Wenatchee, Everett, Kennewick, Longview, Moses Lake, Mt. Vernon, Olympia, Pasco, Pullman, Richland, Seattle, Spokane, Sumner, Tacoma, Vancouver, Yakima, in WV: Charleston, in WI: Belvedere, Milwaukee, Shawano, in WY: Afton, Casper, Cheyenne, Cody, Evanston, Green River, Lovell, Rock Springs, Worland.

When you go to GSU or BLSGU, first ask for the VA international genealogical index microfiche and examine it for the name of your ancestor, then if you are at GSU, request the records. If you are at BLGSU, ask them to borrow the microfilm containing the record from GSU. The cost is only a few dollars, and when your microfilm arrives (usually 4-6 weeks), you will be notified so that you can return and examine it. Second, ask for the surname catalog at GSU or the microfiche copy of it at BLGSU. Examine it for all listings of the surname of your ancestor. If you think any of the references relate to your ancestral line, and if you are at GSU, request the records. If you are at BLGSU, ask them to borrow the record for you. Third;, ask for the VA locality catalog. It will be a card catalog at GSU and a microfiche copy of the card catalog at BLGSU. Examine all listings under the main heading of VIRGINIA. Then examine all listings under the subheading of the county you are interested in. These listings follow those for the state of VA. Toward the end of each of the county listings, there are listed materials relating to cities and towns in the county. Be sure not to overlook them. If you are at GSU, you can request the materials which are of interest to you. If you are at BLGSU, you may have the branch librarian borrow them for you. A large number of the books and records referred to in Chapter 2 and those listed under the counties in Chapter 4 will be found in the VA locality catalog. Fourth, make use of the integrated census indexes, looking for your ancestors' names under the VA heading.

If you happen to be at GSU, there are several other important indexes that you should examine thoroughly. Included among them are the Temple Index Bureau and the Family Group Records Archive (if the Temple Index Bureau indicates). Further details concerning the records in GSU and BLGSU along with instructions for finding and using them will be found in:
  R. Cunningham and E. Evans, A HANDY GUIDE TO THE GENEA-LOGICAL LIBRARY AND CHURCH HISTORICAL DEPARTMENT, Everton Publishers, Logan, UT, 1980.

10. Regional libraries (RL)

In the state of VA there are a number of regional libraries (RL) which have genealogical collections. Their holdings are larger than those of most local libraries (LL), but are smaller than the holdings of VSL&A and VHSL. As might be expected, the materials in each of the RL are best for the immediate and the surrounding counties. Among the best of these RL are:

__Alexandria Public Library, 717 Queen St., Alexandria, VA 22314.

__Blue Ridge Regional Library, 310 East Church St., Martinsville, VA 24112.

__Bristol Public Library, 701 Goode St., Bristol, VA 24201.

__Danville Public Library, 511 Patton St., Danville, VA 24541.

__Fairfax County Public Library, 3915 Chain Bridge Rd., Fairfax, VA 22030.

__Taylor Memorial Public Library, 4205 Victoria Blvd., Hampton, VA 23669.

__Jones Memorial Library, 434 Rivermont Ave., Lynchburg, VA 24504.

__Norfolk Public Library, 301 East City Hall Ave., Norfolk, VA 23510.

__Newport News Public Library, 2400 Washington St., Newport News, VA 23607.

__Roanoke County Public Library, 3131 Electric Rd., SW, Roanoke, VA 24018.

__Roanoke Public Library, 706 South Jefferson St., Roanoke, VA 24011.

__Rockingham Public Library, 45 Newman Rd., Harrisonburg, VA 22801.

__Swem Library, College of William and Mary, Williamsburg, VA 23185.

When a visit is made to any of these libraries, your first endeavor is to search the card catalog. You can remember what to look for with the acronym SLANT. This procedure should give you very good coverage of the library holdings which are indexed in the card catalog.

The second endeavor at any of these libraries is to ask about any special indexes, catalogs, collections, or materials which might be pertinent to your search. You should make it your aim particularly to inquire about Bible, cemetery, church, map, manuscript, military, mortuary, and newspaper materials. In some cases, microform (microfilm, microfiche, microcard) records are not included in the regular card catalog but are separately indexed. It is important that you be alert to this possibility.

In addition to the RL mentioned above, there are several libraries in VA which have highly-specialized

collections which are pertinent to VA genealogy. Many are mentioned in:
__VA Task Force on Higher Education, A DIRECTORY OF VA LIBRARY RESOURCES, VA Council of HIgher Education, Richmond, VA 23219, 1979.

11. Large genealogical libraries (LGL)

Spread around the US there are a number of large genealogical libraries (LGL) which have at least some VA genealogical source materials. In general, those librar- ies nearest VA (DC, KY, MD, NC, PA, TN, WV), are the ones that have the larger VA collections, but there are excep- tions. Among these LGL are:
__In AL: Birmingham Public Library, Library at Samford University in Birmingham, AL Archives and History Dept. in Birmingham, in AZ: Southern AZ Genealogical Society in Tucson, in AR: AR Genealogical Society in Little Rock, AR History Commission in Little Rock, Little Rock Public Library, in CA: CA Genealogical Society in San Francisco, Los Angeles Public Library, San Diego Public Library, San Francisco Public Library, Sutro Library in San Francisco,
__In CO: Denver Public Library, in CT: CT State Library in Hartford, Godfrey Memorial Library in Middletown, in FL: FL State Library in Tallahassee, Miami-Dade Public Library, Tampa Public Library, in GA: Atlanta Public Library, in ID: ID Genealogical Society, in IL: New- berry Library in Chicago, in IN: IN State Library in Indianapolis, Public Library of Fort Wayne, in IA: IA State Department of History and Archives in Des Moines, in KY: KY Historical Society in Frankfort,
__In LA: LA State Library in Baton Rouge, in ME: ME State Library in Augusta, in MD: MD State Library in Annapo- lis, MD Historical Society in Baltimore, in MA: Boston Public Library, New England Historic Genealogical Society in Boston, in MI: Detroit Public Library, in MN: Minneapolis Public Library, in MS: MS Department of Archives and History in Jackson, in MO: Kansas City Public Library, St. Louis Public Library,
__In NE: NE State Historical Society in Lincoln, Omaha Public Library, in NV: Washoe County Library in Reno, in NY: NY City Public Library, NY Genealogical and Biographical Society in NY City, in NC: NC State Li- brary in Raleigh, in OH: Cincinnati Public Library, OH State Library in Columbus, Western Reserve Historical

Society in Cleveland, in OK: OK State Historical Society in Oklahoma City, in OR: Genealogical Forum of Portland, Portland Library Association, in PA: Historical Society of PA in Philadelphia, Carnegie Library of Pittsburgh,
In SC: The South Caroliniana Library in Columbia, in SD: State Historical Society in Pierre, in TN: TN State Library and Archives in Nashville, in TX: Dallas Public Library, Fort Worth Public Library, in UT: Brigham Young University Library in Provo, in WA: Seattle Public Library, in WV: WV Department of Archives and History in Charleston, in WI: Milwaukee Public Library, State Historical Society in Madison.

12. Local libraries (LL)

Listed under the 100 VA counties in Chapter 4 are most of the important local libraries in the state. Libraries of independent cities are listed under encompassing or adjacent counties or under the county the city replaced (see Chapter 1). These libraries are of a very wide variety, some having sizable genealogical materials, some having practically none. However, you should never overlook a LL in a county or city of your interest since quite often they have local records or collections available nowhere else. In addition, local librarians are frequently very knowledgeable concerning genealogical sources in their areas. Further, they are also usually acquainted with the people in the county (city) who are experts in the county's (city's) history and genealogy. Thus, both local libraries and local librarians can be of exceptional value to you.

When you visit a LL, the general procedure described previously should be followed: First, search the card catalog. Look under the headings summarized by SLANT: subject, location, author, name, title, doing them in the order L-N-S-A-T. Then, second, inquire about special indexes, catalogs, collections, materials, and microforms. Also ask about any other local sources of data such as cemetery records, church records, maps and atlases, genealogical and historical societies, mortuary records, and old newspaper records and indexes.

If you choose to write a LL, please remember that the librarians are very busy people. Always send them an

SASE and confine your questions to one straight-forward item. Librarians are usually glad to help you if they can employ indexes to answer your question, but you must not expect them to do research for you. In case research in required, they will usually be able to supply you with a list of researchers which you may hire.

13. Bookshop

In the Washington-Northern-VA area there is an excellent bookshop which specializes in genealogy, local history, and related subjects. This store, one of the few such retail outlets in the country, is HEARTHSTONE BOOKSHOP, Potomac Square, 8405-H Richmond Highway, Alexandria, VA 22309. They stock the publications of all major genealogical publishers, and are dealers for US Geological Survey maps, and Hollinger acid-free paper and containers (for preservation of old documents and photographs). In addition, they carry an extensive line of genealogical accessories, including forms, charts, and notebooks. The store, run by its genial proprietor Stuart Nixon, is located in historic Alexandria. They welcome you from 10-5 Monday through Saturday (with Sunday hours during the summer). Don't fail to visit them when you are in the area, or send $1 for their illustrated catalog, which they publish each year. For ordering materials and/or inquiries, phone them at 1-703-360-6900.

Abbreviations

ALUV	Alderman Library, University of VA
AMS	Anne M. Smalley
BLGSU	Branch Library(ies), Genealogical Society of UT
CH	Court House(s)
DARL	Daughters of American Revolution Library, Washington
GKS	George K. Schweitzer or Genealogy Kinship Sources
GSU	Genealogical Society of UT, Salt Lake City
LL	Local Library(ies)
LOC	Library of Congress
RL	Regional Library(ies)
SLCWM	Swem Library, College of William & Mary, Williamsburg
VHSL	VA Historical Society Library, Richmond
VSL&A	VA State Library and Archives, Richmond

Chapter 4

RESEARCH PROCEDURE & COUNTY LISTINGS

1. Finding the county

Now that you have read Chapters 1-3, you should have a good idea of VA history, its genealogical records, and the locations and availability of these records. Your situation is now that you can begin to use these resources. The single most important thing to discover about a VA ancestor is the county or counties (or perhaps the city) in which he or she lived. This is because the basis of most VA genealogical records is the county or independent city. If your ancestor lived in VA in or after 1900, this information is probably available to you from older members of the family. There are also the completely indexed 1900 and 1910 censuses (section 6, Chapter 2), and the state-wide birth and death records for the period after 1912. However, it is often the case that for a VA ancestor before 1900, all you know is that he or she lived somewhere in the state. If you happen to know the county, you are fortunate because this permits you to proceed without working through the problem of locating it. You may skip directly to section 2 of this chapter. If you don't know the county, discovery of it is your first priority.

If your ancestor's period is 1820-1910, the federal census records for 1820, 1830, 1840, 1850, 1880, 1900, and 1910 will be of a great deal of help (section 6, Chapter 2). Indexes are available for the 1820, 1830, 1840, 1850, 1900, and 1910 censuses, and a partial index for the 1880 census. If this fails to locate your forebear, then you need to look into a number of other state-wide indexes which could list him or her. Among the most useful of these for the period 1820-1910 are:
__Biographies (section 3, Chapter 2).
__Genealogical compilations and indexes (section 18, Chapter 2).
__Marriage indexes in VHSL (section 24, Chapter 2).
__Military records, War of 1812, Mexican War, Civil War, Spanish American War (sections 27-28, Chapter 2).
__Special indexes in VSL&A and VHSL (especially Bible, biography, marriage, manuscript, newspaper, and obituary: sections 3-4, Chapter 3).

If your ancestor's period is 1776-1819, there are excellent tax-based substitutes for the lost 1790 and the partial 1810 censuses (section 6, Chapter 2). These are well indexed. The lost 1800 census records are being substituted for by a series of journal articles in the VA Genealogist (section 6, chapter 2). If these do not locate your ancestor, then you should try the following:

__Biographies (section 3, Chapter 2).

__Genealogical indexes and compilations (section 18, Chapter 2).

__Land records of transfer of ownership from the state to the first owner (section 22, Chapter 2).

__Card indexes to marriages in VHSL (section 24, Chapter 2).

__Revolutionary War military records (section 26, Chapter 2).

__War of 1812 military records (section 27, Chapter 2).

__Indexes in books dealing with regional records (section 33, Chapter 2).

__State-wide will indexes in Torrence and VSL&A (section 35, Chapter 2).

__Special indexes in VSL&A, VHSL, and ALUV (especially Bible, wills and administrations, Revolutionary, War of 1812, public service claims, land office records, manuscripts, newspapers, marriages, obituaries: sections 3-5, Chapter 3).

If your ancestor's period falls within the colonial era (1607-1775), particular attention needs to be paid to the following sources which are the most likely ones to contain references to his or her location:

__Bible records (section 2, Chapter 2).

__Biographies (section 3, Chapter 2).

__Early lists, enumerations, and polls (second paragraph, section 6, Chapter 2).

__Colonial record compilations (section 10, Chapter 2).

__Early immigration lists (section 15, Chapter 2).

__Genealogical indexes and compilations (section 18, Chapter 2).

__Early land grants, patents, certificates, surveys, and warrants (section 22, Chapter 2).

__Military records (especially Colonial, French and Indian, and Dunmore's Wars: section 25, Chapter 2).

__Index to VA's colonial newspaper (section 31, Chapter 2).

___ Published genealogies for the US (section 32, Chapter 2).
___ Regional records (section 33, Chapter 2).
___ Early tithable, tax, poll, and rent lists (section 34, Chapter 2).
___ Indexes to early wills and administrations (section 35, Chapter 2).
___ Special indexes to VSL&A, VHSL, and ALUV (especially colonial papers, wills and administrations, manuscripts, land office records, newspapers, obituaries, marriages, Bible: sections 3-5, Chapter 3).

As you can see from the above considerations, the earlier the period in which you think your ancestor was in VA, the greater your need to look into the resources of VSL&A, VHSL, and ALUV. The key items for the period 1820-1910 are the censuses and their indexes. These are to be found in VSL&A, VHSL, NA, GSU, BLGSU, in many LGL and RL, and in some LL. The key items for the period 1776-1819 are the tax-list substitutes or supplements for the missing 1790, 1800, and 1810 censuses. Again, these are to be found in VSL&A, VHSL, NA, LOC, GSU, BLGSU, in many LGL and RL, and in some LL. The key items for the colonial period, 1607-1775, are the early records of the Land Office. These are all in VSL&A, and the major ones are available at GSU and BLGSU. For the two periods mentioned first (1820-1910 and 1776-1819), you can probably look into the key items in libraries near your home. But, if you need to go beyond these key items or if you need to look into the colonial period (1607-1775), the thing to do is to go to VSL&A and VHSL or GSU or a BLGSU. If none of these is near you, it would be next best for you to hire a researcher in Richmond (VSL&A and VHSL). Instructions for hiring a researcher will be given below. Once you locate in these indexes references to a person you think to be your ancestor, you may then dig into the records of the appropriate county. Sometimes you will need to look into the various county records in order to sort the names out.

2. Recommended approaches

Having identified the county of your ancestor's residence, you are in position to begin to ferret out the details. Turn to the section on that county in the following pages. There you will find a summary of the

most-important readily-accessible records for that county. [A detailed description of the format of these
county record summaries is given in the next section.]
You should make a thorough examination of all the records
which apply to your ancestor's dates in the county, since
this will give you the best chance of finding the maximum
amount of information. Then you should ascertain if
there are any further records at the CH and/or the LL in
the county. If your ancestor's dates extend beyond 1865,
then the answer to this question will always be affirma-
tive. That is because most records kept by county and
city governments after 1865 are only in the CH (probate,
will, deed, some marriage, court, guardian, and survey).
[Please re-read paragraph 2, section 1, Chapter 3 to make
sure you are clear on this important 1865 situation.]
Both before and after 1865 there will inevitably be boxes
and cabinets of folders and loose records which have not
been microfilmed and are therefore not available anywhere
else. The exact approach you choose to take in getting
at the records will most likely depend on where you live.

The best approach is one in which (1) you examine
all the holdings of LL, LGL, and any RL near you, then
(2) you go to Richmond and perhaps Washington and use the
holdings of VSL&A, VHSL, and perhaps NA, LOC, and DARL,
then (3) you go to the county seat or city and look into
the records at the CH and the LL. A modification of this
approach would be to hire researchers to do the work for
you at VSL&A, VHSL, NA, LOC, DARL, CH, and LL.

The second best approach is one in which (1) you
examine all the holdings of LL and LGL near you, then (2)
you go to Salt Lake City and use the holdings of GSU,
then (3) you hire a researcher to examine the materials
in VSL&A-VHSL (and perhaps NA-LOC-DARL) which you have
not seen at GSU, then (4) you hire a researcher to look
into the records at the CH and LL in the county (and/or
city). When you hire a researcher, be very careful to
explain exactly what records you have already seen. This
will avoid needless duplication of effort and extra
expense on your part.

Another approach is one in which (1) you examine all
the holdings of LL, LGL, and perhaps RL near you, then
(2) you go to the nearest BLGSU, order the microfilms you
need, wait for them to come, return to BLGSU to read

them, then (3) you hire a researcher to examine the materials in VSL&A-VHSL (and perhaps NA-LOC-DARL) which you have not seen in BLGSU, then (4) you hire a researcher to look into the records at the CH and LL in the county (and/or city). When you hire a researcher, carefully explain exactly what records you have already examined, so as to avoid unnecessary duplication and expense.

In selecting an approach, whether it be one of the above or one at which you arrive by your own consideration of Chapter 3, you need to think about three items carefully. The first is expense. In visiting VSL&A-VHSL (and perhaps NA-LOC-DARL) or GSU, at least 2 or 3 full working days should be planned for. This means you will have travel costs plus at least 2 nights' lodging. To visit a county seat or city (CH and LL) requires at least 1 day. So travel costs and 1 night's lodging will be involved, although this could be combined with the trip to VSL&A-VHSL (and perhaps NA-LOC-DARL) which might cut the expense somewhat. In visiting a BLGSU, your initial visit for index-checking and microfilm-ordering will require about half a day, but your return visits will take more time depending on how many microfilms you order and whether they come together or piecemeal. Thus, travel and perhaps lodging costs for several trips could be involved, plus the cost of borrowing the films. This will run several dollars per film and, in many cases, between 40 and 80 films might be needed for full coverage. This means that the film cost could easily be a couple of hundred dollars. All of this travel, lodging, and film rental must be weighed over against the cost of hiring a researcher or making a trip to GSU or VSL&A-VHSL-CH-LL. Of course, your own desire to look at the records for yourself may be an important consideration.

The second item is a reminder about interlibrary loans. With the exception of the microfilms of BLGSU, very few libraries and even fewer archives will lend out their genealogical holdings on interlibrary loan. This is almost always the case for microfilms and usually the case for books. This means that the amount of information you may obtain through interlibrary loan is ordinarily quite limited.

The <u>third</u> <u>item</u> is also a reminder, this being a restatement of what was said in Chapter 3. You will have noticed that correspondence with librarians and archivists of VSL&A, VHSL, ALUV, NA, LOC, DARL, GSU-BLGSU, RL, LGL, LL, and county and city employees has not been mentioned in the above procedures. This is because these helpful and hard-working federal, state, local, and private employees seldom have time to do detailed work for you because of the demanding duties of their offices. In many cases, these people are willing to look up one specific item for you (a marriage date, a deed record, a will, an entry in an land grant index, a military pension) <u>if</u> an overall index is available. But please don't ask them for detailed data. If you do write them, enclose a long SASE, a check for $4 with the payee line left blank, a brief (no more than one-third page) request for a specific item, and a request that if they do not have the time, that they hand your letter and check to a researcher who can do the work. In requesting military records from NA (service, pension, or bounty land), a check for $5 for each item requested must be sent.

3. <u>Format of the listings</u>

In the 110 sections to follow, summaries of the most-important readily-available older records of the VA counties and independent cities are given. The older independent city records are listed with the counties from which they were formed or which surround them. Take a look at the Accomack County materials which we will use to illustrate the format employed for these summaries. First, the name of the county is given, then its county seat, then the zip code of the county seat in parentheses. Next comes the date of formation and the territory, county, or counties from which it was formed. This should alert you to track your ancestor back through the parent counties if he or she was living there in the year of formation. Following this, if appropriate, information is given regarding disastrous events in which records were destroyed, regarding county name changes, regarding independent city information and regarding present location of records. Then, a reference to a very useful listing and discussion of the county's records is given. These references are all to a series of articles in the VA Genealogist, a highly-respected periodical. The first figure gives the volume number, the second gives the year in parentheses, and the third figure is the page number on which the article begins.

The next section under each county lists various governmental county records which are available along with dates of availability. The record designations refer in general to labels on various items (books, boxes, files, folders), and to the major contents of these items. A date by itself such as [rent roll (1704)] indicates that the item is available only for that year. A date followed by a dash and another date such as [birth (1854-96)] indicates an essentially continuous year-by-year run of records from 1854-1896, although a few years may be missing. A date followed by only a hyphen such as [chancery court order (1831-)] indicates a continuous run of yearly records from 1831 at least up into the 1860s and usually into the 20th century, even up to the present. In the continuous run, there may be a few missing years. These listings tell you what is available and alert you to what you should look for in VSL&A, GSU, BLGSU, RL, LGL, LL, and CH according to previously given instructions (Chapter 3). The listings have been obtained from card catalogs and/or special indexes in VSL&A, GSU, BLGSU, WPA Surveys, DAR listings, the Stemmons' compendia, books by Brown, Everton, Beard, the VA State Library Staff, Bullock and Potter, Gentry and Salmon, Clay, McKay, Clark and Long, Kaminkow, LeGear, and Schreiner-Yantis, and journal articles by Dorman. Two very important notes regarding these governmental county records need to be recognized. First, you must bear in mind that land records can occur under many titles (for example, assessor, chancery court, circuit court, court, district court, land cause, grant, tax, warrant, plat, rent, superior court, survey), as is the case with estate records (for example, account, administrator, court minute, executor, guardian, inventory, orphan, settlement, will). This emphasizes the importance of examining all records. Second, please remember that the records in VSL&A usually go up only into the middle 1860s. For dates after that, the county or city CH must be visited.

In some of the county listings, a section relating to independent cities now follows. Record listings for these cities follow the same general pattern as those for the counties.

Following this, there appears a section listing other types of records, which are available for the county (and sometimes an enclosed or contiguous independent city) and which can be sought in VSL&A, VHSL, ALUV, NA, LOC, DARL, GSU, BLGSU, RL, LGL, and LL. The listings largely indicate records available before 1900. In the census listings, T indicates a tax list substitute for the census, R indicates a regular population census, A indicates the listing of additional names missed in the 1810 Census, [VA Genealogist 18 (1974) 136], F a farm census, M a manufactures census, D a mortality census, and S a slave-holder census. For example, 1870 RFMD means that the regular, farm, manufactures, and mortality censuses are available for 1870. You will also notice that biography, cemetery, county history, county map, Episcopal parish, landowner map, and Presbyterian records are also available for Accomack County.

The last section under each county gives you the libraries, and genealogical and/or historical societies in each county. When a small hatch mark # appears after the name of a library, this means that the library has notable holdings of genealogically-related materials. When an asterisk * appears after the name of a society, this indicates that the society publishes a periodical dealing with the genealogy and/or history of the area. Also listed are one or a few of the better county histories, if available. For over half the counties there are other county histories which you may want to see.

4. ACCAMACK COUNTY, formed in 1634, one of the 8 original shires (counties), originally made up of the entire Eastern Shore, name changed to Northampton County in 1642, see Northampton County for records, see VA Genealogist 3 (1959) 38.

5. ACCOMACK COUNTY, County Seat: Accomac (23301), formed in 1663 from Northampton County, see VA Genealogist 3 (1959) 38.
Court house records: birth (1854-96), chancery court order (1831-), circuit court order (1850-), common law order (1822-), court minute (1729-30), court order (1663-), death (1853), deed (1663-), district court order (1789-1816), indenture (1798-1835), inventory (1663-), judgment (1778-1801), land cause (1727-), land tax (1782,

1787-), marriage (1774-), military (1785-7), orphan (1741-), overseers of poor (1787-1819), personal property tax (1787, 1816-), procession (1723-84, 1796-1816, 1819-32, 1836-44, 1848-), rent roll (1704), summons (1830-5), superior court minute (1831-55), survey (1784-), tax alteration (1783-6), tithable (1663-95), will (1663). Other records: biography, cemetery, census(1790T, 1800T, 1810RA, 1820R, 1830R, 1840R, 1850RFMS, 1860RFMDS, 1870RFMD, 1880RFMD, 1900R, 1910R), county histories, county map, Episcopal parish, landowner map (1820), Presbyterian. Libraries: Eastern Shore Public Library, Accomac, VA 23301; Eastern Shore of VA Historical Society Collection, Kerr Place, Onancock, VA 23417 (not open to the public). Histories: J. C. Wise, YE KINGDOME OF ACCAWMACKE OR THE EASTERN SHORE OF VA IN THE 17TH CENTURY, Bell Book Co., Richmond, VA, 1911; S. M. Ames, STUDIES OF THE VA EASTERN SHORE IN THE 17TH CENTURY, Dietz Press, Richmond, VA, 1940; C. B. Clark, editor, THE EASTERN SHORE OF MD AND VA, Lewis Historical Publishing Co., New York, NY, 1950, 3 volumes; N. M. Turman, THE EASTERN SHORE OF VA, Eastern Shore News, Onancock, VA, 1964; R. T. Whitelaw, VA'S EASTERN SHORE: A HISTORY OF NORTHAMPTON AND ACCOMACK COUNTIES, P. Smith, Gloucester, MA, 1968 (1951), 2 volumes.

6. ALBEMARLE COUNTY, County Seat: Charlottesville (22902), formed in 1744 from Goochland and Louisa Counties, see VA Genealogist 3 (1959) 86.
Court house records: birth (1853-61), circuit court will (1798-1904), court minute (1830-), court order (1744-8, 1783-5, 1791-1804, 1806-31), death (1853-61), deed (1748-), district court deed (1790-1806), guardian (1783-), land tax (1782, 1787-), marriage (1780-), personal property tax (1782-), petition (1776, 1787), residents (1758), superior court deed (1807-32), tax alteration (1783-6), will (1748-). Other records: Baptist, biography, cemetery, census (1790T, 1800T, 1810RA, 1820R, 1830R, 1840R, 1850RFMS, 1860RFMDS, 1870RFMD, 1880RFMD, 1900R, 1910R), city history, city map, county histories, county map, Episcopal parish, Friends, landowner maps (1864, 1875), Methodist, minister's records, newspaper, Presbyterian. Libraries: Alderman Library,# University of VA, Charlottesville, VA 22904; Jefferson-Madison Regional Library, McIntire Public Library, 2nd and E. Jefferson Sts., Charlottesville, VA 22901, Albemarle County Historical Society Library,# 220 Court Square,

Charlottesville, VA 22901. <u>Societies</u>: Albemarle County
Historical Society,* Alderman Library, University of VA,
Charlottesville, VA 22904; Central VA Genealogical Association, RFD 5, Box 258, Charlottesville, VA 22901.
<u>Histories</u>: E. Woods, ALBEMARLE COUNTY IN VA, C. J. Car-
rier Co., Bridgewater, VA 1964 (1901); M. Rawlings, THE
ALBEMARLE OF OTHER DAYS, Michie Co., Charlottesville, VA,
1925; J. H. Moore, ALBEMARLE: JEFFERSON'S COUNTY, 1726-
1976, Charlottesville, VA, 1976; WPA Writers' Program,
JEFFERSON'S ALBEMARLE, Charlottesville, VA, 1941.

7. <u>ALEXANDRIA COUNTY</u>, formed in 1801 from Fairfax County,
name changed in 1920 to Arlington County, see Arlington
County for details and records, see VA Genealogist <u>3</u>
(1959) 126.

8. <u>ALLEGHENY COUNTY</u>, County Seat: Covington (24226),
formed in 1822 from Bath, Botetourt, and Monroe (WV)
Counties, see VA Genealogist <u>3</u> (1959) 129.
  <u>Court house records</u>: chancery court order (1831-),
court minute (1822-), court order (1822-), deed (1822-),
divorce (1822-), guardian (1825-), land tax (1822-),
marriage (1822-), personal property tax (1822-), settlement (1833-), survey (1822-), will (1822-). <u>Other re-
cords</u>: cemetery, census (1830R, 1840R, 1850RFMS, 1860-
RFMDS, 1870RFMD, 1880RFMD, 1900R, 1910R), city history,
county histories, county map, newspaper. <u>Library</u>: Charles P. Jones Memorial Library, 406 W. Riverside St.,
Covington, VA 24426; Clifton Forge Public Library, PO Box
61, Clifton Forge, VA 24422. <u>History</u>: O. F. Morton, A
CENTENNIAL HISTORY OF ALLEGHENY COUNTY, Ruebush Co.,
Dayton, VA, 1923.

9. <u>AMELIA COUNTY</u>, County Seat: Amelia Court House
(23002), formed in 1735 from Prince George and Brunswick
Counties, see VA Genealogist <u>3</u> (1959) 171.
  <u>Court house records</u>: account (1831-), birth (1853-71),
chancery court papers (1832-), court order (1735-), death
(1853-1871), deed (1734-), divorce (1734-), guardian
(1750-1817), land tax (1782, 1787-), marriage (1735-),
personal property tax (1782-), petition (1768, 1776),
poll (1768), residents (1758), tax alteration (1783-6),
will (1734-). <u>Other records</u>: Baptist, cemetery, census
(1790T, 1800T, 1810RA, 1820R, 1830R, 1840R, 1850RFMS,
1860RFMDS, 1870RFMD, 1880RFMD, 1900R, 1910R), county
history, county map, Episcopal parish, Friends, inventory

of county records, landowner maps (1855, 1864), Metho-
dist. Society: Amelia Historical Society, Church St.,
Amelia Court House, VA 23002. Histories: M. A. Jefferson,
OLD HOMES AND BUILDINGS IN AMELIA COUNTY, The Author,
Amelia, VA, 1964; W. A. Watson, NOTES ON SOUTHSIDE VA,
1977 (1925).

10. AMHERST COUNTY, County Seat: Amherst (24521), formed
in 1761 from Albemarle County, see VA Genealogist 4
(1960) 38.
  Court house records: chancery order (1831-), circuit
court will (1810-97), court order (1766-9, 1773-94,
1799-1802, 1811-24, 1826-31, 1836-40, 1844-), deed (1761-
), divorce (1761-), land tax (1782-3, 1787), land warrant
(1783), marriage (1763), military (1772-82), personal
property tax (1782), petition (1775-6), plat (1761-),
survey (1781-1802), tax alteration (1784-6), will
(1761-). Other records: biography, cemetery, census
(1780T, 1800T, 1810RA, 1820R, 1830R, 1840R, 1850RFMS,
1860RFMDS, 1870RFMD, 1880RMFD, 1900R, 1910R), county
histories, county map, Episcopal parish, Friends, landowner maps (1862, 1864). Library: Amherst County Public
Library,# PO Box 370, Amherst, VA 24521. Histories: Hardesty, HISTORICAL & GEOGRAPHICAL ENCYCLOPEDIA: AMHERST &
BEDFORD COUNTY EDITION, Richmond, VA, 1884; A. Percy, THE
AMHERST COUNTY STORY, Percy Press, Madison Heights, VA,
1961.

11. APPOMATTOX COUNTY, County Seat: Appomattox (24522),
formed in 1845 from Buckingham, Campbell, Charlotte, and
Prince Edward Counties, most records destroyed in 1892 by
fire, see VA Genealogist 4 (1960) 79.
  Court house records: court order (1892-), deed (1892-),
divorce (1892-), land tax (1845-), marriage (1892-),
personal property tax (1845-), suit papers (1892-), will
(1892-). Other records: Baptist, cemetery, census (1850-
RFMS, 1860RFMDS, 1870RFMD, 1880RFMD, 1900R, 1910R),
church, county map, landowner map (1863), town history.
Library: Appomattox Court House National Historical Park
Library, Appomattox, VA 24522. Histories: N. R. Feather-
ston, THE HISTORY OF APPOMATTOX, American Legion, Appomattox, VA, 1948; V. S. Stanley, APPOMATTOX COUNTY, PAST,
PRESENT, FUTURE, Times-Virginian, Appomattox, VA, 1965.

12. ARLINGTON COUNTY, County Seat: Rosslyn (22210),
formed in 1801 from Fairfax County to become part of DC,

returned to VA in 1847, known as Alexandria County from 1847-1920, records in both County Court House and Alexandria Court House, see VA Genealogist 3 (1959) 126.

Court house records: account (1810-50), appraisal (1800-), birth (1853-96), common law order (1847-), court minute (1825-), court order (1801-27), death (1853-96), deed (1785-), estate (1801-47), guardian (1810-50), inventory (1800-), judgment (1783-1846), land (1847-60), land suit (1834-43), levy court (1801-27), marriage (1801-22, 1850-), military (1861-5), orphan (1801-30), personal property tax (1847-57, 1859-), tax (1787-9, 1803-5), tithable (1817), will (1786). Alexandria city records: city census (1799-1800, 1808, 1810, 1816), divorce (1870-), hustings court (1786-1846), hustings court deed (1783-1801), hustings court order (1780-99), hustings court will (1786-1800), land tax (1787-90, 1795-1855, 1862-), marriage (1870-), personal property tax (1787-90), petition (1785-7, 1792), trustee (1669-97, 1749-80, 1794-1800), will (1800-67). Other records: cemetery, census (1810RA, 1820R, 1830R, 1840R, 1850RFMS, 1860RFMDS, 1870RFMD, 1880RFMD, 1900R, 1910R), city atlas, city directories, city histories, city map, county atlas, county history, county map, Episcopal parish, Friends, landowner maps (17--, 1861, 1864, 1900), newspaper, Presbyterian. Libraries: Alexandria Library,# 717 Queen St., Alexandria, VA 22314; Arlington Public Library,# 1015 N. Quincy St., Arlington, VA 22201. Societies: Alexandria Historical Society, 201 S. Washington St., Alexandria, VA 22314; Arlington Historical Society, 1805 S. Arlington Ridge Rd., Arlington, VA 22210. Histories: B. C. Smoot, DAYS IN AN OLD TOWN, Alexandria, VA, 1934; M. G. Powell, THE HISTORY OF OLD ALEXANDRIA, Byrd Press, Richmond, VA, 1928; D. E. Lee, A HISTORY OF ARLINGTON COUNTY, Dietz Press, Richmond, VA, 1946.

13. AUGUSTA COUNTY, County Seat: Staunton (24401), formed in 1738/45 from Orange County, see VA Genealogist 4 (1960) 80.

Court house records: administrator (1776-), birth (1853-1900), chancery court order (1831-), circuit court deed (1789-1813), circuit court will (1745-), circuit superior court (1789-1842), common law order (1831-), court martial (1756-93), court order (1745-), death (1853-1900), deed (1745-), district court (1788-1808), executor (1787-), fee (1748-74), guardian (1809-50, 1855-), judgment (1745-1816), land tax (1782, 1787-), loose papers index (1745-), marriage (1748-74, 1785-), military (1776-1833, 1861-5), militia (1742, 1756), militia court (1807-12), muster roll (1861-5), personal property tax (1782-), petition (1742, 1749, 1779-80), residents (1758), settlers (1748-79), superior court of chancery (1802-31), superior court will (1778-), survey (1744-), tax alteration (1783-6), tithable (1777, 1781--4), will (1745-). Staunton city records: birth (1854-96), council minutes (1796-1865), court minutes (1802-18, 1825-30), court order (1839-), death (1853-92), deed (1802-), marriage (1802-), personal property tax (1802-), will (1802-). Other records: Baptist, cemetery, census (1790T, 1800T, 1810RA, 1820R, 1830R, 1840R, 1850RFMS, 1860RFMDS, 1870RFMD, 1880RFMD, 1900R, 1910R), city histories, county atlas (1885), county histories, county map, Episcopal parish, landowner maps (1736, 1865, 1870), Lutheran, Presbyterian. Libraries: Staunton Public Library,# Fannie Bayly King Library, 19 S. Market St., Staunton, VA 24401; Augusta County Public Library, Route 1, Fisherville, VA 22939; Waynesboro Public Library,# 600 S. Wayne Ave., Waynesboro, VA 22980; Blue Ridge Community College Library,# Weyers Cave, VA 24486. Society: Augusta County Historical Society,* PO Box 686, Staunton, VA 24401. Histories: J. L. Peyton, HISTORY OF AUGUSTA COUNTY, Yost & Son, Bridgewater, VA, 1953 (1882); J. A. Waddell, ANNALS OF AUGUSTA COUNTY, Carrier Co., Bridgewater, VA, 1958 (1902); C. E. Kemper, HISTORICAL NOTES FROM THE RECORDS OF AUGUSTA COUNTY, Lancaster, PA, 1921.

14. BATH COUNTY, County Seat: Warm Springs (24484), formed in 1791 from Augusta, Botetourt, and Greenbrier (WV) Counties, see VA Genealogist 4 (1960) 128.
Court house records: administrator (1808-), birth (1853-70), chancery court order (1831-), circuit court deed (1809-), circuit court will (1809-), court order (1791-), death (1853-70), deed (1791-), divorce (1791-), executor (1793-), land tax (1791-), law & chancery (1791-), marriage (1791-), personal property tax (1791-), survey (1791-), voter (1791-1821), will (1791-). Other records: cemetery, census (1800T, 1810RA, 1820R, 1830R, 1840R, 1850RFMS, 1860RFMDS, 1870RFMD, 1880RFMD, 1900R, 1910R), county history, county map, Presbyterian, town histories. Library: Bath County Regional Library, Warm Springs, VA 24484. Society: Bath County Historical Society, Warm Springs, VA 24484. History: O. F. Morton, ANNALS OF BATH COUNTY, McClure Co., Staunton, VA, 1917.

15. <u>BEDFORD</u> <u>COUNTY</u>, County Seat: Bedford (24523), formed in 1753 from Lunenburg and Albemarle Counties, see VA Genealogist <u>4</u> (1960) 171.

<u>Court house records</u>: birth (1853-97), chancery court order (1831-), court order (1754-), death (1853-97), deed (1754-), divorce (1754-), fiduciary (1754-), heirs (1754-), land tax (1782, 1787-), marriage (1754-), personal property tax (1782-), petition (1774), procession (1796-1812), residents (1758), superior court deed (1810-), superior court will (1810-), survey (1754-), tax alteration (1783-6), trust (1754-), ward (1754-), will (1754-). <u>Other records</u>: Baptist, biography, cemetery, census (1790T, 1800T, 1810RA, 1820R, 1830R, 1840R, 1850-RFMS, 1860RFMDS, 1870RFMD, 1880RFMD, 1900R, 1910R), city history, county histories, county map, Episcopal parish, Friends, landowner map (1864), minister's records, Presbyterian. <u>Library</u>: Bedford Public Library, 321 N. Bridge St., Bedford, VA 24523. <u>Society</u>: Bedford Historical Society, PO Box 602, Bedford, VA 24523. <u>Histories</u>: HISTORICAL SKETCH OF BEDFORD COUNTY, J. P. Bell Co., Lynchburg, VA, 1907; L. E. J. Parker, THE HISTORY OF BEDFORD COUNTY, Bedford Democrat, Bedford, VA, 1954; D. I. Read, NEW LONDON TODAY AND TOMORROW, J. P. Bell Co., Lynchburg, VA, 1950.

16. <u>BLAND</u> <u>COUNTY</u>, County Seat: Bland (24315), formed in 1861 from Giles, Wythe, and Tazewell Counties, some records destroyed in fire in 1885, see VA Genealogist <u>5</u> (1961) 77.

<u>Court house records</u>: bond (1861-), court order (1861-), deed (1861-), divorce (1861-), land tax (1861-), marriage (1861-), personal property tax (1861-), will (1861-). <u>Other records</u>: biography, cemetery, census (1870RFMD, 1880RFMD, 1900R, 1910R), county histories, county map, landowner map (1866), village history. <u>Library</u>: Smythe-Bland Regional Library, PO Box 1068, Marion, VA 24354. <u>Histories</u>: Bland County Centennial Corporation, HISTORY OF BLAND COUNTY, The Corporation, Bland, VA, 1961; D. E. Johnston, HISTORY OF THE MIDDLE NEW RIVER SETTLEMENTS, 1906.

17. <u>BOTETOURT</u> <u>COUNTY</u>, County Seat: Fincastle (24090), formed in 1770 from Augusta and Rockbridge Counties, see VA Genealogist <u>5</u> (1961) 131.

<u>Court house records</u>: birth (1853-70), chancery court order (1831-), circuit court deed (1810-3), circuit court

will (1835-), court order (1770-), death (1853-70), deed (1770-), divorce (1770-), guardian (1799-), land grant (1770-1802), land tax (1783-), marriage (1770-), personal property tax (1784-), survey (1774-), tax alteration (1782), tithable (1770-90), will (1770-). Other records: Baptist, cemetery, census (1790T, 1800T, 1810RA, 1820R, 1830R, 1840R, 1850RFMS, 1860RFMDS, 1870RFMD, 1880RFMD, 1900R, 1910R), county histories, county map, Episcopal parish, landowner maps (1864-5), Presbyterian, town history. Histories: F. B. Kegley, VA FRONTIER, Southwest VA Historical Society, Roanoke, VA, 1938; R. D. Stoner, A SEED-BED OF THE REPUBLIC, Roanoke Historical Society, Roanoke, VA, 1962.

18. BRUNSWICK COUNTY, County Seat: Lawrenceville (23868), formed in 1732, from Prince George, Surry, and Isle of Wight Counties, see VA Genealogist 6 (1962) 34.
   Court house records: account (1782-), birth (1853-7), court minute (1824-35, 1842-52), court order (1732-), death (1853-5), deed (1732-), divorce (1732-), ended chancery causes (1732-), guardian (1732-), land tax (1782-), loose papers (1732-1829), marriage (1750-), orphan (1740-81), personal property tax (1782-), poll (1748, 1778), procession (1795-1816), residents (1758), survey (1737-70), tax alterations (1786, 1797), will (1732-). Other records: cemetery, census (1790T, 1800T, 1810RA, 1820R, 1830R, 1840R, 1850RFMS, 1860RFMDS, 1870-RFMD, 1880RFMD, 1900R, 1910R), county history, county map, Episcopal parish, inventory of county records, landowner maps (1820, 1864), Methodist. Libraries: Brunswick-Greensville Regional Library,# 234 Main St., Lawrenceville, VA 23868; St. Paul's College, Russell Memorial Library,# Lawrenceville, VA 23868. Society: Brunswick County Historical Society, PO Box 1776, Law-renceville, VA 23868. History: E. R. Bell and W. L. Heartwell, THE BRUNSWICK STORY, Brunswick Times-Gazette, Lawrenceville,VA, 1957.

19. BUCHANAN COUNTY, County Seat: Grundy (24614), formed in 1858 from Tazewell and Russell Counties, most records destroyed in 1885 by fire, many records damaged in 1977 by flood, see VA Genealogist 6 (1962) 81.
   Court house records: birth (1912-22), chancery court order (1885-), common law order (1925-), deed (1885-), divorce (1885-), grants (1787-), judgment (1917-), land tax (1859-), marriage (1885-), personal property tax

(1859-), will (1886-).   Other records: cemetery, census
(1860RFMDS, 1870RFMD, 1880RFMD, 1900R, 1910R), county
map.   Library: Buchanan County Public Library,# Route 2,
Box 59-E-1, Grundy, Va 24614. Histories: A. S. Richard-
son, HISTORY OF BUCHANAN COUNTY, Grundy, VA, 1958; H. A.
Compton, LOOKING BACK 100 YEARS: A BRIEF STORY OF BUCHAN-
AN COUNTY AND ITS PEOPLE, Centennial Committee, Grundy,
VA, 1958.

20. BUCKINGHAM COUNTY, County Seat: Buckingham (23921),
formed in 1761 from Albemarle County and later Appomattox
County, most records destroyed in 1869 by fire, see VA
Genealogist 6 (1962) 121.
   Court house records: birth (1869-94), chancery court
order (1869-), common law order (1869), court martial
(1832-44), death (1869-96), deed (1864-), divorce
(1869-), fiduciary (1905-), land tax (1782, 1787-),
marriage (1784-94, 1869-), military (1814-8), personal
property tax (1782-), petition (1776), plat (1762-1814),
survey (1762-1814), tax alteration (1783-6), tithable
(1773-4), will (1869-). Other records: Baptist, census
(1790T, 1800T, 1810RA, 1820R, 1830R, 1840R, 1850RFMS,
1860RFMDS, 1870RFMD, 1880RFMD, 1900R, 1910R), county
history, county map, Episcopal parish, landowner map
(1863), Methodist, Presbyterian.   History: Farmville
Herald, TODAY AND YESTERDAY IN THE HEART OF VA, The
Herald, Farmville, VA, 1935.

21. CAMPBELL COUNTY, County Seat: Rustburg (24588),
formed in 1782 from Bedford County, see VA Genealogist 6
(1962) 176.
   Court house records: birth (1853-68, 1912-8), chancery
court order (1831-), circuit court deed (1809-), circuit
court will (1816-), court order (1782-), death (1853-68,
1912-8), deed (1782-), divorce (1782-), land tax (1782-
1844), 1851-), marriage (1782-), personal property tax
(1785-), procession (1804-42), residents (1782-3), survey
(1783-), tax alteration (1784, 1786), will (1782-).
Lynchburg city records: accounts (1809-23), birth (1853-
68), chancery & law order (1828-), chancery court order
(1814-), circuit court will (1809-), council (1826-38),
court order (1805-17), death (1853-68), deed (1805-),
guardian (1809-23), marriage (1805-), military (1861-5),
personal property tax (1809-10, 1817-), trustee (1787-),
will (1809-17). Other records: Baptist, Bible, cemetery,
census (1790T, 1800T, 1810RA, 1820R, 1830R, 1840R, 1850-

RFMS, 1860RFMDS, 1870RRMD, 1880RFMD, 1900R, 1910R), city histories, county history, county map, Episcopal parish, Friends, landowner maps (1864-5), Presbyterian, Roman Catholic, town history. <u>Libraries</u>: Campbell County Public Library,# PO Box 310, Rustburg, VA 24588; Jones Memorial Library,# 434 Rivermont Ave., Lynchburg, VA 24504; Lynchburg Public Library, 914 Main St., Lynchburg, VA 24503. <u>Society</u>: Lynchburg Historical Foundation,* PO Box 3154, Lynchburg, VA 24503. <u>History</u>: R. H. Early, CAMPBELL CHRONICLES AND FAMILY SKETCHES, Bell Co., Lynchburg, VA, 1927.

22. <u>CAROLINE COUNTY</u>, County Seat: Bowling Green (22427), formed in 1728 from Essex, King and Queen, and King William Counties, most records prior to 1836 destroyed in the Civil War, see VA Genealogist 7 (1963) 30.
  <u>Court house records</u>: administrator (1732-),appeal (1777-1807), birth (1864-7), committee of safety (1774-6), court minute (1770-81, 1787-91, 1794-6, 1815-9, 1847-51, 1858-), court order (1732-89, 1799-1809, 1822-4, 1862-), death (1865-7), deed (1758-), executor (1806-24), guardian (1806-), inventory (1732-), land cause (1777-1807, 1835-), land tax (1787-), marriage (1787-), personal property tax (1783-), plat (1777-1840), procession (1846-), superior court order (1820-6), 1836-), survey (1729-62), tax alteration (1787-1817), will (1732-). <u>Other records</u>: cemetery, census (1790T, 1800T, 1810RA, 1820R, 1830R, 1840R, 1850RFMS, 1860RFMDS, 1870RFMD, 1880RFMD, 1900R, 1910R), county histories, county map, Episcopal parish, Friends, landowner maps (1862, 1865), town history. <u>Histories</u>: M. Wingfield, A HISTORY OF CAROLINE COUNTY, Regional Publishing Co., Baltimore, MD, 1969 (1924); T. E. Campbell, COLONIAL CAROLINE, Dietz Press, Richmond, VA, 1954.

23. <u>CARROLL COUNTY</u>, County Seat: Hillsville (24343), formed in 1842 from Grayson County and later Patrick County, see VA Genealogist 7 (1963) 33.
  <u>Court house records</u>: birth (1853-91), court order (1842-), death (1853-70), deed (1842-), divorce (1842-), land tax (1842-), marriage (1854-), personal property tax (1842-), survey (1842-), will (1842-). <u>Other records</u>: Baptist, cemetery, census (1850RFMS, 1860RFMDS, 1870RFMD, 1880RFMD, 1900R, 1910R), county map. <u>Library</u>: Vaughn Memorial Library, Galax Public Library, 608 W. Stuart

Dr., Galax, VA 24333. History: W. R. Morris, FOLKLORE OF
BLUE RIDGE MOUNTAIN, Fancy Gap, VA, 1953/62.

24. CHARLES CITY COUNTY, County Seat: Charles City
(23030), formed in 1634 as one of the 8 original counties
(shires), many records destroyed, damaged, or lost in the
Civil War, see VA Genealogist 7 (1963) 75.
   Court house records: birth (1853-1912), circuit court
minute (1853-), circuit court order (1831-), circuit
court will (1862-), court minute (1762, 1769, 1785-9,
1823-7, 1838-), court order (1655-65, 1677-9, 1687-95,
1737-62, 1788-9, 1823-), death (1853-1912), deed (1655-
65, 1689-90, 1763-74, 1789-), fiduciary (1789), land tax
(1783), marriage (1853-), military (1861-5), miscellaneous (1762-1855), personal property tax (1783-), petition
(1710), rent roll (1704), tax delinquency (1801-11), will
(1655-65, 1689-90, 1763-74, 1789-). Other records: cemetery, census (1790T, 1800T, 1810RA, 1820R, 1830R, 1840R,
1850RFMS, 1860RMFDS, 1870RFMD, 1880RFMD, 1900R, 1910R),
city history, county history, county map, Episcopal
parish, Friends [Quakers], inventory of county records,
landowner map (1865), minister's records. Histories: A.
Hardesty, HISTORICAL AND GEOGRAPHICAL ENCYCLOPEDIA:
CHARLES CITY, ISLE OF WIGHT, NEW KENT, & SURRY COUNTIES,
Richmond, VA, 1884; G. L. Christian, CHARLES CITY, Richmond, VA, 1910.

25. CHARLES RIVER COUNTY, formed in 1634 as one of the 8
original counties (shires), name changed in 1642 to York
County, see York County for records.

26. CHARLOTTE COUNTY, County Seat: Charlotte Court House
(23923), formed in 1765 from Lunenburg County, see VA
Genealogist 7 (1963) 115.
   Court house records: birth (1853-70), court order
(1765-), death (1853-70), deed (1765-), guardian (1765-),
land tax (1782, 1787-), land cause (1818), marriage
(1782-), personal property tax (1782-), tax alteration
(1783-), will (1765-). Other records: Baptist, cemetery,
census (1790T, 1800T, 1810RA, 1820R, 1830R, 1840R, 1850-
RFMS, 1860RFMDS, 1870RFMD, 1880RFMD, 1900R, 1910R),
county histories, county map, Episcopal parish, landowner's maps (1864, 1865), minister's records, Presbyterian. Library: Charlotte County Free Library, Charlotte Court House, VA 23923. Histories: P. Bouldin, THE
OLD TRUNK, Andrews, Baptist & Clemmitt, Richmond, VA,

1888; J. C. Carrington, CHARLOTTE COUNTY, Heritage Press, Richmond, VA, 1907; R. V. Gaines, HANDBOOK OF CHARLOTTE COUNTY, Waddey, Richmond, VA, 1889.

27. CHESTERFIELD COUNTY, County Seat: Chesterfield (23832), formed in 1749 from Henrico County, see VA Genealogist 7 (1963) 174.

Court house records: court order (1749-), deed (1749-), land tax (1791-), land grant (1748-), marriage (1771-), military (1812, 1861-5), personal property tax (1786, 1788, 1790-), petition (1775), sheriff (1736), survey (1801-11), will (1749-). Other records: Baptist, cemetery, census (1790T, 1800T, 1810RA, 1820R, 1830R, 1840R, 1850RFMS, 1860RFMDS, 1870RFMD, 1880RFMD, 1900R, 1910R), county histories, county map, Episcopal parish, Friends, inventory of county records, landowner maps (1863-4, 1888), Methodist, minister's records, Presbyterian, village history. Library: Chesterfield County Free Library, PO Box 29, Chesterfield, VA 23832. Histories: F.E. Lutz, CHESTERFIELD, AN OLD VA COUNTY, Byrd Press, Richmond, VA, 1954; B. W. Weaver, CHESTERFIELD COUNTY: A HISTORY, Richmond, VA, 1970.

28. CLARKE COUNTY, County Seat: Berryville (22611), formed in 1836 from Frederick County and later Warren County, see VA Genealogist 8 (1964) 23.

Court house records: bond (1836-50), chancery court order (1836-), circuit court will (1841-), court order (1836-), deed (1836-), divorce (1836-), guardian (1836-), land tax (1836-), marriage (1836-), muster rolls (1861-5), personal property tax (1836-), will (1836-). Other records: Baptist, cemetery, census (1840R, 1850RFMS, 1860RFMDS, 1870RFMD, 1880RFMD, 1900R, 1910R), county histories, county map, Episcopal parish, landowner map (1834). Society: Clarke County Historical Association,* Berryville, VA 22611. Histories: R. M. E. McDonald, CLARKE COUNTY, Blue Ridge Press, Berryville, VA, 1943; T. D. Gold, HISTORY OF CLARKE COUNTY, Chesapeake Book Co., Berryville, VA, 1962; T. K. Cartmell, SHENANDOAH VALLEY PIONEERS AND THEIR DESCENDANTS, VA Book Co., Berryville, VA, 1972 (1908); J. E. Norris, HISTORY OF THE LOWER SHENANDOAH VALLEY, VA Book Co., Berryville, VA, 1973 (1890).

29. CRAIG COUNTY, County Seat: New Castle (24127), formed in 1851 from Botetourt, Giles, Monroe (WV), and Roanoke

Counties, and later Montgomery and Allegheny Counties, see VA Genealogist 8 (1964) 26.

Court house records: birth (1864-96), court order (1851-), deed (1851-), divorce (1851-), land tax (1851-), marriage (1865-), military (1861-5), personal property tax (1851-), plat (1851-), will (1851-). Other records: cemetery, census (1860RFMDS, 1870RFMD, 1880RFMD, 1900R, 1910R), Christian Church, county map.

30. CULPEPER COUNTY, County Seat: Culpeper (22701), formed in 1748 from Orange County, see VA Genealogist 8 (1964) 63.

Court house records: birth (1864-96, 1912-7), chancery court order (1831-), circuit superior court will (1811-27, 1831-), court minute (1763-4, 1798-1811, 1814-32, 1835-), death (1864-96), deed (1749-), land cause (1810-26, 1831-), land tax (1782, 1787-1804, 1811-), marriage (1751-4, 1781-), military (1781, 1815), personal property tax (1783-1804, 1811-), rent roll (1764), residents (1758), tax alteration (1783-6), will (1749-1813, 1817-27, 1833-). Other records: Baptist, Bible, cemetery, census (1790T, 1800T, 1810RA, 1820R, 1830R, 1840R, 1850-RFMS, 1860RFMDS, 1870RFMD, 1880RFMD, 1900R, 1910R), church, county histories, county map, Episcopal parish, landowner maps (1863-4), Lutheran, town history. Library: Culpeper Town and County Library,# Main and Mason Sts., Culpeper, VA 22701. Society: Culpeper Historical Society, Culpeper, VA 22701. Histories: R. T. Green, GENEALOGICAL AND HISTORICAL NOTES ON CULPEPER COUNTY, Southern Book Co., Baltimore, MD, 1958 (1900); Culpeper Historical Society, HISTORIC CULPEPER, The Society, Culpeper, VA, 1972.

31. CUMBERLAND COUNTY, County Seat: Cumberland (23040), formed in 1749 from Goochland County and later Buckingham County, see VA Genealogist 8 (1964) 122.

Court house records: birth (1853-70), court order (1749-), death (1853-70), deed (1749-), divorce (1749-), guardian (1769-), land tax (1782, 1784, 1787-), marriage (1854-), personal property tax (1782-), petition (1776-89), superior court deed (1809-27), tithable (1776), will (1749-). Other records: Baptist, cemetery, census (1790T, 1800T, 1810RA, 1820R, 1830R, 1840R, 1850RFMS, 1860RFMDS, 1870RFMD, 1880RFMD, 1900R, 1910R), county histories, county map, Episcopal parish, landowner map (1864), Presbyterian, village history. Histories: Farm-

ville Herald, TODAY AND YESTERDAY IN THE HEART OF VA, The
Herald, Farmville, VA, 1935; G. E. Hopkins, THE STORY OF
CUMBERLAND COUNTY, The Author, Winchester, VA, 1942.

32. DICKENSON COUNTY, County Seat: Clintwood (24228),
formed 1880 from Russell, Wise, and Buchanan Counties,
see VA Genealogist 8 (1964) 124.
Court house records: chancery court order (1880-),
court order (1880-), deed (1880-), divorce (1880-), fiduciary (1880-), law orders (1880-), marriage (1880-),
supervisors (1880-), will (1880-). Other records: Baptist, cemetery, census (1880RFMD, 1900R, 1910R), county
history, county map. Library: Dickenson County Public
Library, Clintwood, VA 24228. History: E. J. Sutherland,
MEET VA'S BABY: A BRIEF PICTORIAL HISTORY OF DICKENSON
COUNTY, Clintwood, VA, 1955.

33. DINWIDDIE COUNTY, County Seat: Dinwiddie (23841),
formed in 1752 from Prince George County, most records
prior to 1833 destroyed in 1864, see VA Genealogist 8
(1964) 170.
Court house records: birth (1853-96), chancery court
order (1832-), circuit superior court (1819-41), circuit
superior court will (1830-), court minute (1855-), court
order (1789-91), death (1853-96), deed (1833-), divorce
(1870-), fiduciary (1850-), guardian (1844-), land tax
(1782, 1787-), marriage (1850-), military (1853-5),
personal property tax (1782-), plat (1755-), sheriff
(1841-56), superior court (1819-56), survey (1755-), will
(1830-). Petersburg city records: accounts (1806-),
birth (1853-96), burial (1843-), circuit court will
(1831-), death (1853-96), deed (1784-), fiduciary (1806),
hustings court bonds (1850-), hustings court deed
(1784-), hustings court minute (1784-), hustings court
order (1784-96), hustings court will (1784-), land tax
(1787, 1790, 1820-42), marriage (1784-), militia (1853-
5), personal property tax (1804-). Other records: Bible,
cemetery, census (1790T, 1800T, 1810RA, 1820R, 1830R,
1840R, 1850RFMS, 1860RFMDS, 1870RFMD, 1880RFMD, 1900R,
1910R), city history, county history, county map, Episcopal parish, inventory of county records, Jewish, landowner maps (1854, 1864), minister's records. Libraries:
Colonial Heights Public Library, 326 Royal Oak Ave.,
Colonial Heights, VA 23834; Petersburg Public Library,#
137 S. Sycamore St., Petersburg, VA 23803; Petersburg
National Battlefield Library,# PO Box 549, Petersburg, VA

23803; Richard Bland College Library,# Petersburg, VA 23803. History: Writers Program of VA, DINWIDDIE COUNTY, Whittet & Shepperson, Richmond, VA, 1942.

34. DUNMORE COUNTY, formed in 1772 from Frederick County, in 1778 name changed to Shenandoah County, see Shenandoah County for records.

35. ELIZABETH CITY COUNTY, County Seat: Hampton (23369), formed in 1634 as one of the 8 original counties (shires), many records destroyed in Revolutionary War, War of 1812, and Civil War, in 1952 became the City of Hampton, see VA Genealogist 9 (1965) 16.
Court house records: bond (1730-56), circuit court order (1747-55, 1784-8, 1798-1802, 1809-31), Court minute (1756-69, 1803-9, 1819-24, 1844-), court order (1715-69, 1784-8, 1798-), deed (1684-99, 1715-30, 1737-56, 1758-1816, 1819-24, 1844-), execution (1814-37), guardian (1737-48, 1827-43), inventory (1715-23), judgment (1809-30, 1832-47), land cause (1809-13, 1833-6), land tax (1782-4, 1787-98, 1801-21, 1835-40, 1846-), marriage (1865-), personal property tax (1782-98, 1801-), petition (1803, 1830, 1836-7, 1839), plat (1761-), poll (1758), process (1837-), rent roll (1704), survey (1761-), tax alteration (1785-6), will (1684-99, 1715-30, 1737-56, 1758-). Other records: cemetery, census (1790T, 1800T, 1810RA, 1820R, 1830R, 1840R, 1850RFMS, 1860 RFMDS, 1870 RFMD, 1880RFMD, 1900R, 1910R), city histories, county histories, county map, Episcopal parish, landowner map (1892). Libraries: Charles H. Taylor Memorial Library,# Hampton Public Library, 4205 Victoria Blvd., Hampton, VA 23669; Fort Monroe Casemate Museum Library,# PO Box 341, Fort Monroe, VA 23651. Society: Genealogical Society of Tidewater, VA,* Thomas Nelson Community College, PO Box 9407, Hampton, VA 23670. Histories: M. L. Starkey, THE FIRST PLANTATION: A HISTORY OF HAMPTON AND ELIZABETH CITY COUNTY, Houston Printing & Publishing House, Hampton, VA, 1936; R. D. Whichard, THE HISTORY OF LOWER TIDEWATER VA, Lewis Historical Publishing Co., New York, NY, 1959, 3 volumes; L. G. Tyler, HISTORY OF HAMPTON AND ELIZABETH CITY COUNTY, Board of Supervisors, Hampton, VA, 1922.

36. ESSEX COUNTY, County Seat: Tappahannock (22560), formed in 1692 from Old Rappahannock County, see VA Genealogist 9 (1965) 59.

Court house records: account (1834-), birth (1856-1916), bond (1834-), circuit court (1834-), court order (1692-), death (1856-1916), deed (1691-), divorce (1865-), execution (1745-1850), guardian (1761-), index of records of Old Rappahannock County (1654-92), inventory (1834-), judgment (1752-1857), land tax (1782, 1787-), land trials (1741-60, 1790-1818), marriage (1804-), military (1861-5), miscellaneous (1752-), orphan (1731-), personal property tax (1782-), petition (1758), poll (1741), procession (1796-1820, 1824-5, 1831, 1834, 1837, 1843-56), quit rent (1704, 1714-5), rent roll (1704, 1715), school board (1823-50), survey (1792-7), tax alteration (1783-6), will (1691-). Other records: Baptist, cemetery, census (1790T, 1800T, 1810RA, 1820R, 1830R, 1840R, 1850RFMS, 1860RFMDS, 1870RFMD, 1880RFMD, 1900R, 1910R), Christian Church, county histories, county map, Episcopal parish, landowner map (1863), town history. Histories: P. P. Warner, HISTORY OF ESSEX COUNTY, 1607-92, Sentinel Print, Urbanna, VA, 1926; W. C. Garnett, TIDEWATER TALES, Tidewater Publishing Co., Dunnsville, VA, 1927; T. H. Warner, HISTORY OF OLD RAPPAHANNOCK COUNTY, Warner, Tappahannock, VA, 1965.

37. FAIRFAX COUNTY, County Seat: Fairfax (22030), formed in 1742 from Prince William County and later Loudoun County, see VA Genealogist 9 (1965) 124.

Court house records: birth (1853-1912), bond (1752-82), court minute (1749-74, 1783-93, 1799-1800, 1807-8, 1822-31, 1835-), court order (1749-74, 1783-93, 1799-1800, 1807-8, 1824-31, 1835-), death (1853-69), deed (1742-), divorce (1850-), land (1742-70), land cause (1742-70, 1788-1832), land tax (1782, 1787-), marriage (1853-), military (1861-5), personal property tax (1782-), residents (1758), superior court will (1804-), survey (1742-1856), tax alteration (1783-6), voter (1744), will (1742-). Other records: Baptist, cemetery, census (1790T, 1800T, 1810RA, 1820R, 1830R, 1840R, 1850RFMS, 1860RFMDS, 1870RFMD, 1880RFMD, 1900R, 1910R), city histories, county atlas (1879), county histories, county map, Episcopal parish, Friends, landowner (1861, 1864), Methodist, Presbyterian, Roman Catholic, town histories. Libraries: Fairfax County Public Central Library,# 3915 Chain Bridge Road, Fairfax, VA 22030; Mary Riley Styles Public Library,# 120 N. Virginia Avenue, Falls Church, VA 22046; George Mason University, Charles Rogers Fenwick Library,# 4400 University Dr., Fairfax, VA 22030. Societies: Historical Society of Fairfax County,* PO Box 415, Fairfax, VA 22030; Fairfax County Park Authority, Division of History, 4030 Hummer Rd., Annandale, VA 22003; Fairfax County History Commission,* 4100 Chain Bridge Rd., Fairfax, VA 22030; Falls Church Historical Commission, 120 N. Virginia Ave., Falls Church, VA 22046. Histories: J. Geddes, FAIRFAX COUNTY, Denlingers, Middleburg, VA, 1967; Fairfax History Program, FAIRFAX COUNTY IN VA, The Program, Fairfax, VA, 1974; Fairfax County Board of Supervisors, FAIRFAX COUNTY, A HISTORY, Fairfax County Publications Center, Fairfax, VA, 1978.

38. FAUQUIER COUNTY, County Seat: Warrenton (22186), formed in 1759 from Prince William County, see VA Genealogist 9 (1965) 176.

Court house records: birth (1853-96), chancery court order (1831-), circuit superior court will (1821-), court minute (1759-), death (1853-96), deed (1759-), divorce (1925-), land cause (1809-50), land tax (1783-), marriage (1759-), militia (1807-51, 1861-5), miscellaneous (1759-1807), personal property tax (1782-), rent roll (1770, 1777, 1789-91), superior court deed (1809-29), superior court will (1809-29), tithable (1759-1800), will (1759-). Other records: Baptist, cemetery, census (1790T, 1800T, 1810RA, 1820R, 1830R, 1840R, 1850RFMS, 1860RFMDS, 1870-RFMD, 1880RFMD, 1900R, 1910R), county histories, county maps, Episcopal parish, landowner maps (1863, 1865), Methodist, Presbyterian, town histories. Library: Fauquier County Public Library,# 2 Court House Square, Warrenton, VA 22186. Society: Fauquier Historical Society,* PO Box 675, Warrenton, VA 22186. Histories: Fauquier County Bicentennial Commission, FAUQUIER COUNTY, The Committee, Warrenton, VA, 1959; M. L. Evans, AN OLD TIMER IN WARRENTON AND FAUQUIER COUNTY, VA Publishers, Warrenton, VA, 1955; C. S. McCarty, THE FOOTHILLS OF THE BLUE RIDGE IN FAUQUIER COUNTY, Fauquier Democrat, Warrenton, VA, 1874.

39. FINCASTLE COUNTY, formed in 1772 from Botetourt County, became extinct in 1777 when it was divided into Montgomery and Washington Counties, see these counties for records, especially Montgomery County.

40. FLOYD COUNTY, County Seat: Floyd (24091), formed in 1831 from Montgomery County and later Franklin County, see VA Genealogist 10 (1966) 74.

Court house records: birth (1853-72), chancery court order (1831-), court order (1831-), death (1853-72), deed (1831-), divorce (1831-), land tax (1831-), personal property tax (1831-), will (1831-). Other records: Baptist, cemetery, census (1840R, 1850RFMS, 1860RFMDS, 1870RFMD, 1880RFMD, 1900R, 1910R), county map, Lutheran. Histories: A. D. Wood, FLOYD COUNTY, A HISTORY OF ITS PEOPLE AND PLACES, Floyd County Historical Society, Willis, VA, 1981 (1923); S. J. Shelor, PIONEERS AND THEIR COATS OF ARMS OF FLOYD COUNTY, Hunter Publishing Co., Winston-Salem, NC, 1961.

41. FLUVANNA COUNTY, County Seat: Palmyra (22963), formed in 1777 from Albemarle County, see VA Genealogist 10 (1966) 76.
Court house records: account (1777-), birth (1853-96), circuit court will (1831-), court order (1777-), death (1853-96), deed (1777-), divorce (1777-), guardian (1794-1852), inventory (1777-), land tax (1787-), marriage (1777-), personal property tax (1782-), will (1777-). Other records: Baptist, cemetery, census (1790T, 1800T, 1810RA, 1820R, 1830R, 1840R, 1850RFMS, 1860RFMDS, 1870-RFMD, 1880RFMD, 1900R, 1910R), county history, county map, Episcopal parish, landowner map (1863), Methodist. Library: Fluvanna County Library, PO Box 102, Palmyra, VA 22963. Society: Fluvanna County Historical Society,* Palmyra, VA 22963. History: V. J. Snead, FLUVANNA COUNTY SKETCHBOOK, Whittet and Shepperson, Richmond, VA, 1963.

42. FRANKLIN COUNTY, County Seat: Rocky Mount (24151), formed in 1786 from Bedford and Henry Counties and later Patrick County, see VA Genealogist 10 (1966) 123.
Court house records: birth (1853-1912), chancery court order (1831-), circuit court will (1804-), court order (1786-), death (1853-1912), deed (1786-), district court deed (1789-1814), district court order (1789-1809), land suit (1805-18), land tax (1786-), personal property tax (1786-), plat (1792-), will (1786-). Other records: Baptist, biography, cemetery, census (1790T, 1800T, 1810RA, 1820R, 1830R, 1840R, 1850RFMS, 1860RFMDS, 1870 RFMD, 1880RFMD, 1900R, 1910R), county atlas (1885), county histories, county map, Friends [Quakers]. Libraries: Franklin County Library, East Court St., Rocky Mount, VA 24151; Ferrum College, Thomas Stanley Library,# Ferrum, VA 24088 (local history and Methodist Collection). Society: Franklin County Historical Society, PO

Box 86, Rocky Mount, VA 24151. Histories: M. Wingfield, FRANKLIN COUNTY, A HISTORY, Chesapeake Book Co., Berryville, VA, 1964; M. Wingfield, PIONEER FAMILIES OF FRANKLIN COUNTY, Chesapeake Book Co., Berryville, VA, 1964.

43. FREDERICK COUNTY, County Seat: Winchester (22601), formed in 1743 from Orange County and later Augusta County, see VA Genealogist 10 (1966) 174.

Court house records: birth (1853-1912), chancery court order (1812-58), court minute (1801-41), court order (1743-1806, 1841-56), death (1853-96), deed (1743-), district court order (1789-1809), divorce (1870-), guardian (1792-), inventory (1743-), land (1799-1825), land cause (1758-1832), land tax (1782, 1787-), marriage (1771-), militia (1756, 1796-1821, 1861-5), personal property tax (1782-), petition (1775), rent roll (1746-64), residents (1758), suit papers (1742-), superior court deed (1793-1826), superior court of chancery (1784-1825), superior court order (1809-29), superior court will (1790-1859), survey (1736-58, 1782-), tax alteration (1783-6), will (1743-). Winchester city records: land tax (1797, 1817-), personal property tax (1788-). Other records: Baptist, Bible, cemetery, census (1790T, 1800T, 1810RA, 1820R, 1830R, 1840R, 1850RFMS, 1860RFMDS, 1870-RFMD, 1880RFMD, 1900R, 1910R), city histories, county atlas (1885), county histories, county map, Episcopal parish, family, Friends [Quakers], German Reformed, landowner maps (1809, 1820, 1865), Lutheran, Methodist, minister's records, newspaper, Presbyterian, town history. Libraries: Handley Library,# Braddock and Piccadilly Sts., Winchester, VA 22601; Shenandoah College, Howe Library,# Millwood Pike, Winchester, VA 22601 (Evangelical United Brethren records). Society: Winchester-Frederick County Historical Society,* 610 Tennyson Ave., Winchester, VA 22601. Histories: T. K. Cartmell, SHENANDOAH VALLEY PIONEERS AND THEIR DESCENDANTS: A HISTORY OF FREDERICK COUNTY, Eddy Press, Winchester, VA, 1909; J. E. Norris, HISTORY OF THE LOWER SHENANDOAH VALLEY COUNTIES, Warner and Co., Chicago, IL, 1890.

44. GILES COUNTY, County Seat: Pearisburg (24134), formed in 1806 from Montgomery, Monroe (WV), and Tazewell Counties and later Wythe, Mercer (WV), and Craig Counties, see VA Genealogist 11 (1967) 12.

Court house records: birth (1858-96), bond (1806-), chancery court order (1831-), circuit court will (1856-),

court order (1806-), death (1858-96), deed (1806-), land
tax (1806-), marriage (1806-), personal property tax
(1806-), sheriff (1833-), survey (1807-), will (1806-).
Other records: cemetery, census (1810RA, 1820R, 1830R,
1840R, 1850RFMS, 1860RFMDS, 1870RFMD, 1880RFMD, 1900R,
1910R), county history, county map, minister's records.
Libraries: Pearisburg Public Library,# 112 S. Tazewell
St., Pearisburg, VA 24134; Narrows Public Library, Narrows, VA 24124. History: R. C. Friend, GILES COUNTY,
Giles County Chamber of Commerce, Pearisburg, VA, 1956.

45. GLOUCESTER COUNTY, County Seat: Gloucester (23061),
formed in 1651 from York County, most records destroyed
by fires in 1821 and 1865, see VA Genealogist 11 (1967)
81.
   Court house records: birth (1863-90, 1912-6), carriage
owner (1784), court minute (1820-5, 1833-42, 1858-),
death (1865-90), deed (1865-), divorce (1865-), land tax
(1782, 1784, 1786-), marriage (1777-8, 1853-), military
(Revolutionary War lists), personal property tax (1782-),
rent roll (1704), residents (1782-3), survey (1733-1810,
1817-52), tax (1770-91), tithable (1770-1, 1774-5), will
(1865-).   Other records: cemetery, census (1790T, 1800T,
1810RA, 1820R, 1830R, 1840R, 1850RFMS, 1860RFMDS, 1870-
RFMD, 1880RFMD, 1900R, 1910R), county history, county
map, Episcopal parish, Methodist. Library: Gloucester
Public Library, PO Box 367, Gloucester, VA 23061. History: M. W. Gray, GLOUCESTER COUNTY, Cottrell and Cooke,
Richmond, VA, 1936.

46. GOOCHLAND COUNTY, County Seat: Goochland (23063),
formed in 1728 from Henrico County, see VA Genealogist 11
(1967) 132.
   Court house records: birth (1852-1901), bond (1805-17),
court minute (1779-82, 1803-7, 1811-8), court order
(1728-), death (1852-1901), deed (1728-), divorce
(1800-), guardian (1794-1822), inventory (1728-), marriage (1730-), military (1861-5), personal property tax
(1782-1803), procession (1795-1820), road orders (1728-
44), tithable (1747, 1751), will (1728-). Other records:
Baptist, cemetery, census (1790T, 1800T, 1810RA, 1820R,
1830R, 1840R, 1850RFMS, 1860RFMDS, 1870RFMD, 1880RFMD,
1900R, 1910R), county histories, county map, Episcopal
parish, Friends, Huguenot, landowner maps (1820, 1863,
1881), minister's records, Presbyterian, town history.
Society: Goochland County Historical Society, River Rd.,

Route 6, Goochland, VA 23063.   Histories: H. B. Agee,
FACETS OF GOOCHLAND COUNTY'S HISTORY, Dietz Press, Rich-
mond, VA, 1962; R. C. Wight, THE STORY OF GOOCHLAND,
Richmond Press, Richmond, VA, 1973 (1935).

47. GRAYSON COUNTY, County Seat: Independence (24348),
formed in 1793 from Wythe County and later Patrick County, see VA Genealogist 11 (1967) 157.
   Court house records, birth (1853-70), chancery court
order (1832-), circuit court will (1848-), court order
(1793-4, 1806-), death (1853-70), deed (1793-), divorce
(1796-), land tax (1794-), marriage (1793-), personal
property tax (1794-), plat (1793-), will (1796-). Other
records: Baptist, Bible, cemetery, census (1800T, 1810R,
1820R, 1830R, 1840R, 1850RFMS, 1860RFMDS, 1870RFMD,
1880RFMD, 1900R, 1910R), county histories, county map,
landowner map (1897). Library: Wythe-Grayson Regional
Library, PO Box 159, Independence, VA 24348. History: B.
F. Nuckolls, PIONEER SETTLERS OF GRAYSON COUNTY, Genealogical Publishing Co., Baltimore, MD, 1975 (1914).

48. GREENE COUNTY, County Seat: Stanardsville (22973),
formed in 1838 from Orange County, first deed book lost
in the Civil War, see VA Genealogist 12 (1968) 106.
   Court house records: birth (1853-1919), circuit court
minute (1842-), circuit court order (1838-), court order
(1841-), death (1853-1912), deed (1841-), divorce
(1838-), land tax (1838-), marriage (1838-), military
(1900-), pension (1900-), personal property tax (1838-),
will (1838-). Other records: Baptist, cemetery, census
(1840R, 1850RFMS, 1860RFMDS, 1870RFMD, 1880RFMD, 1900R,
1910R), county map, landowner maps (1863, 1865, 1866).
Library: Greene County Regional Branch Library, Stanardsville, VA 22973.   Society: Greene County Historical
Society, PO Box 185, Stanardsville, VA 22973.

49. GREENSVILLE COUNTY, County Seat: Emporia (23847),
formed in 1781 from Brunswick County and later Sussex
County, some records lost in a fire of unknown date, see
VA Genealogist 12 (1968) 107.
   Court house records: birth (1853-60), common law will
(1824-), court minute (1816-22, 1840-), court order
(1781-), death (1853-60), deed (1781-), divorce (1781-),
guardian (1801-20, 1847-), inventory (1781-), land tax
(1782, 1787-), marriage (1781-1853, 1861-), personal
property tax (1782-), procession (1796-1832, 1848-57),

will (1781-). Other records: biography, cemetery, census (1790T, 1800T, 1810RA, 1820R, 1830R, 1840R, 1850RFMS, 1860RFMDS, 1870RFMD, 1880RFMD, 1900R, 1910R), county histories, county map, Episcopal parish, landowner map (1864), minister's records. Library: Richardson Memorial Branch Regional Library, Emporia, VA 23847. History: D. S. Brown, HISTORICAL AND BIOGRAPHICAL SKETCHES OF GREENS-VILLE COUNTY, Riparian Woman's Club, Emporia, VA, 1968.

50. HALIFAX COUNTY, County Seat: Halifax (24558), formed in 1752 from Lunenburg County, see VA Genealogist 12 (1968) 184.
Court house records: birth (1853-71), circuit court minute (1821-4, 1829-), circuit court order (1752-1816, 1818-21), court minute (1821-), court order (1752-1821), death (1853-71), deed (1752-), fiduciary (1752-), land tax (1782, 1787-), marriage (1753-), military (1774-7), personal property tax (1782-), residents (1758), superior court deed (1909-22), superior court will (1833-57), survey (1751-), tithable (1763, 1770), will (1752-).
Other records: Baptist, cemetery, census (1790T, 1800T, 1810RA, 1820R, 1830R, 1840R, 1850RFMS, 1860RFMDS, 1870-RFMD, 1880RFMD, 1900R, 1910R), county histories, county map, Episcopal parish, family, Friends, minister's records, Presbyterian. Library: Halifax-South Boston Regional Library, 720 Mountain Rd., Halifax, VA 24558. Histories: W. J. Carrington, A HISTORY OF HALIFAX COUNTY, Regional Publishing Co., Baltimore, MD, 1924; H. R. Mathis, ALONG THE BORDER, Coble Press, Oxford, NC, 1964.

51. HANOVER COUNTY, County Seat: Hanover (23069), formed in 1721 from New Kent County, most records destroyed in 1865 by fire, see VA Genealogist 13 (1969) 125.
Court house records: birth (1853-79), circuit court will (1852-), court (1733-5), court of equity order (1840-65), court miscellaneous (1739-), death (1853-71), deed (1733-5, 1742-59, 1783-92, 1865-), justice of peace (1837-41), land grant (1721-1800), land tax (1782, 1787-), marriage (1777-81, 1831-47, 1863-), miscellaneous (1727-1858), personal property tax (1782-), petition (1774), tax alteration (1783-6), tax payers (17821815), tithable (1763, 1770), will (1733-5, 1783-), witness (1838-56). Other records: Baptist, cemetery, census (1790T, 1800T, 1810RA, 1820R, 1830R, 1840R, 1850 RFMS, 1860RFMDS, 1870RFMD, 1880RFMD, 1900R, 1910R), county histories, county map, Episcopal parish, Friends, land-

owner maps (1820, 1865), Methodist, minister's records. Libraries: Pamunkey Regional Library,# PO Box 119, Hanover, VA 23069; Randolph-Macon College, Walter Hines Page Library,# Ashland, VA 23005 (Methodist collection). Society: Hanover County Historical Society,* PO Box 91, Hanover, VA 23069. Histories: R. Page, HANOVER COUNTY, ITS HISTORY AND LEGENDS, Richmond, VA, 1926; Herald-Progress, HISTORIC HANOVER COUNTY, The Herald-Progress, Ashland, VA, 1938; Herald-Progress, SIXTIETH ANNIVERSARY, HANOVER COUNTY, The Herald-Progress, Ashland, VA, 1957; Herald-Progress, HANOVER COUNTY, The Herald Progress, Ashland, VA, 1971.

52. HENRICO COUNTY: County Seat: Richmond (23261), formed in 1634 as one of the original 8 counties (shires), records before 1655 and most records before 1677 destroyed in Revolutionary War, see VA Genealogist 14 (1970) 71.
   Court house records: assessor (1803-13), birth (1853-70), court minute (1816-), court order (1678-1701, 1707-14, 1719-24, 1737-46, 1752-69, 1781-1816), death (1853-70), deed (1677-1718, 1725-37, 1744-74, 1781-), grand jury (1690, 1692), guardian (1813-), land tax (1782, 1799-), marriage (1781-), military (1869, 1894-), miscellaneous (1650-1877), orphan (1677-1739), personal property tax (1782-), petition (1774), procession (1795-1839), rent roll (1704), tax alteration (1786), tithable (1679), will (1677-1718, 1725-37, 1744-67, 1781-). Richmond city records: birth (1900-12), circuit court will (1852-65), common council (1782-), death (1900-12), divorce (1870-), hustings court deed (1782-), hustings court minute (1793-), hustings court order (1782-1817), hustings court will (1810-), marriage (1780-), personal property tax (1787, 1811-), will (1810). Other records: Baptist, cemetery, census (1790T, 1800T, 1810RA, 1820R, 1830R, 1840R, 1850RFMS, 1860RFMDS, 1870RFMD, 1880RFMD, 1900R, 1910R), Christian Church, city atlases (1876-7, 1899), city directories, city histories, county atlas (1901), county histories, county map, Episcopal parish, Friends, Jewish, landowner maps (1819-20, 1853, 1862, 1864-65, 1887), Methodist, minister's records, newspaper, Presbyterian, Roman Catholic. Libraries: County of Henrico Public Library, 1000 N. Laburnum Ave., Richmond, VA 23223; Museum of the Confederacy Library,# 1201 E. Clay St., Richmond, VA 23219; Richmond Public Library, 101 E. Franklin St., Richmond, VA 23219; Union Theologi-

cal Seminary Library,# 3401 Brook Rd., Richmond, VA 23227 (Presbyterian records); University of Richmond, Boat-wright Memorial Library,# Richmond, VA 23173 (Baptist records); Valentine Museum Library,# 1015 E. Clay St., Richmond, VA 23219 (history of Richmond); VA Historical Society Library,# 428 North Blvd., Richmond, VA 23221; VA State Library and Archives,# 12th and Capitol Sts., Rich-mond, VA 23219; Richmond National Battlefield Park Libra-ry,# 3215 E. Broad St., Richmond, VA 23223; Richmond Newspapers, Inc., Library,# 333 E. Grace St., Richmond, VA 23219; United Daughters of the Confederacy, Caroline Meriwether Goodlett Library,# 328 North Blvd., Richmond, VA 23220 (not open to the public). Societies: VA Genea-logical Society,* PO Box 1397, Richmond, VA 23211; VA Historical Society,* PO Box 7311, Richmond, VA 23211. Histories: L. H. Manarin and C. Dowdy, HISTORY OF HENRICO COUNTY, Univ. Press of VA, Charlottesville, VA, 1984; P. P. Warner, THE COUNTY OF HENRICO, A HISTORY, Richmond, VA, 1959; W. A. Christian, RICHMOND, HER PAST AND PRE-SENT, Jenkins, Richmond, VA, 1912; S. Mordecai, RICHMOND IN BYGONE DAYS, Dietz Press, Richmond, VA, 1946.

53. HENRY COUNTY, County Seat: Martinsville (24112), formed in 1777 from Pittsylvania County and later Patrick County, see VA Genealogist 14 (1970) 117.
  Court house records: birth (1853-71), chancery court order (1831-), court minute (1820-), court order (1777-1820), criminal orders (1777-), death (1853-71), deed (1777-), divorce (1909-), ended law and chancery (1777-), land grant (1779-1853), land tax (1782-), marriage (1778-), militia (1776-81), oath of allegiance (1777-80), personal property tax (1782-), survey (1778-), tax alter-ation (1778-80), will (1777-). Other records: Baptist, biography, cemetery, census (1790T, 1800T, 1810RA, 1820R, 1830R, 1840R, 1850RFMS, 1860RFMDS, 1870RFMD, 1880RFMD, 1900R, 1910R), city history, county histories, county map, Friends. Library: Blue Ridge Regional Library,# 310 E. Church St., Martinsville, VA 24112. Society: Henry County Historical Society, Bassett, VA 24055. Histories: J. P. A. Hill, A HISTORY OF HENRY COUNTY, Martinsville, VA, 1925; V. G. and L. G. Pedigo, HISTORY OF PATRICK AND HENRY COUNTIES, Stone Publishing Co., Roanoke, VA, 1933; M. D. Coe, OUR PROUD HERITAGE, Bassett Publishing Corp., Bassett, VA, 1969.

54. <u>HIGHLAND</u> <u>COUNTY</u>, County Seat: Monterey (24465), formed in 1847 from Pendleton (WV) and Bath Counties, a few records lost in a 1947 fire, see VA Genealogist <u>14</u> (1970) 119.

 <u>Court</u> <u>house</u> <u>records</u>: appraisal (1847-), birth (1850-78), chancery court order (1848-), court order (1847-), death (1853-62), deed (1847-), inventory (1847-), land tax (1847-), marriage (1847-), personal property tax (1847-), will (1847-). <u>Other</u> <u>records</u>: cemetery, census (1850RFMS, 1860RFMDS, 1870RFMD, 1880RFMD, 1900R, 1910R), county histories, county map. <u>Library</u>: Highland County Regional Branch Library, Monterey, VA 24465. <u>Histories</u>: O. F. Morton, A HANDBOOK OF HIGHLAND COUNTY, Highland Recorder, Monterey, VA, 1922; O. F. Morton, A HISTORY OF HIGHLAND COUNTY, The Author, Monterey, VA, 1911.

55. <u>ISLE</u> <u>OF</u> <u>WIGHT</u> <u>COUNTY</u>, County Seat: Isle of Wight (23397), formed in 1634 as one of the 8 original counties (shires) under the name Warrosquoyoake, name changed to Isle of Wight in 1637, later additions from Upper Norfolk and Nansemond Counties, see VA Genealogist <u>14</u> (1970) 160.

 <u>Court</u> <u>house</u> <u>records</u>: assessment (1777), birth (1853-76), common law will (1833-), court order (1693-5, 1746-83, 1795-), death (1853-74), deed (1688-), divorce (1853--), guardian (1741-), land tax (1782, 1787-), marriage (1771-), personal property tax (1782-), rent roll (1704), tax alteration (1783-6), will (1636-). <u>Other</u> <u>records</u>: Baptist, cemetery, census (1790T, 1800T, 1810RA, 1820R, 1830R, 1840R, 1850RFMS, 1860RFMDS, 1870RFMD, 1880RFMD, 1900R, 1910R), county histories, county map, Episcopal Parish, Friends, inventory of county records, landowner map (1864), town history, village history. <u>Library</u>: Franklin Library Association, 800 W. Second Ave., Franklin, VA 23851. <u>Histories</u>: J. B. Boddie, SEVENTEENTH CENTURY ISLE OF WIGHT, Chicago Law Printing Co., Chicago, IL, 1938; R. D. Whichard, THE HISTORY OF LOWER TIDEWATER VA, Lewis Historical Publishing Co., New York, NY, 1959.

56. <u>JAMES</u> <u>CITY</u> <u>COUNTY</u>: County Seat: Williamsburg (23185), formed in 1634 as one of the 8 original counties (shires), later additions from New Kent and York Counties, most records destroyed in 1865, see VA Genealogist <u>15</u> (1971) 15.

 <u>Court</u> <u>house</u> <u>records</u>: birth (1865-83), court order (1865-), death (1864-84), deed (1865-), divorce (1865-), land (1619-1779), land tax (1782-3, 1787-), marriage

(1865-), personal property tax (1782-), rent roll (1704), sheriff (1768), tax alteration (1783-6), tithable (1768-9), will (1865-). Williamsburg city records: land tax (1782, 1784-5, 1787-), owners of lots (1783), personal property tax (1784-), tax list (1783). Other records: Baptist, cemetery, census (1790T, 1800T, 1810RA, 1820R, 1830R, 1840R, 1850RFMS, 1860RFMDS, 1870RFMD, 1880RFMD, 1900R, 1910R), city histories, city map, county histories, county map, Episcopal Parish, Friends, landowner maps (1865). Libraries: College of William and Mary, Earl Gregg Swem Library,# Williamsburg, VA 23185; Colonial Williamsburg Research Center Library, Francis and Henry Sts., Williamsburg, VA 23185; Williamsburg Regional Library, 515 Scotland St., Williamsburg, VA 23185. Histories: L. G. Tyler, WILLIAMSBURG, THE OLD COLONIAL CAPITAL, Whittet and Shepperson, Richmond, VA, 1907; E. S. Meirs, BLOOD OF FREEDOM: THE STORY OF JAMESTOWN, WILLIAMSBURG, AND YORKTOWN, Colonial Williamsburg, Williamsburg, VA, 1958; H. Hawthorne, WILLIAMSBURG OLD AND NEW, Appleton-Century, New York, NY, 1941; P. Rouse, COWS ON CAMPUS, WILLIAMSBURG IN BYGONE DAYS, Dietz Press, Richmond, VA, 1973; L. G. Tyler, THE CRADLE OF THE REPUBLIC, Hermitage Press, Richmond, VA, 1906.

57. KING AND QUEEN COUNTY, County Seat: King and Queen Court House (23085), formed in 1691 from New Kent County, many records destroyed by fires in 1825 and 1865, see VA Genealogist 15 (1971) 191.

Court house records: birth (1865-98), circuit court chancery order (1859-), court minute (1858-), death (1865-98), divorce (1864-), land tax (1782, 1787-), marriage (1864-), personal property tax (1782-), plat (1823-), rent roll (1704), superior court (1831-), superior court minute (1858-), superior court order (1854-), survey (1851-), tax alteration (1783-6), will (1864-). Other records: Baptist, cemetery, census (1790T, 1800T, 1810RA, 1820R, 1830R, 1840R, 1850RFMS, 1860RFMDS, 1870-RFMD, 1880RFMD, 1900R, 1910R), Christian Church, county history, county map, Episcopal Parish, landowner map (1863), Methodist. Society: King and Queen County Historical Society,* Court House, Newton, VA 23126. History: A. Bagby, KING AND QUEEN COUNTY, Neale Publishing Co., New York, NY, 1908.

58. KING GEORGE COUNTY, County Seat: King George (22485), formed 1721 from Richmond County and later Westmoreland

County, first will book missing, see VA Genealogist 15 (1971) 193.

Court house records: birth (1871–1915), bond (1765–), chancery court order (1831–), court of inquiry (1789–1812), court order (1721–), death (1871–1912), deed (1721–), divorce (1721–), fiduciary (1721–), inventory (1721–65, 1794–), land cause (1792–1813, 1831–3), land tax (1782, 1787–), land transfer index (1721–), marriage (1786–1850, 1856–), militia (1824–60), orphan (1740–61), personal property tax (1782–), will (1721–). Other records: cemetery, census (1790T, 1800T, 1810RA, 1820R, 1830R, 1840R, 1850RFMS, 1860RFMDS, 1870RFMD, 1880RFMD, 1900R, 1910R), county history, county map, Episcopal Parish. Library: Lewis Egerton Smoot Regional Library, # Route 3, King George, VA 22485. History: VA and the VA County, August, 1950.

59. KING WILLIAM COUNTY, County Seat: King William (23086), formed in 1702 from King and Queen County, most records destroyed in 1385 by fire, see VA Genealogist 15 (1971) 191.

Court house order: court order (1885–), deed (1885–), divorce (1885–), land tax (1782–9, 1793–), marriage (1885–), miscellaneous (1702–7, 1721–2, 1785–6, 1793–1822, 1835–53, 1858–71, 1877–84), personal property tax (1782–5, 1787–), rent roll (1704), residents (1722, 1727), tax alteration (1786, 1791), tithable (1730–8), will (1885–). Other records: Baptist, cemetery, census (1790T, 1800T, 1810RA, 1820R, 1830R, 1840R, 1850RFMS, 1860RFMDS, 1870RFMD, 1880RFMD, 1900R, 1910R), county histories, county map, Episcopal Parish, family, land-owner maps (1863, 1865), town history. History: E. H. Ryland, KING WILLIAM COUNTY FROM OLD NEWSPAPERS AND FILES, Dietz Press, Richmond, VA, 1955.

60. LANCASTER COUNTY: County Seat: Lancaster (22503), formed in 1651 from Northumberland County, see VA Genealogist 15 (1971) 273.

Court house records: appeal (1795–), birth (1853–70), chancery court order (1831–60), court order (1652–), death (1853–70), deed (1652–), divorce (1800–), estate (1796–), fiduciary (1750–), land cause (1795–), land tax (1787–), marriage (1652–), military (1775–83, 1812), orphan (1824–42), personal property tax (1782–), property settlements (1841–), record books (1652–66), settlement (1796–), tax alteration (1783–6), tithable (1653–1720,

1745-81), will (1652-60, 1674-). Other records: Baptist, cemetery, census (1790T, 1800T, 1810RA, 1820R, 1830R, 1840R, 1850RFMS, 1860RFMDS, 1870RFMD, 1880RFMD, 1900R, 1910R), county history, county map, Episcopal Parish, Methodist. Libraries: Mary Ball Washington Museum and Library, Inc.,# Route 3, Lancaster, VA 22503; Lancaster County Public Library, Kilmarnock, VA 22482. History: VA and the VA County, August, 1950.

61. LEE COUNTY, County Seat: Jonesville (24263), formed in 1793 from Russell County and later Scott County, see VA Genealogist 15 (1971) 275.
  Court house records: birth (1853-77), circuit court will (1846-), claims (1825-30), court order (1808-18, 1826-), death (1853-77), deed (1793-), divorce (1832-), estray (1858-), land tax (1795-), marriage (1830-6, 1850-), overseers of poor (1838-), personal property tax (1795-1813, 1827-), petition (1876-7), survey (1794-1815, 1822-), will (1794-). Other records: Baptist, Bible, cemetery, census (1800T, 1810RA, 1820R, 1830R, 1840R, 1850RFMS, 1860RFMDS, 1870RFMD, 1880RFMD, 1900R, 1910R), county history, county map. Library: Lee County Public Library, 406 Joslyn Ave., Pennington Gap, VA 24277. Histories: Boone Trail Historians, HISTORICAL FACTS OF LEE COUNTY, The Historians, Pennington Gap, VA, 1930; A. W. Laningham and H. M. Bales, THE EARLY SETTLERS OF LEE COUNTY, Media, 1977.

62. LOUDOUN COUNTY, County Seat: Leesburg (22075), formed in 1757 from Fairfax County, see VA Genealogist 16 (1972) 126.
  Court house records: administrator (1757-), birth (1853-9, 1864-6), chancery court order (1831-), circuit court order (1831-), circuit court will (1810-), court (1757-), court minute (1812-), court order (1757-1812), death (1853-66), deed (1757-), divorce (1757-), guardian (1759-1823, 1838-), inventory (1757-), land (1809-45), land cause (1757-73, 1780-7), land tax (1782, 1787-), marriage (1760-), military (1861-5), militia (1793-1827), personal property tax (1782-), petition (1774), poll (1801-21), rent roll (1769-71), superior court deed (1809-44), tax alteration (1783-6), tithable (1758-99), will (1757-). Other records: Baptist, cemetery, census (1790T, 1800T, 1810RA, 1820R, 1830R, 1840R, 1850RFMS, 1860RFMDS, 1870RFMD, 1880RFMD, 1900R, 1910R), county histories, county map, Episcopal Parish, Friends, German

Reformed, landowner maps (1853, 1863-5), Lutheran, Methodist, minister's records, newspaper, Presbyterian, town
history. Library: Loudoun County Public Library,# 52 W.
Market St., Leesburg, VA 22075. Society: Loudoun County
Historical Society,* PO Box 344, Leesburg, VA 22075.
Histories: J. W. Head, HISTORY AND COMPREHENSIVE DESCRIP-
TION OF LOUDOUN COUNTY, Park View Press, Washington, DC,
1908; H. Williams, LEGENDS OF LOUDOUN, Garrett and Massie, Richmond, VA, 1938.

63. LOUISA COUNTY, County Seat: (23093), formed in 1742
from Hanover County, see VA Genealogist 16 (1972) 216.
   Court house records: birth (1867-96), circuit court
will (1810-), court order (1742-8, 1760-82, 1790-), death
(1864-70), deed (1742-), divorce (1742-), guardian (1767-
-1819), inventory (1743-90), land tax (1782, 1787-),
marriage (1766-), military (1861-5), militia (1812),
orphan (1743-1814), personal property tax (1782-), petition (1775), road orders (1742-8), sheriff (1785-91,
1796-1812), survey (1805-), tax alteration (1783-7),
tithable (1767-86), will (1743-61, 1767-). Other records: Baptist, Bible, biography, cemetery, census (1790T,
1800T, 1810RA, 1820R, 1830R, 1840R, 1850RFMS, 1860RFMDS,
1870RFMD, 1880RFMD, 1900R, 1910R), county histories,
county map, Episcopal Parish, Friends, landowner maps
(1863-5), Presbyterian. Library: Louisa County Regional
Branch Library, Louisa, VA 23093. History: M. H. Harris,
HISTORY OF LOUISA COUNTY, Dietz Press, Richmond, VA,
1963.

64. LOWER NORFOLK COUNTY, formed in 1637 from New Norfolk
County, became extinct later in 1691 when it was split
into Princess Anne and Norfolk Counties, records in
Princess Anne and Norfolk Counties.

65. LUNENBURG COUNTY, County Seat: Lunenburg (23952),
formed in 1746 from Brunswick County and later Charlotte
County, see VA Genealogist 16 (1972) 219.
   Court house records: account (1746-), birth (1853-89),
circuit court deed (1811-), circuit court will (1811-),
court minute (1817-9, 1822-32, 1842-), court order
(1746-), death (1853-70), deed (1746-), divorce (1746-),
guardian (1791-), inventory (1746-), land tax (1782,
1787-), marriage (1746-), personal property tax (1782-),
procession (1808-), residents (1758), tax alteration
(1783-6), tithable (1748-83), will (1746-). Other rec-

ords: Baptist, cemetery, census (1790T, 1800T, 1810RA, 1820R, 1830R, 1840R, 1850RFMS, 1860RFMDS, 1870RFMD, 1880RFMD, 1900R, 1910R), county histories, county map, Episcopal Parish, landowner maps (1864, 1871). History: L. C. Bell, THE OLD FREE STATE, William Byrd Press, Richmond, VA, 1927.

66. MADISON COUNTY, County Seat: Madison (22727), formed in 1793 from Culpeper County, see VA Genealogist 17 (1973) 50.

Court house records: circuit court will (1820-), court order (1793-), deed (1793-), divorce (1793-), land tax (1793-), land warrant (1805-), marriage (1793-), military (1861-5), militia (1812), personal property tax (1793-), procession (1796-1800), survey (1792-), will (1793-). Other records: Baptist, cemetery, census (1800T, 1810RA, 1820R, 1830R, 1840R, 1850RFMS, 1860RFMDS, 1870RFMD, 1880RFMD, 1900R, 1910R), county histories, county map, Episcopal Parish, landowner maps (1863-6), Lutheran. Library: Madison County Library, PO Box 243, Madison, VA 22727. History: C. L. Yowell, A HISTORY OF MADISON COUNTY, Shenandoah Publishing House, Strasburg, VA, 1926.

67. MATHEWS COUNTY, County Seat: Mathews (23104), formed in 1791 from Gloucester County, most records destroyed in 1865 by fire, see VA Genealogist 17 (1973) 302.

Court house records: chancery court docket (1805-58), circuit court execution (1842-), circuit court fee (1852-6, 1859, 1861, 1868-), circuit court minute (1831-62), circuit court process (1831-40), circuit court subpoena (1854-63), circuit court suit (1865-), circuit court writ docket (1840-3), circuit superior court fee (1822-4, 1836-9, 1843-8), court order (1865-), court process book (1831-61), court rule docket (1796-1853), deed (1865-), divorce (1865-), executor (1795-1825), fee (22 years 1795-1858), guardian (1806-22), land tax (1791-), marriage (1865-), personal property tax (1791-5, 1809-), plat (1817-), sheriff (1840-1), superior court execution (1809-31), superior court plea (1814-30), superior court rule docket (1809-30), survey (1817-), tithable (1774-5), will (1865-). Other records: cemetery, census (1800T, 1810RA, 1820R, 1830R, 1840R, 1850RFMS, 1860RFMDS, 1870-RFMD, 1880RFMD, 1900R, 1910R), county history, county map, Episcopal Parish, Methodist. Library: Mathews Memorial Library, PO Box 988, Mathews, VA 231109. Society:

Mathews County Historical Society, Mathews, VA 23109. History: VA and the VA County, September, 1951.

68. MECKLENBURG COUNTY, County Seat: Boydton (23917), formed in 1765 from Lunenburg County, see VA Genealogist 18 (1974) 41.

Court house records: court order (1765-1843), deed (1765-), fiduciary (1765-1850), free blacks (1809-65), guardian (1765-), land tax (1782, 1787-), marriage (1765-), military (1775-82), personal property tax (1782-), superior court will (1810-22, 1831-), tax alteration (1783-6), tithable (1745, 1752, 1764), will (1765-). Other records: Baptist, Bible, cemetery, census (1790T, 1800T, 1810RA, 1820R, 1830R, 1840R, 1850RFMS, 1860RFMDS, 1870RFMD, 1880RFMD, 1900R, 1910R), county histories, county map, Episcopal parish, Friends, landowner maps (1864-5, 1870), minister's records, Presbyterian. Library: Southside Regional Library,# Boydtown, VA 23917. Histories: H. R. Mathis, ALONG THE BORDER, Coble Press, Oxford, NC, 1964; W. B. Hill, LAND BY THE ROANOKE: AN ALBUM OF MECKLENBURG COUNTY, Whittet and Shepperson, Richmond, VA 1957.

69. MIDDLESEX COUNTY, County Seat: Saluda (23149), formed in 1669 from Lancaster County, see VA Genealogist 18 (1974) 120.

Court house records: administrator (1767-1810, 1821-35), birth (1853-96), chancery court order (1831-52), circuit superior court order (1843-57), circuit superior court will (1819-44), common law order (1831-43), common law will (1844-), court fee (1832-47), court minute (1823-7), court order (1673-1726, 1732-7, 1740-1804, 1807, 1811-5, 1821, 1829-), death (1853-96), deed (1673-1720), execution (1799-1802, 1820-4, 1831-45), guardian (1760-1857), inventory (1675-), land tax (1782, 1787-), marriage (1740-), military (1861-5), militia (1676, 1687), miscellaneous (1807), orphan (1760-1820), personal property tax (1782-), procession (1826-50), rent roll (1704), superior court order (1813-25), survey (1735-1807), 1832-47), tax alteration (1783-5), will (1673-). Other records: cemetery, census (1790T, 1800T, 1810RA, 1820R, 1830R, 1840R, 1850RFMS, 1860RFMDS, 1870RFMD, 1880RFMD, 1900R, 1910R), county history, county map, Episcopal parish, inventory of county records, Methodist, plantation. Library: Urbanna Public Library,# Urbanna,

VA 23175. History: VA and the VA County, September, 1951.

70. MONTGOMERY COUNTY, County Seat: Christiansburg (24073), formed in 1777 from Fincastle County and later Botetourt and Pulaski Counties, see VA Genealogist 18 (1974) 298.

Court house records: birth (1853-68), chancery court order (1831-), circuit court will (1831-), court order (1773-1855, 1859-), death (1853-68), deed (1773-), divorce (1773-), land tax (1782, 1783-), marriage (1777-), military (1818-39), oath of allegiance (1776, 1784), personal property tax (1786-), plat (1773-), survey (1774-91), warrant (1774-80), will (1773-). Other records: Baptist, casket records, cemetery, census (1790T, 1800T, 1810RA, 1820R, 1830R, 1840R, 1850RFMS, 1860RFMDS, 1870RFMD, 1880RFMD, 1900R, 1910R), county histories, county map, family, landowner maps (1821, 1864-5), Lutheran, town history. Libraries: Montgomery-Floyd Regional Library, 201 Radford St., Christiansburg. VA 24073; VA Polytechnic Institute and State University, Carol M. Newman Library,# Blacksburg, VA 24061; Radford Public Library, Recreation Building, Radford, VA 24141; Radford College, John Preston McConnell Library,# Radford, VA 24142. Society: New River Historical Society,* PO Box 711, Radford, VA 24141. Histories: C. W. Crush, THE MONTGOMERY COUNTY STORY, Montgomery County Jamestown Festival Committee, Christiansburg, VA, 1957; R. L. Lucas, A VALLEY AND ITS PEOPLE IN MONTGOMERY COUNTY, Southern Printing Co., Blacksburg, VA, 1973.

71. NANSEMOND COUNTY, County Seat: Suffolk (23434), formed in 1637 as Upper Norfolk County, name changed in 1642 to Nansemond County, most records destroyed in 1866 by fire, in 1972-4 became City of Suffolk, see VA Genealogist 19 (1975) 59.

Court house records: court order (1866-), deed (1866-), fee (1789-1818), land tax (1782-3, 1787-9, 1794-), marriage (1866-), personal property tax (1815-61), petition (1778-84), rent roll (1704), tax alteration (1784-6, 1790, 1792-3), will (1866-). Other records: Baptist, Bible, cemetery, census (1790T, 1800T, 1810RA, 1820R, 1830R, 1840R, 1850RFMS, 1860RFMDS, 1870RFMD, 1880RFMD, 1900R, 1910R), city history, county histories, county map, Episcopal parish, farms, Friends, landowner maps (16--, 1820, 64). Libraries: Morgan Memorial Library,

118 Bosley Ave., Suffolk, VA 23434. Societies: Suffolk-
Nansemond Historical Society, Box 1255, Suffolk, VA
23434. Histories: J. B. Dunn, THE HISTORY OF NANSEMOND
COUNTY, 1907; R. D. Whichard, THE HISTORY OF LOWER TIDE-
WATER VA, Lewis Historical Publishing Co., New York, NY,
1959; A. Burton, HISTORY OF SUFFOLK AND NANSEMOND COUNTY,
Phelps Ideas, Suffolk, VA, 1970.

72. NELSON COUNTY, County Seat: Lovingston (22949),
formed in 1808 from Amherst County, see VA Genealogist 19
(1975) 61.
   Court house records: account (1808-), birth (1853-72),
circuit court deed (1811-31), circuit court will (1832-),
court order (1808-), death (1853-72), deed (1808-),
divorce (1808-), inventory (1808-), land tax (1809-),
marriage (1808-), personal property tax (1809-), will
(1808-). Other records: Baptist, cemetery, census (1810-
RA, 1820R, 1830R, 1840R, 1850RFMS, 1860RFMDS, 1870RFMD,
1880RFMD, 1900R, 1910R), county histories, county map,
Episcopal parish, landowner maps (1864, 5, 6), Presbyterian. Library: Nelson County Regional Branch, Lovingston,
VA 22949. Histories: J. G. Claiborne, NELSON COUNTY,
Brown-Morrison Co., Lynchburg, VA, 1925; J. B. Coincom,
COLONIAL HISTORY OF NELSON COUNTY, 1734-1807, Amherst
Publishing Co., Amherst, VA, no date.

73. NEW KENT COUNTY, County Seat: New Kent (23124),
formed in 1654 from York and later James City Counties,
most records destroyed by fires in 1787 and 1865, see VA
Genealogist 19 (1975) 63.
   Court house records: birth (1865-88), court order
(1865-), death (1865-88), deed (1865-), divorce (1865-),
land tax (1783-4, 1786-), marriage (1865-), military
(1775-82), personal property tax (1783-), petition
(1683), rent roll (1704), tax alteration (1785), tax
conveyances (1782). Other records: Baptist, cemetery,
census (1790T, 1800T, 1810RA, 1820R, 1830R, 1840R, 1850-
RFMS, 1860RFMDS, 1870RFMD, 1880RFMD, 1900R, 1910R),
county map, Episcopal parish, Friends, landowner map
(1865), Methodist, minister's records.

74. NEW NORFOLK COUNTY, formed in 1636 from Elizabeth
City County, became extinct in 1637 when split into Lower
Norfolk and Upper Norfolk, records now in Norfolk, Prin-
cess Anne and Nansemond Counties.

75. <u>NORFOLK COUNTY</u>, County Seat: Norfolk (23510), formed in 1691 from Lower Norfolk County, in 1963 became the Cities of Chesapeake, Norfolk, and Portsmouth, see VA Genealogist <u>19</u> (1975) 139.

<u>Court house records</u>: appraisal (1755-), audit (1755-), birth (1853-1917), chancery court order (1831-), circuit court will (1831-), court minute (1743-54, 1773-85, 1793-), court order (1637-95, 1710-35, 1742-1810), death (1853-97), deed (1637-), divorce (1637-), guardian (1751-), head rights (1638-66), inventory (1755-91), land tax (1786-), loose wills (1778-1845), marriage (1706-99, 1817-), military (1861-5), personal property tax (1782-), rent roll (1704), residents (1637-65), superior court deed (1809-31), survey (1790-), tax alteration (1782, 1784-5), tithable (1730-80), will (1646-). <u>Norfolk city records</u>: accounts (1851-), appraisals (1851-), birth (1792-1912), borough order (1736-98), borough register (1756-1810), circuit court accounts (1851-), circuit court appraisal (1851-), circuit court chancery (1833-), circuit court inventory (1851-), circuit court law (1833), circuit court reports (1852-), circuit court will (1834-), city atlas (1889), court order (1761-), death (1853-1912), deed (1784-), estate (1850-), fiduciary (1850-), guardian (1804-), hustings court order (1761-), inventory (1851-), land tax (1787-), marriage (1803-), personal property tax (1782-), tax alteration (1782-6), will (1784-). <u>Portsmouth city records</u>: birth (1868-96), chancery court order (1866-), death (1858-96), deed (1858-), inventory (1858-), marriage (1858-), personal property tax (1831-64), will (1855-). <u>Other records</u>: Baptist, biography, cemetery, census (1790T, 1800T, 1810RA, 1820R, 1830R, 1840R, 1850RFMS, 1860RFMDS, 1870-RFMD, 1880RFMD, 1900R, 1910R), city directories, city histories, city maps, county histories, county map, Episcopal parish, family, Friends, landowner maps (16--, 1781, 1887), Methodist, minister's records, newspaper. <u>Libraries</u>: Chesapeake Public Library,# 300 Cedar Road, Chesapeake, VA 23320; Norfolk Public Library,# 301 E. City Hall Ave., Norfolk, VA 23510; Portsmouth Public Library,# 601 Court St., Portsmouth, VA 23704. <u>Societies</u>: Norfolk Historical Society,* 708 Professional Arts Bldg., Norfolk, VA 23510; Portsmouth Historical Association, 221 Worth St., Portsmouth, VA 23704; Portsmouth Genealogical Society, 4505 Caroline Ave., Portsmouth, VA 23707; Norfolk County Historical Society of Chesapeake, PO Box 15205, Chesapeake, VA 23320. <u>Histories</u>: W. H.

Stewart, HISTORY OF NORFOLK COUNTY, 1637-1900, Biographical Publishing Co., Chicago, IL, 1902; R. D. Whichard, THE HISTORY OF LOWER TIDEWATER VA, Lewis Historical Publishing Co., New York, NY, 1959; W. S. Forrest, HISTORICAL AND DESCRIPTIVE SKETCHES OF NORFOLK AND VICINITY, Lindsay and Blakiston, Philadelphia, PA, 1853.

76. NORTHAMPTON COUNTY, County Seat: Eastville (23347), formed in 1634 as one of the 8 original counties (shires), called Accawmack, name changed to Northampton in 1643, see VA Genealogist 19 (1975) 203.
   Court house records: birth (1853-70), court minute (1754-83), court order (1632-), death (1853-70), deed (1632-), district court (1789-1809), fee (1718-49, 1785), inventory (1740-50, 1799-1833, 1854-), land cause (1754-71, 1815-), land tax (1782-1844, 1860-), marriage (1706-), military (1775-82, 1812), orphan (1731-1850), personal property tax (1782-), petition (1723, 1726), poll (1789), procession (1795-1828, 1831-), rent roll(1704), residents (1640-60), superior court (1819-28, 1843-), superior court will (1811-), survey (1784-1833), tax alteration (1784-90), tithable (1662-6, 1675-7), will (1632-). Other records: Baptist, biography, cemetery, census (1790T, 1800T, 1810RA, 1820R, 1830R, 1840R, 1850-RFMS, 1860RFMDS, 1870RFMD, 1880RFMD, 1900R, 1910R), county histories, county map, Episcopal parish, Methodist, Presbyterian. Library: Eastern Shore Public Library,# Accomac, VA 23301. Histories: N. M. Turman, THE EASTERN SHORE OF VA, Eastern Shore News, Onancock, VA, 1964; R. T. Whitelaw, VA'S EASTERN SHORE, A HISTORY OF NORTHAMPTON AND ACCOMACK COUNTIES, P. Smith, Gloucester, MA, 1968 (1951).

77. NORTHUMBERLAND COUNTY, County Seat: Heathville (22473), formed in 1648 from the Indian District of Chickacoan, many records destroyed in 1710 fire, see VA Genealogist 19 (1975) 205.
   Court house records: birth (1853-96), chancery court order (1831-), circuit court order (1831-54), court minute (1797-1807), court order (1650-1797, 1807-), death (1853-95), deed (1650-72, 1706-29, 1738-), district court deed (1789-1849), district court order (1789-1849), district court will (1789-1849), estate (1652-72, 1706-29, 1738-), fee (1718-49, 1785), fiduciary (1749-), guardian (1788-), inventory (1652-72, 1706-), land cause (1846-73), land tax (1782, 1787-), marriage (1735-),

personal property tax (1782-), procession (1795-1839), tax alteration (1783-6), will (1652-72, 1706-29, 1738-). Other records: Baptist, cemetery, census (1790T, 1800T, 1810RA, 1820R, 1830R, 1840R, 1850RFMS, 1860RFMDS, 1870-RFMD, 1880RFMD, 1900R, 1910R), church vital statistics, county histories, county map, Episcopal parish, Methodist. Library: Northumberland Memorial Library, Heath-ville, VA 22473. History: VA and the VA County, August, 1950.

78. NOTTOWAY COUNTY, County Seat: Nottoway (23955), formed in 1789 from Amelia County, see VA Genealogist 19 (1975) 208.

Court house records: court minute (1840-), court order (1789, 1793-1854), deed (1789-1816, 1824-9, 1836-), divorce (1865-), inventory (1789-), land tax (1789-), marriage (1856-), personal property tax (1789-), tithable (1771), will (1789-). Other records: biography, cemetery, census (1790T, 1800T, 1810RA, 1820R, 1830R, 1840R, 1850RFMS, 1860RFMDS, 1870RFMD, 1880RFMD, 1900R, 1910R), county histories, county map, Episcopal parish, family, landowner map (1864), Methodist, Presbyterian. Library: Nottoway County Library, Nottoway, VA 23955. Society: Nottoway County Historical Association, 100 Bird Rd., Blackstone, VA 23824. Histories: W. R. Turner, OLD HOMES AND FAMILIES IN NOTTOWAY, Nottoway Publishing Co., Blackstone, VA, 1950, to be used with R. B. Batte, INDEX TO OLD HOMES AND FAMILIES IN NOTTOWAY, VA Genealogical Society, Richmond, VA, 1961; A. B. Cummins, NOTTOWAY COUNTY: FOUNDING AND DEVELOPMENT, Nottoway Publishing Co., Blackstone, VA, 1970.

79. OLD RAPPAHANNOCK COUNTY, formed in 1656 from Lancaster County, became extinct in 1692 when it split into Essex and Richmond Counties, records in Essex and Richmond Counties, see VA Genealogist 21 (1977) 219.

Court house records: court records (1654-91), deed (1654-91), index to records (1654-92), will (1654-91). Other records: county histories, county map, Episcopal parish. History: T. H. Warner, HISTORY OF OLD RAPPAHAN-NOCK COUNTY, Warner, Tappahannock, VA, 1965.

80. ORANGE COUNTY, County Seat: Orange (22960), formed in 1734 from Spotsylvania County, see VA Genealogist 19 (1975) 283.

Court house records: birth (1751-78, 1866-95), court minute (1764-1806, 1825-52, 1856-), court order (1734-77, 1801-11, 1816-24, 1852-6), death (1866-95), deed (1734-), guardian (1827-52), judgment (1735-6), land tax (1782, 1787-), marriage (1757-), militia court (1813-53), personal property tax (1782-), procession (1795-1804), superior court minute (1809-), tax alteration (1783-6), tithable (1734-58), will (1735-). Other records: Baptist, cemetery, census (1790T, 1800T, 1810RA, 1820R, 1830R, 1840R, 1850RFMS, 1860RFMDS, 1870RFMD, 1880RFMD, 1900R, 1910R), county histories, county map, Episcopal parish, family, Friends, town history. Library: Orange County Public Library, 127 Belleview Ave., Orange, VA 22960. Society: Orange County Historical Society,* 104 W. Main St., Orange, VA 22960. History: W. W. Scott, A HISTORY OF ORANGE COUNTY, Waddey Co., Richmond, VA 1907.

81. PAGE COUNTY, County Seat: Luray (22835), formed in 1831 from Rockingham and Shenandoah Counties, see VA Genealogist 20 (1976) 51.

Court house records: administrator (1850-65), birth (1865-72), chancery court order (1831-59), common law order (1831-59), court minute (1831-), death (1864-72), deed (1831-), divorce (1831-), executor (1850-), guardian (1850-70), land cause (1843-56), marriage (1831-), survey (1831-), will (1831-). Other records: Baptist, cemetery, census (1840R, 1850RFMS, 1860RFMDS, 1870RFMD, 1880RFMD, 1900R, 1910R), county atlas (1885), county histories, county map, Evangelical, German Reformed, landowner map (1866), Lutheran. History: H. M. Strickler, A SHORT HISTORY OF PAGE COUNTY, Dietz Press, Richmond, VA, 1952.

82. PATRICK COUNTY, County Seat: Stuart (24171), formed in 1791 from Henry County, see VA Genealogist 20 (1976) 52.

Court house records: account (1791-1823), birth (1853-96), chancery court order (1832-), court order (1791-), death (1853-70), deed (1791-), divorce (1791-), inventory (1791-1823), land grant (1793-), land tax (1791-), marriage (1791-), military (1861-5), personal property tax (1791-), will (1791-). Other records: Baptist, bibliography, cemetery, census (1800T, 1810RA, 1820R, 1830R, 1840R, 1850RFMS, 1860RFMDS, 1870RFMD, 1880RFMD, 1900R, 1910R), county history, county map, Friends, landowner map (1821). Library: Patrick County Regional Branch Library, Blue Ridge St., Stuart, VA 24171. History: V.

G. and L. G. Pedigo, HISTORY OF PATRICK AND HENRY COUN-
TIES, Stone Printing Co., Roanoke, VA,1933.

83. PITTSYLVANIA COUNTY, County Seat: Chatham (24531),
formed in 1767 from Halifax County, see VA Genealogist 20
(1976) 119.

Court house records: account (1770-), birth (1853-96),
circuit court will (1809-), court order (1767-), death
(1853-96), deed (1767-), divorce (1767-), estate (1767-),
inventory (1767-), land (1737-70), land tax (1782, 1786-
), marriage (1767-), military (1861-5), personal property
tax (1782-), procession (1812-34), survey (1741-), tax
alteration (1783-5), tithable (1767), will (1767-).
Danville city records: birth (1874-9), bond (1875-),
chancery court order (1871-), common law order (1874-),
corporation court (1859-63), court order (1860-), deed
(1841-), land (1851-), land tax (1851-), marriage (1841-
), personal property tax (1851-), will (1857-). Other
records: Baptist, cemetery, census (1790T, 1800T, 1810RA,
1820R, 1830R, 1840R, 1850RFMS, 1860RFMDS, 1870 RFMD,
1880RFMD, 1900R, 1910R), city histories, city map, county
histories, county map, Episcopal parish, Friends, inventory of county records, minister's records, Presbyterian,
town history. Libraries: Pittsylvania County Public
Library, PO Box 1049, Chatham, VA 24531; Danville Public
Library,# 511 Patton St., Danville, VA 24541. Societies:
VA-NC Piedmont Genealogical Society,* PO Box 2272, Danville, VA 24541; Pittsylvania Historical Society, Route
2, Box 26-A, Chatham, VA 24531; Danville Historical
Society, PO Box 2291, Danville, VA 24541. History: M. C.
Clement, THE HISTORY OF PITTSYLVANIA COUNTY, Bell Co.,
Lynchburg, VA, 1929.

84. POWHATAN COUNTY, County Seat: Powhatan (23139),
formed in 1777 from Cumberland County and later Chesterfield County, see VA Genealogist 20 (1976) 212.

Court house records: appeal (1790-2), birth (1853-71),
circuit court deed (1809-), circuit court will (1809-),
court order (1777-), death (1853-71), deed (1777-), divorce (1777-), land tax (1782, 1787-), marriage (1777-),
personal property tax (1782-), sheriff (1811-28), tax
alteration (1784-6), will (1777-). Other records: cemetery, census (1790T, 1800T, 1810RA, 1820R, 1830R, 1840R,
1850RFMS, 1860RFMDS, 1870RFMD, 1880RFMD, 1900R, 1910R),
county histories, county map, Episcopal parish, inventory

of county records, landowner map (1864), Methodist. History: VA Cavalcade, Winter, 1968.

85. PRINCE EDWARD COUNTY, County Seat: Farmville (23901),
formed in 1754 from Amelia County, see VA Genealogist 20
(1976) 291.
   Court house records: birth (1853-96), circuit court
will (1833-), court order (1754-), death (1853-68), deed
(1754-), district court deed (1789-1816), district court
order (1789-1830), district court will (1789-1829),
divorce (1754-), guardian (1764-), land tax (1782-),
marriage (1754-), military (1861-5), personal property
tax (1782-), petition (1776), settlers (before 1753),
superior court (1789-98), superior court order (1831-58),
tax alteration (1783-6), will (1754-). Other records:
Baptist, cemetery, census (1790T, 1800T, 1810RA, 1820R,
1830R, 1840R, 1850RFMS, 1860RFMDS, 1870RFMD, 1880RFMD,
1900R, 1910R), county histories, county map, Episcopal
parish, family, landowner maps (1820, 1864, 1879), minister's records, Presbyterian. Libraries: Farmville
Reading Room Library, PO Box 424, Farmville, VA 23901;
Longwood College, Dabney S. Lancaster Library, Farmville,
VA 23901. Histories: H. C. Bradshaw, HISTORY OF PRINCE
EDWARD COUNTY, Dietz Press, Richmond, VA, 1955; C. E.
Burrell, A HISTORY OF PRINCE EDWARD COUNTY, Williams
Printing Co., Richmond, VA, 1922; Farmville Herald, TODAY
AND YESTERDAY IN THE HEART OF VA, The Farmville Herald,
Farmville, VA, 1935.

86. PRINCE GEORGE COUNTY, County Seat: Prince George
(23875), formed in 1703 from Charles City County, most
records destroyed by fire in the Civil War, see VA Genealogist 20 (1976) 294.
   Court house records: account (1835-41), birth (1865-
96), claims (1817-37), court minute (1737-40), court
order (1714-20, 1811, 1814, 1835-41), death (1865-73),
deed (1713-28, 1759-60, 1787-92, 1842-6, 1851-8, 1865-),
divorce (1865-), execution (1801-3), inventory (1835-41),
land patents (1666-1719), land tax (1782-3, 1787-), marriage (1865-), military (1861-5), personal property tax
(1782-), rent roll (1704), survey (1711-24, 1794-), tax
alteration (1784-6), will (1711-28, 1759-60, 1787-92,
1865-). Other records: Baptist, Bible, cemetery, census
(1790T, 1800T, 1810RA, 1820R, 1830R, 1840R, 1850RFMS,
1860RFMDS, 1870RFMD, 1880RFMD, 1900R, 1910R), city histories, county histories, county map, Episcopal parish,

Friends, inventory of county records, landowner maps (1863-5). Library: Appomattox Regional Library, Maude Langhorne Nelson Library, 220 Appomattox St., Hopewell, VA 23860. History: E. Lutz, THE PRINCE GEORGE-HOPEWELL STORY, William Byrd Press, Richmond, VA, 1957.

87. PRINCE WILLIAM COUNTY, County Seat: Manassas (22110), formed in 1731 from Stafford and King George Counties, many records destroyed, damaged, lost, or stolen in Revolutionary and Civil Wars, see VA Genealogist 21 (1977) 54.

Court house records: administrator (1753-86), birth (1864-70), bond (1753-86, 1815-47, 1852-), chancery court order (1837-70), court minute (1752-, many missing years), court order (1752-, many missing years), death (1864-70), deed (1731-, many missing years), district court deed (1795-9), district court order (1793-9, 1804-17), divorce (1734-), executor (1753-86, 1813-47, 1852-), land (1835-43), land cause (1789-1849), land tax (1782, 1784, 1787-), marriage (1859-), personal property tax (1782-), petition (1776), plat (1789-1858), tax alteration (1783-6), tithable (1747), will (1734-44, 1778-). Other records: Baptist, cemetery, census (1790T, 1800T, 1810RA, 1820R, 1830R, 1840R, 1850RFMS, 1860RFMDS, 1870RFMD, 1880RFMD, 1900R, 1910R), county histories, county map, Episcopal parish, landowner maps (1864-5), Presbyterian. Library: Prince William Public Library,# 8601 Mathis Ave., Manassas, VA 22110. Society: Prince William County Historical Commission, Courthouse, Manassas, VA 22110. Histories: WPA Writers, PRINCE WILLIAM, THE STORY OF ITS PEOPLE AND ITS PLACES, Whittet and Shepperson, Richmond, VA, 1941; A. M. Ewell, A VA SCENE, OR LIFE IN OLD PRINCE WILLIAM, Bell, Lynchburg, VA, 1931; F. Harrison, LANDMARKS OF OLD PRINCE WILLIAM, Chesapeake Book Co., Berryville, VA, 1964.

88. PRINCESS ANNE COUNTY, County Seat: Princess Anne (23456), formed in 1691 from Lower Norfolk County, in 1963 replaced by the City of VA Beach, see VA Genealogist 21 (1977) 56.

Court house records: audit (1783-1862), birth (1853-70), chancery court order (1831-58), chancery reports (1814-49), claims (1816-27), court minute (1691-), court order (1691-), death (1864-70), deed (1691-), guardian (1736-), inventory (1783-1862), land patent (1666-79), marriage (1749-), military (1861-5), miscellaneous

(1700–89), personal property tax (1782–), petition (1770, 1772), procession (1796–1858), rent roll (1704), slave owner (1810), suitpapers (1700–89), superior court (1812–31), superior court deed (1812–31), superior court will (1831–), tax alteration (1784–5), will (1691–). Other records: Baptist, cemetery, census (1790T, 1800T, 1810RA, 1820R, 1830R, 1840R, 1850RFMS, 1860RFMDS, 1870RFMD, 1880RFMD, 1900R, 1910R), county history, county map, Episcopal parish, Friends, landowner map (1781), Methodist, minister's records. Library: VA Beach Public Library,# Municipal Center, VA Beach, VA 23456. Society: Princess Anne County Historical Society, 609 Bay Colony Dr., VA Beach, VA 23451. History: R. D. Whichard, THE HISTORY OF LOWER TIDEWATER VA, Lewis Historical Publishing Co., New York, NY, 1959.

89. PULASKI COUNTY, County Seat: Pulaski (24301), formed in 1839 from Montgomery and Wythe Counties, see VA Genealogist 21 (1977) 122.
    Court house records: birth (1853–70), chancery court order (1839–), circuit court order (1839–), circuit court will (1848–), court order (1839–), death (1853–70), deed (1839–), divorce (1839–), land tax (1839–), marriage (1839–), personal property tax (1839–), will (1839–). Other records: Bible, cemetery, census (1840R, 1850RFMS, 1860RFMDS, 1870RFMD, 1880RFMD, 1900R, 1910R), county histories, county map, family, landowner map (1890), Presbyterian. Library: Pulaski County Library, 60 W. Third St., Pulaski, VA 24301. Histories: Pulaski County Commission, JAMESTOWN EXPOSITION, 1907, Southwest Publishing Co., Pulaski, VA, 1907; C. H. Smith, COLONIAL DAYS IN THE LAND THAT BECAME PULASKI COUNTY, Library Board, Pulaski, VA, 1975.

90. RAPPAHANNOCK COUNTY, County Seat: Washington (22747), formed in 1833 from Culpeper County, see VA Genealogist 21 (1977) 220.
    Court house records: administrator (1833–50), birth (1853–70), bond (1833–50), chancery court order (1833–), circuit court minute (1833–46), circuit court will (1833–), court minute (1833–) deed (1833–), divorce (1833–), executor (1833–50), guardian (1833–50), land cause (1839–49), land tax (1833–), land division (1833–47), marriage (1833–), personal property tax (1833–), superior court order (1833–56), will (1833–). Other records: Baptist, cemetery, census (1840R,

1850RFMS, 1860RFMDS, 1870RFMD, 1880RFMD, 1900R, 1910R),
county history, county map, landowner maps (1863-6), town
history. Library: Rappahannock County Library, PO Box
55, Washington, VA 22747. History: M. E. Hite, MY
RAPPAHANNOCK STORY BOOK, Dietz Press, Richmond, VA, 1950.

91. RICHMOND COUNTY, County Seat: Warsaw (22572), formed
in 1692 from Old Rappahannock County, see VA Genealogist
21 (1977) 222.
    Court house records: account (1724-), birth (1853-96,
1912-4), chancery court order (1815-28, 1848-9, 1856),
circuit superior court (1841-50), circuit court law order
(1831-40), circuit court chancery order (1831-61), court
order (1692-5, 1699-), criminal trial (1710-54), death
(1853-95, 1912-7), deed(1692-), divorce (1693-), execution (1786-97), freeholders (1701), guardian (1824-50),
land tax (1782, 1787-), marriage (1709-16, 1824-50,
1853-), miscellaneous (1699-1724), overseers of poor
(1843-56), personal property tax (1782-), poll (1771),
procession (1796-1817), rule books (1786-1805, 1816-41,
1850-), superior court order (1809-31), tax alteration
(1783-6), will (1699-). Other records: Bible, cemetery,
census (1790T, 1800T, 1810RA, 1820R, 1830R, 1840R, 1850
RFMS, 1860RFMDS, 1870RFMD, 1880RFMD, 1900R, 1910R),
county histories, county map, Episcopal parish, family,
Methodist. Library: Rappahannock Community College,
North Campus Library, Warsaw, VA 22572. Histories: E. L.
Ryland, RICHMOND COUNTY, 1776-1976, Warsaw, VA, 1976; T.
H. Warner, HISTORY OF OLD RAPPAHANNOCK COUNTY, INCLUDING
THE PRESENT COUNTIES OF ESSEX AND RICHMOND, Warner,
Tappahannock, VA, 1965.

92. ROANOKE COUNTY, County Seat: Salem (24153), formed in
1838 from Botetourt County and later Montgomery County,
see VA Genealogist 21 (1977) 285.
    Court house records: appraisal (1838-), birth (1853-
85), chancery court order (1838-), circuit court will
(1841-), court order (1838-), death (1853-81), deed
(1838-), divorce (1838-), inventory (1838-), land tax
(1838-), personal property tax (1838-), survey (1840-),
will (1838-). Roanoke city records: birth (1884-96),
court order (1884-), deed (1884-), divorce (1884-),
marriage (1884-), will (1884-). Other records: Bible,
biography, cemetery, census (1840R,1850RFMS, 1860RFMDS,
1870RFMD, 1880RFMD, 1900R, 1910R), city directories, city
histories, city maps, county histories, county map,

family, landowner maps (1864-5), Presbyterian. Libraries: Salem Public Library,# 28 E. Main St., Salem, VA
24153; Roanoke County Public Library,# 3131 Electric Rd.,
SW, Roanoke, VA 24018; Roanoke Public Library,# 706 S.
Jefferson St., Roanoke, VA 24011. Societies: Roanoke
Valley Historical Society,* PO Box 1904, Roanoke, VA
24008; Southwestern VA Genealogical Society,* 2609 Hill-
crest Ave., NW, Roanoke, VA 24012. Histories: G. S.
Jack, HISTORY OF ROANOKE COUNTY, Stone, Roanoke, VA,
1912; W. McCauley, HISTORY OF ROANOKE COUNTY, SALEM, &
ROANOKE, Biographical Publishing Co., Chicago, IL 1902;
Times-Register, AN HISTORICAL RECORD OF ROANOKE COUNTY,
Times-Register, Salem, VA, 1938; WPA Writers Program,
ROANOKE, STORY OF COUNTY AND CITY, Stone Printing Co.,
Roanoke, VA, 1942.

93. ROCKBRIDGE COUNTY, County Seat: Lexington (24450),
formed in 1778 from Augusta and Botetourt Counties, see
VA Genealogist 22 (1978) 51.
    Court house records: birth (1853-96), chancery court
order (1831-), circuit court deed (1809-14), circuit
court minute (1825-), circuit court order (1821-41),
circuit court will (1809-), claims (1824-35), court
minute (1825-), court order (1778-), death (1853-70),
decided causes (1778-), deed (1778-), divorce (1778-),
estray (1831-56), fee (1841-2), land tax (1782, 1784-5,
1787-), marriage (1778-), military (1778-1833, 1861-5),
militia (1796), miscellaneous (1794-9, 1875-), pension
(1778-1833), personal property tax (1782-), plat (1787-
99), suit papers (1778-), survey (1779-1806), tax alteration (1783, 1786), tithable (1778-9), will (1778-).
Other records: Baptist, cemetery, census (1790T, 1800T,
1810RA, 1820R, 1830R, 1840R, 1850RFMS, 1860RFMDS,
1870RFMD, 1880RFMD, 1900R, 1910R), city histories, county
histories, county map, landowner maps (1860, 1865-6),
Presbyterian. Libraries: Rockbridge Regional Library,
312 S. Main St., Lexington, VA 24450; Buena Vista Regional Branch Library, 2110 Magnolia Ave., Buena Vista,
VA 24416; Washington and Lee University Library,# Lex-
ington, VA 24450 (VA Valley manuscripts); VA Military
Institute, J. T. L.Preston Library,# Lexington, VA 24450;
Rockbridge Historical Society Library,# 101 E. Washington
St., Lexington, VA 24450. Society: Rockbridge Historical
Society,* 101 E. Washington St., Lexington, VA 24450.
Histories: O. F. Morton, A HISTORY OF ROCKBRIDGE COUNTY,
McClure Co., Staunton, VA, 1920; E. P. Tompkins, ROCK-

BRIDGE COUNTY, AN INFORMAL HISTORY, Whittet and Shepperson, Richmond, VA, 1952; J. W. McClung, HISTORICAL SIGNIFICANCE OF ROCKBRIDGE COUNTY, McClure Co., Staunton, VA, 1939.

94. ROCKINGHAM COUNTY, County Seat: Harrisonburg (22801), formed 1778 from Augusta County, some records destroyed in 1864 fire, see VA Genealogist 22 (1978) 54.

Court house records: administrator (1778-1836, 1852-), birth (1862-94), chancery court (1831-65), common law minute (1831-45), common law (1842-54), court minute (1778-), court order (1778-1804), death (1862-70, 1890-4), deed (1778-), executor (1778-1815, 1819-54), guardian (1779-), judgment (1778-1804), land cause (1810-48), land grant (1761-91), land tax (1782, 1787-), marriage (1778-1852, 1864-), military (1861-5), overseers of poor (1782-), personal property tax (1781-), superior court deed (1809-52), survey (1761-), tax alteration (1783-6), tithable (1792), will (incomplete before 1865, 1865-). Other records: Baptist, biography, cemetery, census (1790T, 1800T, 1810RA, 1820R, 1830R, 1840R, 1850RFMS, 1860RFMDS, 1870RFMD, 1880RFMD, 1900R, 1910R), city histories, county atlas (1885), county histories, county map, German Reformed, inventory of county records, landowner map (1866), Lutheran, town history. Libraries: Eastern Mennonite College Library,# Harrisonburg, VA 22801 (Mennonite collection), Rockingham Public Library,# 45 Newman Ave., Harrisonburg, VA 22801; Bridgewater College, Alexander Mack Memorial Library,# Bridgewater, VA 22812 (Brethren collection). Society: Harrisonburg-Rockingham Historical Society,* Harrisonburg, VA 22801. History: J. W. Wayland, A HISTORY OF ROCKINGHAM COUNTY, Ruebush-Elkins Co., Dayton, VA, 1912.

95. RUSSELL COUNTY, County Seat: Lebanon (24266), formed in 1785 from Washington County, a few records lost in 1853 fire, see VA Genealogist 22 (1978) 131.

Court house records: birth (1853-66, 1912-22), chancery court order (1821-), circuit court will (1809-), court order (1786-), death (1853-66), deed (1787-), divorce (1786-), fiduciary (1803-), land cause (1814, 1817, 1822), land tax (1786-), law orders (1786-), marriage (1853-), personal property tax (1787-), superior court deed (1809-17), survey (1786-), will (1803-). Other records: Baptist, cemetery, census (1790T, 1800T, 1810RA, 1820R, 1830R, 1840R, 1850RFMS, 1860RFMDS, 1870RFMD, 1880

RFMD, 1900R, 1910R), county histories, county map. Library: Russell County Public Library, PO Box 297, Lebanon, VA 24266. History: D. C. Pratt, RUSSELL COUNTY, VA'S BLUE GRASS EMPIRE, King Printing Co., Bristol, TN, 1968.

96. SCOTT COUNTY, County Seat: Gate City (24251), formed in 1814 from Lee, Russell, and Washington Counties, see VA Genealogist 22 (1978) 133.

Court house records: birth (1853-70), bond (1832-), chancery court (1837-47), chancery court order (1831-), court minute (1815-), court order (1831-), death (1853-70), deed (1815-), divorce (1815-), docket cases (1815-), entry (1816-58), land tax (1815-), land title (1816-58), law and chancery (1815-), marriage (1815-), personal property tax (1815-), superior court order (1825-31), survey (1816-), will (1816-). Other records: Baptist, biography, cemetery, census (1820R, 1830R, 1840R, 1850 RFMS, 1860RFMDS, 1870RFMD, 1880RFMD, 1900R, 1910R), county histories, county map, minister's records. Library: Scott County Public Library, Gate City, VA 24251. History: R. M. Addington, HISTORY OF SCOTT COUNTY, Kingsport Press, Bristol, TN, 1932.

97. SHENANDOAH COUNTY, County Seat: Woodstock (22664), formed in 1772 from Frederick County, first called Dunmore County, name changed in 1778 to Shenandoah County, see VA Genealogist 22 (1978) 210.

Court house records: account (1809-), birth (1853-71), chancery court order (1831-), circuit court will (1856-), court minute (1774-80, 1785-96, 1810-), court order (1772-4, 1781-6, 1795-1811), death (1853-71), deed (1772), divorce (1772-), land tax (1782, 1787-), marriage (1772-), personal property tax (1782-), rent roll (1774), settlement (1856-), superior court will (1809-), survey (1785-), tax alteration (1783-6), will (1772-). Other records: Baptist, biography, cemetery, census (1790T, 1800T, 1810RA, 1820R, 1830R, 1840R, 1850RFMS, 1860RFMDS, 1870RFMD, 1880RFMD, 1900R, 1910R), Christian Church, county atlas (1885), county histories, county map, Episcopal parish, German Reformed, Lutheran, minister's records, Presbyterian, town histories. Library: Edinburgh Community Library,# Piccadilly St., Edinburg, VA 22824. History: J. W. Wayland, A HISTORY OF SHENANDOAH VALLEY, Shenandoah Publishing House, Strasburg, VA, 1927.

98. <u>SMYTH COUNTY</u>, County Seat: Marion (24354), formed in 1832 from Washington and Wythe Counties, a few records lost in fire of unknown date, see VA Genealogist <u>22</u> (1978) 213.

<u>Court house records</u>: census (1840R, 1850RFMS, 1860 RFMDS, 1870RFMD,1880RFMD, 1900R, 1910R), county histories, county map, landowner map (1899). <u>Library</u>: Smyth-Bland Regional Library, PO Box 1068, Marion, VA 24354. <u>Society</u>: Smyth County Historical and Museum Society, 230 N. Church St., Marion, VA 24354. <u>History</u>: G. Wilson, SMYTH COUNTY HISTORY AND TRADITIONS, Kingsport Press, Kingsport, TN, 1932.

99. <u>SOUTHAMPTON COUNTY</u>, County Seat: Courtland (23837), formed in 1749 from Isle of Wight and Nansemond Counties, see VA Genealogist <u>22</u> (1978) 287.

<u>Court house records</u>: birth (1853-70), court minute (1775-8, 1786-90,1793-), court order (1749-89, 1802-7, 1811-24, 1835-49), death (1853-70), deed (1749-), guardian (1751-72), land tax (1782-4, 1792-), marriage (1750-), personal property tax (1782-), plat (1826-36), procession (1836-), tax alteration (1785-93), tithable (1770), will (1749-). <u>Other records</u>: Baptist, cemetery, census (1790T, 1800T, 1810RA, 1820R, 1830R, 1840R, 1850 RFMS, 1860RFMDS, 1870RFMD, 1880RFMD, 1900R, 1910R), Christian Church, city history, county histories, county map, Episcopal parish, Friends, inventory of county records, landowner maps (1863, 1865), minister's records. <u>Libraries</u>: Walter Cecil Rawls Regional Library System, PO Box 318, Courtland, VA 23837; Franklin Library Association, 800 W. Second Ave., Franklin, VA 23851. <u>Society</u>: Southampton County Historical Society,* Courtland, VA 23837. <u>Histories</u>: R. D. Whichard, THE HISTORY OF LOWER TIDEWATER VA, Lewis Publishing Co., New York, NY, 1959; T. C. Parramore, SOUTHAMPTON COUNTY, 1978.

100. <u>SPOTSYLVANIA COUNTY</u>, County Seat: Spotsylvania (22553), formed in 1721 from Essex, King William, and King and Queen Counties, see VA Genealogist <u>22</u> (1978) 290.

<u>Court house records</u>: court docket (1846-73, 1881-), court minute (1722-65,1768-), court order (1722-65, 1768-), deed (1722-), divorce (1875-), execution (1756-71), judgment (1843-), land tax (1782, 1784-), marriage (incomplete 1721-94, 1795-), personal property tax (1782-), procession (1796-1831), slaveowners (1783), will

(1722-1824, 1830-). <u>Fredericksburg city records</u>: chancery court (1814-), deed (1782-), district court (1790-1831), district court deed (1789-1816), hustings court bond (1782-1850), hustings court order (1789-), hustings court will (1782-), land causes (1808-23), land tax (1787-), marriage (1771-), personal property tax (1787-), superior court (1812-31), will (1782-). <u>Other records</u>: Baptist, cemetery, census (1790T, 1800T, 1810RA, 1820R, 1830R, 1840R, 1850RFMS, 1860RFMDS, 1870RFMD, 1880RFMD, 1900R, 1910R), city history, county histories, county map, Episcopal parish, landowner maps (1820, 1862-5), minister's records, newspaper. <u>Libraries</u>: Central Rappahannock Regional Library,# Wallace Memorial Library, 1201 Caroline St., Fredericksburg, VA 22401; Fredericksburg National Military Park, Civil War Library,# 1013 Lafayette Blvd., Fredericksburg, VA 22401. <u>Societies</u>: Historic Fredericksburg Foundation,* 623 Caroline Ave., Fredericksburg, VA 22401; Spotsylvania Historical Association, PO Box 64, Spotsylvania, VA 22553. <u>Histories</u>: J. R. Mansfield, A HISTORY OF EARLY SPOTSYLVANIA COUNTY, VA Book Co., Berryville, VA, 1977; W. A. Crozier, SPOTSYLVANIA COUNTY, Genealogical Publishing Co., Baltimore, MD, 1978 (1905).

101. <u>STAFFORD COUNTY</u>, County Seat: Stafford (22554), formed in 1664 from Westmoreland County, many records lost or stolen during Civil War, see VA Genealogist <u>23</u> (1979) 55.

<u>Court house records</u>: birth (1853-73), court minute (1830-5, 1852-67), court order (1664-8, 1689-93, 1790-3, 1806-9), death (1715-30, 1853-73), deed (1722-, many missing years), divorce (1664-), estate (1827-34, 1852-), land tax (1782-3,1786-), marriage (1854-), military (1861-5), personal property tax (1782-), petition (1774), tax alteration (1784-5), tithable (1768, 1773), will (1699-, many missing years). <u>Other records</u>: Baptist, cemetery, census (1790T, 1800T, 1810RA, 1820R, 1830R, 1840R, 1850RFMS, 1860RFMDS, 1870RFMD, 1880RFMD, 1900R, 1910R), county history, county map, Episcopal parish, landowner maps (1820, 1863-5). <u>History</u>: J. T. Goolrick, THE STORY OF STAFFORD, Tackitt, Concord, CA, 1976 (1939).

102. <u>SURRY COUNTY</u>, County Seat: Surry (23883), formed in 1652 from James City County, see VA Genealogist <u>23</u> (1979) 125.

Court house records: birth (1853-96), chancery court order (1831-), circuit court order (1671-1718, 1741-), circuit court will (1809-), court order (1671-), death (1853-96), deed (1652-), executor (1798-), fiduciary (1831-), guardian (1672-), land tax (1782-3, 1787-), marriage (1768-), militia (1687, 1840-61), orphan (1744-, incomplete), personal property tax (1782-), petition (1676), plat (1810-), procession (1796-1826, 1832-44), rent roll (1704), tax alteration (1785-6), tithable (1668, 1674-5, 1677-8, 1683, 1688, 1694, 1698-9, 1701-3), will (1652-). Other records: cemetery, census (1790T, 1800T, 1810RA, 1820R, 1830R, 1840R, 1850RFMS, 1860RFMDS, 1870RFMD, 1880RFMD, 1900R, 1910R), county histories, county map, Episcopal parish, Friends, land-owner maps (1863, 1865), Methodist, minister's records. History: J. B. Boddie, COLONIAL SURRY, Dietz Press, Richmond, VA, 1948.

103. SUSSEX COUNTY, County Seat: Sussex (23884), formed in 1754 from Surry County, see VA Genealogist 23 (1979) 127.
Court house records: birth (1853-69), court of oyer and terminer orders (1754-1807), court papers (1754-1816), court minute (1818-27), court order (1754-), death (1853-69), deed (1754-), guardian (1754-), land tax (1782, 1787-), marriage (1754-), personal property tax (1782-), superior court order (1812-31), tax alteration (1783-6), will (1754-). Other records: Baptist, cemetery, census (1790T, 1800T, 1810RA, 1820R, 1830R, 1840R, 1850RFMS, 1860RFMDS, 1870RFMD, 1880RFMD, 1900R, 1910R), county histories, county map, Episcopal parish, Friends, land-owner maps (1863, 1865). History: WPA Writers Program, SUSSEX COUNTY, A TALE OF THREE CENTURIES, Whittet and Shepperson, Richmond, VA, 1942.

104. TAZEWELL COUNTY, County Seat: Tazewell (24651), formed in 1800 from Wythe and Russell Counties and later from Washington and Logan (WV) Counties, see VA Genealogist 23 (1979) 218.
Court house records: birth (1853-70), court order (1800-), death (1853-71), deed (1800-), justice of peace (1800-52), land grant (1800-20), land tax (1801-), law & chancery order (1832-), marriage (1800-), personal property tax (1801-), superior court order (1809-31), survey (1801-), will (1800-). Other records: cemetery, census (1790T, 1800T, 1810RA, 1820R, 1830R, 1840R, 1850RFMS,

1860RFMDS, 1870RFMD, 1880RFMD, 1900R, 1910R), county histories, county map, village history. Library: Tazewell County Public Library, Main St., Tazewell, VA 24651. Society: Tazewell County Archeological and Historical Resources, Tazewell County Public Library, Main St., Tazewell, VA 24651. Histories: J. N. Harman, ANNALS OF TAZEWELL COUNTY, 1800-1922, Hill Printing Co., Richmond, VA, 1922-5, 2 volumes; W. C. Pendleton, HISTORY OF TAZEWELL COUNTY AND SOUTHWEST VA, 1748-1920, Hill Printing Co., Richmond, VA, 1920.

105. UPPER NORFOLK COUNTY, formed in 1637 from New Norfolk County, name changed in 1642 to Nansemond County, see Nansemond County for records.

106. WARREN COUNTY, County Seat: Front Royal (22630), formed in 1836 from Shenandoah and Frederick Counties, see VA Genealogist 23 (1979) 284.
  Court house records: administrator (1850-), birth (1853- 1917), bond (1850-), chancery court order (1836-), circuit court will (1838-), court minute (1836-), death (1853-74), deed (1836-), divorce (1836-), land (1842-6), land tax (1836-), marriage (1836-), military (1861-5), personal property tax (1836-),will (1836-). Other records: Baptist, cemetery, census (1840R, 1850RFMS, 1860 RFMDS, 1870RFMD, 1880RFMD, 1900R, 1910R), county map, Friends, landowner maps (1834, 1866). Library: Samuels Public Library, 101 Chester St., Front Royal, VA 22630. History: J. L. Dickinson, THE FAIRFAX PROPRIETARY, Warren Press, Front Royal, VA, 1959.

107. WARROSQUOYOAKE COUNTY, formed in 1634 as one of the original 8 counties (shires), renamed Isle of Wight in 1637.

108. WARWICK COUNTY, County Seat: Newport News (23601), formed in 1634 as one of the original 8 counties (shires), originally named Warwick River, changed to Warwick in 1642, most records destroyed in Civil War, in 1952-8 replaced by City of Newport News, see VA Genealogist 24 (1980) 57.
  Court house records: court minute (1748-62), court order (1647, 1713-4), land patents (1666-79), land tax (1782-), overseers of poor (1786-), personal property tax (1782-), records (1663), rent roll (1704). Other records: cemetery, census (1790T, 1800T, 1810RA, 1820R,

1830R, 1840R, 1850RFMS, 1860RFMDS, 1870RFMD, 1880RFMD, 1900R, 1910R), city histories, city maps, county history, county map, Episcopal parish, landowner map (1862), Mennonite, Lutheran, Methodist. Library: Newport News Public Library System,# 2400 Washington Ave., Newport News, VA 23607. History: R. D. Whichard, THE HISTORY OF LOWER TIDEWATER VA, Lewis Historical Publishing Co., New York, NY, 1959.

109. WASHINGTON COUNTY, County Seat: Abingdon (24210), formed in 1777 from Fincastle County and later Montgomery County, see VA Genealogist 24 (1980) 58.
    Court house records: birth (1853-92), chancery court order (1831-), circuit court will (1840-), court minute (1777-87, 1819-21, 1837-), court order (1777-), death (1853-92), deed (1777-), district court deed (1789-1840), divorce (1777-), land tax (1782, 1786-), marriage (1785-), military (1861-5), overseers of poor (1826-), personal property tax (1782-), survey (1781-), will (1777-). Other records: cemetery, census (1790T, 1800T, 1810RA, 1820R, 1830R, 1840R, 1850RFMS, 1860RFMDS, 1870 RFMD, 1880RFMD, 1900R, 1910R), city history, county histories, county map, landowner maps (1821, 1890-1), town history. Libraries: Historical Society of Washington County Library,# E. Main St., Abingdon, VA 24210; Washington County Public Library, Valley and Oak Hill Sts., Abingdon, VA 24210; Bristol Public Library, 701 Goode St., Bristol, VA 24201. Society: Historical Society of Washington County,# PO Box 484, Abingdon, VA 24210. Histories: T. L. Preston, HISTORICAL SKETCHES AND REMINISCENCES OF AN OCTOGENARIAN, Johnson Publishing Co., Richmond, VA, 1900; L. P. Summers, HISTORY OF SOUTHWEST VA, 1746-86, WASHINGTON COUNTY, 1777-1870, Genealogical Publishing Co., Baltimore, MD, 1979 (1903).

110. WESTMORELAND COUNTY, County Seat: Montross (22520), formed in 1653 from Northumberland County and later King George County, see VA Genealogist 24 (1980)120.
    Court house records: birth (1858-95), chancery court order (1831-), court order (1662-4, 1675-), death (1853, 1857-96), deed (1653-77, 1691-), divorce (1850-), fiduciary (1742-89), free blacks (1828-49), inventory and settlement (1653-71, 1691-1709, 1723-), land cause (1827-37), land tax (1782, 1787-), marriage (1786-), personal property tax (1782-), petition (1776-7), slave owners (1782), superior court (1809-31), superior court

order (1809-57), tax alteration (1783-6), tithable (1776), will (1653-77, 1691-). Other records: Baptist, cemetery, census (1790T, 1800T, 1810RA, 1820R, 1830R, 1840R, 1850RFMS, 1860RFMDS, 1870RFMD, 1880RFMD, 1900R, 1910R), county atlas, county histories, county map, Episcopal parish, Methodist, town history. Society: Northern Neck Historical Society,* Montross, VA 22520. Histories: T. R. B. Wright, WESTMORELAND COUNTY, Whittet and Shepperson, Richmond, VA, 1912; W. A. Crozier, WESTMORELAND COUNTY, Genealogical Publishing Co., Baltimore, MD, 1971 (1913).

111. WISE COUNTY, County Seat: Wise (24293), formed in 1856 from Lee, Scott, and Russell Counties, see VA Genealogist 24 (1980) 203.

Court house records: birth (1856-71), court order (1856-61, 1865-), death (1856-94), deed (1856-), divorce (1856-), land tax (1856-), marriage (1856-), personal property tax (1857-), survey (1856-), will (1856-). Other records: Baptist, cemetery, census (1860RFMDS, 1870RFMD, 1880RFMD, 1900R, 1910R), city history, county histories, county map. Libraries: Wise County Public Library, Wise, VA 24293; Clinch Valley College, John Cook Wyllie Library,# Wise, VA 24293. Society: Southwest VA Historical Society, PO Box 1128, Wise, VA 24293. Histories: L. F. Addington, THE STORY OF WISE COUNTY, Centennial Commission and School Board, Wise, VA, 1956; C. A. Johnson, A NARRATIVE HISTORY OF WISE COUNTY, Norton Press, Norton, VA, 1938; L. F. Addington, HISTORY OF WISE COUNTY, Norton, VA, 1975.

112. WYTHE COUNTY, County Seat: Wytheville (24382), formed in 1790 from Montgomery County and later Grayson County, see VA Genealogist 25 (1981) 49.

Court house records: birth (1853-72), chancery court (1832-47), chancery court order (1831-), circuit court (1832-47), circuit court will (1833-), court martial (1797-1808), court order (1790, 1795-), death (1853-70), deed (1790-), divorce (1790-), land tax (1793-), marriage (1790-), military (1861-5), miscellaneous (1824-38), personal property tax (1793-), superior court (1832-45), survey (1790-), tax (1800), will (1790-). Other records: cemetery, census (1790T, 1800T, 1810RA, 1820R, 1830R, 1840R, 1850RFMS, 1860RFMDS,1870RFMD, 1880RFMD, 1900R, 1910R), county histories, county map, German Reformed, landowner maps (1821, 1865, 1890), Lutheran. Libraries:

Wytheville Community College Library,# 1000 E. Main St.,
Wytheville, VA 24382; Wythe-Grayson Regional Library, PO
Box 159, Independence, VA 24348. Society: Wythe County
Historical Society,* Monroe and Tazewell Sts., Wythe-
ville, VA 24382. Histories: HARDESTY'S HISTORICAL AND
GEOGRAPHICAL ENCYCLOPEDIA, New York, NY, 1884; L. M.
Kincer, GLIMPSES OF WYTHE COUNTY HISTORY, HISTORIC
CHURCHES, Wytheville, VA, 1967; J. S. Presgraves, WYTHE
COUNTY CHAPTERS, Wytheville, VA, 1972.

113. YORK COUNTY, County Seat: Yorktown (23490), formed
in 1634 as one of the 8 original counties (shires),
originally named Charles River County, name changed to
York County in 1642, see VA Genealogist 25 (1981) 51.
  Court house records: administrator (1831-), chancery
court order (1831-), claims (1781), court (1687-8), court
minute (1851-), court order (1633-), deed (1633-),
guardian (1736-1846), inventory (1745-1811), land cause
(1746-69, 1795-), land tax (1782-), marriage (1772-1849,
1854-), military (1776-81), personal property tax
(1782-), petition (1776-1858), rent roll (1704), tax
alteration (1786, 1789), will (1633-). Other records:
cemetery, census (1790T,1800T, 1810RA, 1820R, 1830R,
1840R, 1850RFMS, 1860RFMDS, 1870RFMD, 1880RFMD, 1900R,
1910R), city histories, county histories, county map,
Episcopal parish, Friends, landowner maps (1862, 1865),
Methodist, minister's records. Library: York County
Public Library, Grafton S/Ctr., Grafton, VA 23692.
Histories: E. S. Miers, BLOOD OF FREEDOM: THE STORY OF
JAMESTOWN, WILLIAMSBURG, AND YORKTOWN, Colonial Williams-
burg, Williamsburg, VA, 1958; M. P. Smith, OLD YORKTOWN
AND ITS HISTORY, Richmond Press, Richmond, VA, 1920.

Books by George K. Schweitzer

CIVIL WAR GENEALOGY. A 74-paged book of 316 sources for tracing your Civil War ancestor. Chapters include I: The Civil War, II: The Archives, III: National Publications, IV: State Publications, V: Local Sources, VI: Military Unit Histories, VII: Civil War Events.

GENEALOGICAL SOURCE HANDBOOK. A 100-paged book describing all major and many minor sources of genealogical information with precise and detailed instructions for obtaining data from them.

GEORGIA GENEALOGICAL RESEARCH. A 235-paged book containing 1303 sources for tracing your GA ancestor along with detailed instructions. Chapters include I: GA Background, II: Types of Records, III: Record Locations, IV: Research Procedure and County Listings (detailed listing of records available for each of the 159 GA counties).

KENTUCKY GENEALOGICAL RESEARCH. A 154-paged book containing 1191 sources for tracing your KY ancestor along with detailed instructions. Chapters include I: KY Background, II: Types of Records, III: Record Locations, IV: Research Procedure and County Listings (detailed listing of records available for each of the 120 KY counties).

NORTH CAROLINA GENEALOGICAL RESEARCH. A 190-paged book containing 1233 sources for tracing your NC ancestor along with detailed instructions. Chapters include I: NC Background, II: Types of Records, III: Record Locations, IV: Research Procedure and County Listings (detailed listing of records available for each of the 100 NC counties).

PENNSYLVANIA GENEALOGICAL RESEARCH. A 225-paged book containing 1309 sources for tracing your PA ancestor along with detailed instructions. Chapters include I: PA Background, II: Types of Records, III: Record Locations, IV: Research Procedure and County Listings (detailed listing of records available for each of the 67 PA counties).

REVOLUTIONARY WAR GENEALOGY. A 110-paged book containing 407 sources for tracing your Revolutionary War ancestor. Chapters include I: Revolutionary War History, II: The Archives, III: National Publications, IV: State Publications, V: Local Sources, VI: Military Unit Histories, VII: Sites and Museums.

SOUTH CAROLINA GENEALOGICAL RESEARCH. A 190-paged book containing 1107 sources for tracing your SC ancestor along with detailed instructions. Chapters include I: SC Background, II: Types of Records, III: Record Locations, IV: Research Procedure and County Listings (detailed listing of records available for each of the 47 SC counties and districts).

TENNESSEE GENEALOGICAL RESEARCH. A 136-paged book containing 1073 sources for tracing your TN ancestor along with detailed instructions. Chapters include I: TN Background, II: Types of Records, III: Record Locations, IV: Research Procedure and County Listings (detailed listing of records available for each of the 96 TN counties).

VIRGINIA GENEALOGICAL RESEARCH. A 187-paged book containing 1273 sources for tracing your VA ancestor along with detailed instructions. Chapters include I: VA Background, II: Types of Records, III: Record Locations, IV: Research Procedure and County Listings (detailed listing of records available for each of the 100 VA counties and 41 major cities).

WAR OF 1812 GENEALOGY. A 69-paged book of 289 sources for tracing your War of 1812 ancestor. Chapters include I: History of the War, II: Service Records, III: Bounty Land and Pension Records, IV: National and State Publications, V: Local Sources, VI: Military Unit Histories, VII: Sites and Events.

All of the above books may be ordered from Dr. George K. Schweitzer at the address given on the title page. Or send a long SASE for a FREE descriptive leaflet on any or all of the books.